IMPOSSIBLE PLAYS

KEITH DEWHURST has been a yarn tester in a cotton mill, a football journalist, a TV presenter, an arts columnist for the *Guardian*, writer in residence at Western Australian Academy of Performing Arts, and a member of the production board of the British Film Institute. Of his eighteen stage plays, six, including *Lark Rise*, were premiered by the National Theatre and three by the English Stage Company at the Royal Court Theatre. His extensive TV work includes a further eighteen plays and many episodes for series, including the original *Z-Cars*, *The Edwardians*, *Fall of Eagles*, *Van der Valk* and *Casualty*. In cinema he scripted *The Empty Beach* and with David Leland co-wrote *Land Girls*. He has published two novels and his latest play, *King Arthur*, was produced by Shapeshifter Productions at the Arcola Theatre, London, in November 2006.

JACK SHEPHERD was born in Leeds and studied art at King's College Newcastle, after which he went to Central School of Speech and Drama. As an actor he has enjoyed a successful career at the Royal Court and National Theatre, as well as on the screen where he is best remembered for the series *Blind Justice* and *Wycliffe*. More recently he appeared in Michael Winterbottom's film *Wonderland* and in *Charlotte Grey*. His many directing credits include *The Honest Whore* at the Globe; *King Lear* at Southwark Playhouse, and *Measure for Measure* at the Arcola Theatre. His first play, *In Lambeth*, won the Time Out Award for best directing and writing in 1989, and he has since written a number of plays for stage and screen. He is currently filming the first book of Phillip Pullman's *His Dark Materials* trilogy and writing a play for the Globe Theatre.

IMPOSSIBLE PLAYS

Adventures with the Cottesloe Company

Keith Dewhurst and Jack Shepherd

Methuen Drama

Published by Methuen Drama 2006

1 3 5 7 9 10 8 6 4 2

First published 2006
Methuen Drama
A & C Black Publishers Limited
38 Soho Square
London W1D 3HB
www.acblack.com

ISBN-10: 0-413-77585-2
ISBN-13: 978-0-413-77585-6

A CIP catalogue record for this book is available from the British Library

Cover photograph: The Crucifixion Play on National Theatre terraces, Easter
1977. L to r: Derek Newark, Tom Wilkinson, Mark McManus, Trevor Ray and
Gavin Grainger. Copyright © Nobby Clark

Typeset in Plantin by SX Composing DTP, Rayleigh, Essex
Printed and bound in Great Britain
by St Edmundsbury Press

DISCLAIMER

The authors and publisher gratefully acknowledge the permissions granted
to reproduce quoted extracts within this work. Every effort has been made
to trace the current copyright holders of the extracts included in this work.
The publishers apologise for any unintended omissions and would be pleased
to receive any information that would enable them to amend
any inaccuracies or omissions in future editions.

Contents

Foreword: Impossible Plays   *Jack Shepherd*   xi

Introduction: A Theatrical Ideal   *Keith Dewhurst*   xiii

PART ONE: AT THE ROYAL COURT

1. The French Connection   *Jack Shepherd*   3

2. A Royal Court Actor   9

    The Royal Court Studio   *Jack Shepherd*   9

    A word on the acting   *Jack Shepherd*   11

    Transforming the space   *Jack Shepherd*   15

3. Bill Bryden   17

    The Greenock dreamer   *Keith Dewhurst*   17

    The Journey of the Fifth Horse   *Jack Shepherd*   22

    A vision of the future   *Jack Shepherd*   24

4. Pirate Black   26

    Staging *Pirates*   *Keith Dewhurst*   26

    The actors   *Jack Shepherd*   31

5. Victor Henry: The Company Member Who
    Never was   *Jack Shepherd*   33

6. *The Baby Elephant*   *Keith Dewhurst*   40

7. *Corruna!*   43

    Writing for a company   *Keith Dewhurst*   43

    Why 'Impossible'?   *Jack Shepherd*   47

    The flower path   *Jack Shepherd*   48

    The alienation effect   *Jack Shepherd*   49

    Corruna! on tour   *Keith Dewhurst*   52

The mysteries of the wrestlers' hotel
Jack Shepherd   53

A *Corruna!* summary   *Keith Dewhurst*   55

8. The Royal Court: Publicity and Personalities
Keith Dewhurst   57

Tony Richardson: 'Can No One Clear the
Peacock Shit off this Terrace?'   *Keith Dewhurst*   61

PART TWO: SCOTLAND

9. *Willie Rough*   *Keith Dewhurst*   65

10. *The Misanthrope*   *Jack Shepherd*   67

11. Life at the Lyceum   69

The acting company   *Keith Dewhurst*   69

Kidnapped   *Keith Dewhurst*   70

The integrity of the space   *Keith Dewhurst*   72

The Miser   *Keith Dewhurst*   76

12. *The Magic Island*   *Keith Dewhurst*   77

PART THREE: THE NATIONAL THEATRE

13. The Early Days of the NT   81

Watch It Come Down   *Keith Dewhurst*   81

Social life   *Keith Dewhurst*   83

Il Campiello   *Keith Dewhurst*   85

14. Medieval Mysteries   89

The Passion   *Keith Dewhurst*   89

Seeing *The Passion*   *Jack Shepherd*   91

Impact   *Keith Dewhurst*   93

Judas   *Jack Shepherd*   93

The poet's revenge   *Jack Shepherd*   95

The Crucifixion play   *Jack Shepherd*   96

15. *Lark Rise*   98

    Luggage   Keith Dewhurst   98

    Lark Rise   Keith Dewhurst   98

    Writing *Lark Rise   Keith Dewhurst*   102

    Casting 'Mrs Timms'   *Keith Dewhurst*   104

    Rehearsing *Lark Rise   Keith Dewhurst*   106

    Lessons of *Lark Rise   Keith Dewhurst*   109

16. *American Buffalo*   112

    Two questions to ponder   *Keith Dewhurst*   112

    Playing *American Buffalo   Jack Shepherd*   112

    Dave King   *Jack Shepherd*   116

17. *The World Turned Upside Down*   121

    Civil war, mutinies and strikes   *Keith Dewhurst*   121

    The epic challenge of the brambles   *Jack Shepherd*   127

18. *Dispatches   Jack Shepherd*   129

19. Opportunities and Dilemmas   137

    The Long Riders   Keith Dewhurst   137

    Candleford   Keith Dewhurst   138

    Plans and a dilemma   *Keith Dewhurst*   140

    Summer manoeuvres   *Keith Dewhurst*   142

20. The O'Neill Season   144

    The Sea Plays   *Jack Shepherd*   144

    Hughie and Stacey   *Jack Shepherd*   145

    The Iceman Cometh   Jack Shepherd   147

    The demon drink   *Jack Shepherd*   148

    J. G. Devlin   *Jack Shepherd*   152

    Derek Newark   *Jack Shepherd*   152

20. Extending the Cycle   157

    Creation   Jack Shepherd   157

A popular success   *Jack Shepherd*   159

The outdoor performances   *Jack Shepherd*   160

Sixty crop pruners   *Jack Shepherd*   161

Men without women   *Jack Shepherd*   163

Brian Glover   *Jack Shepherd*   164

22. Choices and Changes   169

Crazy Horse   *Jack Shepherd*   169

Bill's choice   *Keith Dewhurst*   171

Cologne and Rome   *Jack Shepherd*   174

Enforced changes   *Keith Dewhurst*   177

23. Endings   178

Don Quixote   *Keith Dewhurst*   178

A difficult stage   *Jack Shepherd*   181

Departure   *Keith Dewhurst*   182

A threat to family life   *Jack Shepherd*   183

24. *A Midsummer Night's Dream*   184

Playing the *Dream*   *Jack Shepherd*   184

Mechanicals and Princess Margaret   *Jack Shepherd* 186

A flashback   *Keith Dewhurst*   189

25. *Glengarry Glen Ross*   *Jack Shepherd*   190

26. *Cinderella*   *Jack Shepherd*   194

27. The Boxing   *Jack Shepherd*   198

28. *Doomsday*   201

Following the score   *Jack Shepherd*   201

Rehearsal strategies   *Jack Shepherd*   204

A furious row   *Jack Shepherd*   205

'Death' takes the stage   *Jack Shepherd*   206

PART FOUR: REPUTATIONS

28. The Wrap-up   *Keith Dewhurst*   211

29. Reputations   *Jack Shepherd*   213

30. Something Happier   *Keith Dewhurst*   218

Epilogue: What's the Score?   *Keith Dewhurst*   220

A Glossary of Terms   *Keith Dewhurst*   224

Acknowledgements   236

Foreword: Impossible Plays

Jack Shepherd

This book is about a theatre company. It was slow to evolve, beginning in the early 1970s as a search for popular theatre, reaching its peak ten years or so later at the Cottesloe Theatre and ending in the summer of 1986, after the final performance of *The Mysteries* at the Lyceum.

It was known variously throughout this time as the 'Cottesloe Company', the 'Bill Bryden company', and a few other less complimentary names besides.

The company was not in the mainstream of the British theatrical tradition. For one thing, we were essentially a working-class company. And the key influences on our work came from abroad: France and Germany mainly, but also from America.

The search was always to find a *popular* theatre, a form of theatre that would draw into it people from all backgrounds, not just the cultured and the educated.

If plays couldn't be found to inspire the company, books were adapted instead. The scale of these adaptations was epic. Music was integrated into the action, popular music, and in such a way that a scene would lead inevitably to a song – which in turn would point the way to the next scene, and so on. The actors would sing when required to and on occasions the musicians would act. The staging of these productions was often original: the structure of the theatre was adapted to the needs of the drama, rather than the other way around.

Keith tells me that I coined the phrase 'Impossible Plays' but I have only the haziest recollection of the circumstances.

We were in an Italian restaurant, I remember, in 1970 or thereabouts. A summer lunchtime. White tablecloths. Sunlight streaming in from outside. Keith, Bill Bryden and I, dreaming up plans for the future, the way that you do after a bottle or two of red wine. And as we talked long into the afternoon, we started suggesting the books we'd most like to adapt for the stage – our favourite books: *Jude the Obscure*, *The Last of the Mohicans*. Some of these books seemed to lend themselves to adaptation, others did not. And as the afternoon wore on, the wine continued to flow, the laughter intensified and the suggestions got sillier and sillier: *Mrs Beeton's Household Management*, the Telephone Directory. The kind of desultory substances-induced conversation, familiar to rock musicians during their endless hours on the road.

This must have been the moment I came up with the suggestion. 'What you're talking about is "Impossible Plays", isn't it?' It was probably meant as a joke. But the idea stayed with us.

Over the years, Impossible Plays became a kind of shorthand, referring to the kind of project, so epic in its scale that didn't readily lend itself to a stage adaptation. A project so big that the creative effort required to get it moving would be akin to teaching a dinosaur to fly. An idea so outrageous that the difference between success and failure was always going to be wafer-thin.

Introduction: A Theatrical Ideal

Keith Dewhurst

The story of Bill Bryden and the people who ventured with him is one of success and failure; of the ways in which society creates and extinguishes possibilities; of bravery and stupidity; of friendship so hot that it was bound to scorch; and of a passionate belief in a theatrical standard that is as hard to sustain for an evening as it has been persistent over many centuries. Two of us will narrate: I am the theorist and playwright collaborator, and Jack Shepherd is an actor who made vital contributions to the notion of the adventure. We will tell the story alternately because there were times when one of us was involved but not the other. There will be some overlaps, and some divergent opinions; some anecdotes and pen-portraits may seem to digress, but they are there for a purpose, which is to re-create an ambience and to give a flavour of theatrical lives that were not those of today. Each generation, after all, has its attitudes and assumptions.

It must be said at once that the story of the Cottesloe Company does not begin at the Cottesloe itself but at the Royal Court. It is the story of a line of work that was refined in other places before the then Director of the National Theatre, Peter Hall, gave it a perfect home in the Cottesloe; and the roots of the story grow from momentous events in British social history.

When death is near, minds turn to serious matters, and the Second World War stimulated an interest in painting, classical music and theatre of all kinds. It was a war to defend civilisation against barbarism, and people sought to define their values. In Britain there was a sense of shame about the social conditions which many people had endured in the

1930s, and a better society became a definite war aim. Market forces, it was felt, had to be tempered. Men like Maynard Keynes and Kenneth Clark persuaded politicians that there was a positive social value in supporting the arts. Wartime organisations like the Council for Education, Music and the Arts (CEMA), and the Entertainments National Service Association (ENSA) led to the formation of the Arts Council; the Beveridge Report defined the ideals of a welfare state; and Churchill's coalition government passed the Butler Education Act of 1944, creating the Eleven Plus, the selection of bright pupils, and a system of state scholarships.

A characteristic fruit of these events ripened soon after George Devine founded the English Stage Company at the Royal Court in 1955. Devine himself was an old-fashioned, gentlemanly English intellectual who, during the inter-war years, pursued high-minded theatrical ideals despite knowing that society at large was not much interested in what he did. The young men who joined him in the mid-1950s were different, because the Second World War, and the consensus whereby both Labour and Conservative governments put money into the arts, had changed the world of Devine's youth, if only for a few decades. The English Stage Company's commitment was to put on new plays, rediscover the best of the old ones and to establish the theatre's *right to fail*.

Two of Devine's aides, Tony Richardson, the son of a retail chemist, and Bill Gaskill, the son of a schoolmaster, came from Bradford, where they were exposed during the war to government-assisted theatre, and both were educated at Oxford. John Dexter was a working-class autodidact, and John Osborne was the wild card: a lower-middle-class boy from Fulham whose parents had scraped to send him to boarding school, he became a rep actor and from within the old theatre was the force that shook it. Lindsay Anderson and Anthony Page were from traditional military backgrounds but had rejected the easy-going philistinism of their class. Beyond the Court, Peter Hall was the son of a railway signalman, was educated at Cambridge, and went on to turn subsidised theatres into artistic empires. For most of the new writers and actors of this generation, assisted educations, at grammar, arts and drama schools as well as universities, were a vital step.

These people invaded all the arts, and the expanding TV networks, as a new class whose voice had not been heard before. England had never developed a specific intellectual class, as had countries on the Continent. Artistic individuals had always climbed the social ladder and men such as H. G. Wells, D. H. Lawrence, Arnold Bennett and J. B. Priestley had spoken for the provinces and the unconsidered, but not with the confidence that they were part of a new order, or could actually change the cultural scene and remake it in their own image. Now there was a firm notion that public money should be spent for the public good, whatever that is, and that what T. S. Eliot and Dr Leavis had called 'high seriousness' should be allowed to exist in the arts.

What the new class articulated were the feelings of large numbers of people who wanted change. They wanted a debate about the condition of England. They appreciated the old literary culture and at the same time were a mass audience, schooled in the drama by movie-going. With old forms such as the music hall dying and new ones like television and records booming, showbusiness had one of those historic moments when it embodies in itself the state of the nation, and the theatre became the cockpit of debate. There had been such a tradition, in the work of George Bernard Shaw, Harley Granville-Barker, John Galsworthy and Priestley, but for a moment the new theatre went beyond that. It became hot. People were obsessed. Even reviewers were stars.

The Royal Court became the focus of this heat, and made a huge difference in the theatre, not so much because it committed itself to new writing as because it had an intellectual position. There had been harbingers for years, from Eliot and Christopher Fry to Rodney Ackland, John Whiting and Terence Rattigan, but they were metropolitan voices and had tried to work within the commercial ethos of the West End. The Court, as Jack Shepherd will show, came from another direction.

Attempts have been made to prove that the Royal Court was

a committed left-wing theatre that supported socialist writing, but they are wrong. 'What I am required to do', said Chekhov, 'is to know what is significant,' and that attitude, I guess, would have united Devine, Richardson, Dexter, Gaskill, Anderson, Page and a later director like Peter Gill. Tell the specific truth, they would say, and implications will take care of themselves. Similarly, Bertolt Brecht's influence upon the Court was huge, but it was far more in matters of staging than content, and if writers employed his devices it was to present their own ideas.

The practical political triumph of the Court came in 1967 when Gaskill's production of plays by Edward Bond became the trigger for the ending of centuries of direct theatre censorship; a small but excellent example of the sort of change that the new people of the 1950s wanted.

But all new classes are looters, and although this one was not as greedy as the privatisers who followed, they did splurge public money on private careers. Many of them were hypocrites who moralised about poverty and so forth from very affluent armchairs. They were vain, as people are in the little world of the arts, and they took both their situations and their audience for granted.

I spotted recently in a newspaper an archive photograph of Michael Howard, Ken Clarke and others in their formal dress as officers of the Cambridge University Union in 1962. This was the year that *Z Cars* was created, the very ideal of TV social realism that could unite audiences and be both popular and profound, and yet there in the photo, in the first glow of their ambitions, were the students who as politicians would sit in the Cabinets, and approve the policies, that castrated public service television. What we in the theatre thought were perpetual gains for our nation as a whole were no such thing.

No one understood these things more clearly than Margaret Thatcher, the beneficiary in 1979 of the sea-change in the audience; and even if she was more extreme than many of her voters thought she would be, her attack upon the arts is one that no subsequent government has sought to reverse.

Thatcher recognised the importance of the arts, said

Norman St John Stevas in her defence, but she didn't want to pay for them. But really it was *because* she knew their importance that she didn't want to pay. Art defines our dreams, and Thatcher did not want that liberal-minded state-educated class to be heard. One way or another, she destroyed their power bases in television, in Arts Council committees, in art schools and subsidised theatre companies. All she had to do was to refuse to increase subsidies in line with inflation, make it hard for local councils to give grants, and refuse to wipe out deficits without reorganisation. In television her appointees destroyed that proven BBC culture where individual producers had artistic power, and ITV's profits were subjected to levies, in return for which the quality controls were relaxed. Risks became very hard to take, anywhere in showbusiness, and in the end both managements and audiences lost sight of their importance.

At the same time middle-class intellectuals opposed to Thatcher were sidelined. On the one hand they became beneficiaries of what they affected to despise: tax cuts, privatisation windfalls and property booms. On the other the streams that fed their liberal emotions had run dry: socialism didn't work, religious duty was a thing of the past, and the working class had jettisoned its visions for consumerism, and its political agendas for – well, for what, actually? What price Jerusalem, when what would be built in England's green and pleasant land were supermarkets?

One of the things most damaged by cost-cutting market values is the notion of doing things properly for their own sake, and this affects the professional procedures and the accumulated wisdom of any craft. If all you need to attract an audience is a short-term celebrity actor in the lead, why worry about Stanislavski? There is a huge gap between today's theatrical world and the old Royal Court. A theatre of that kind no longer exists. Its intellectual vigour flourished in a period of theatrical and, indeed, social history that came to an end.

What, within that period and for the future, is the significance of 'Impossible Plays' and the companies led by Bill Bryden? Jack Shepherd here lays more stress than I do upon the explicitly political nature of our work. It is true that many of the actors, and Bill Bryden himself, were working class, but Bill did after all marry the daughter of a Lord. His feelings are with the people but his passion is showbusiness, and for him as for me, popular theatre is like the films of John Ford because it demonstrates that what is artistically very serious can also be liked and understood as entertainment. The highest standards of writing, acting and directing can enhance, not deaden, the enjoyment. The audience can be united, even if they have different levels of appreciation, but there must be no cheap short-cuts to attract them. In that sense, popular theatre does imply a struggle for artistic integrity and a conflict with advertising-influenced low-common-denominator market values.

What we never realised at the time was that, with the collapse of Britain's post-war consensus, the world we inhabited was about to end. We behaved wastefully, and without heed, and when the crunch came most of our notions were left high and dry, and the projects we had worked on became expensive to remount. And we had never been universally popular.

However, and here is the irony, and the light in which the ensuing story should be read. Bill and I *always* realised that theatre itself was, in the modern world, an artform under pressure. Verbal culture generally reels under the assault of the visual. How will the theatre survive against comic books, rock concerts, SFX movies, the internet, the iPod, DVD, and international sport on TV? In its great times, theatre interests many. In its slack times, it either becomes trivial for the masses, or effete for the privileged, and today's privileged youth spend as much time on computer games and mobile phones as the disenfranchised. Our notion, vainglorious maybe, was to create an experience that could compete, somehow, because it did not compromise and could only be had through a live show. The reader must be the judge. What is certain is that, for many reasons, meaningful theatre is more threatened as we write than it was when we made our first stab at it, in *Pirates*, a Royal Court Sunday-night performance, without décor, in December 1970.

Part One:

At the Royal Court

1. The French Connection

Jack Shepherd

Looking back, it seems to me now that the first steps of our adventure into popular theatre were taken in the autumn of 1970 with the Sunday-night production of *Pirates* at the Royal Court. It was the prototype of what we soon came to call an Impossible Play, and the cast of actors and musicians contained the seed (the germ some would say) of what was to grow into the Cottesloe Company at the National Theatre a few years later.

This, for me, was the moment when the backbone of that future company was formed. Bill Bryden was the director, Keith Dewhurst the writer, the cast included both Brian Glover and myself, and the live music in the play was performed on stage by folk musicians. This juxtaposition of narrative action and folk music was an idea, or rather the beginnings of an idea, Bill was to develop in many more celebrated productions in the years to come.

Sunday-night productions at the Royal Court were advertised as 'productions without décor'. The budgets were limited. What they were there for was to give writers a fighting chance to show they had something to say.

It was clear from the beginning, therefore, that *Pirates* wasn't going to be an easy ride. The epic scale of the narrative clearly didn't match the very limited resources at our disposal. The costumes were minimal and it required a very large cast, willing to work for little more than expenses. The unadorned space of the Royal Court Theatre was going to have to be *transformed*, not through the ingenuity of a designer but (as in the Elizabethan theatre) through the imagination of the performers and their ability to project the 'world of the play' into the minds of the audience.

During rehearsals there was a lot of talk about the kind of theatre we all believed in: what we all thought we were doing and whom exactly we were doing it for. (This was the time of the student 'sit-ins', and the Workers' Revolutionary Party was at the height of its influence within the acting profession.) Keith would often hold forth about popular theatre: a theatre for everyone, with an epic view of our history. Bill Bryden too. They'd thought about the notion of a *popular theatre* much more than I had, but it wasn't the first time I'd come across such ideas.

Ten years previously, I had been studying Fine Art at Kings College Newcastle, then a subsidiary of Durham University. The Art Department was at that time dominated by Victor Pasmore and his ruthlessly constructivist view of art, and possibly as a reaction against this, I'd been increasingly drawn towards the theatre. I joined the university's Drama Society and became a member of the People's Theatre, a celebrated amateur group with its origins in a distant socialist past. In the summer of 1959, everyone at the People's Theatre was talking about a production of *The Three Musketeers* at the Edinburgh Festival, directed by Roger Planchon.

Planchon was one of four directors who had been sent to form provincial *Centres Dramatiques* by Charles de Gaulle's Minister of Culture, André Malraux: Michel Saint-Denis at St Etienne, Planchon near Lyon, Patrice Chéreau at Nanterre, and Jean Vilar in Paris and, during the summer, at the Palais des Papes in Avignon.

I hadn't been able to see Planchon's production, but I did talk to people who had, and what impressed me was the fact that he hadn't used a set. The company, under Planchon's direction, had elegantly *transformed the space* through the use of wit and invention. I learned, for example, that when they needed to create the English Channel, they had simply brought on a huge blue cloth and rolled it across the floor. It's important to remember that no one had seen anything quite like it before. To an audience accustomed to naturalism and literalness in the theatre, it was a breathtaking idea.

But memory is a very unreliable thing and, talking to these same people forty years later, it now transpires that the English Channel hadn't been created by a roll of cloth, but through the use of blue flags, which were dipped down to stage level and then fluttered in a wave-like motion.

Fortunately, however, both versions of the event make the same point: the ingenious use of a piece of cloth had created the illusion of an expanse of water and transformed the stage. It can't be entirely a coincidence that, when Bill came to create the River Jordan in the promenade production of *The Passion* in 1977, it was a blue cloth that unfurled. And then, with members of the audience encouraged to hold the edge, it was gently fluttered to create an image of the surface of the water in which Christ was shortly to be baptised. Whether the influence of French epic theatre was direct or indirect, it was clearly there.

There was another influence, too, found in the story (probably apocryphal) of how Planchon's production came into being. The tale I heard goes like this: when he arrived in Lyon, Planchon was determined to make his theatre a popular one and duly canvassed people as to what play they would most like to see performed. As he might well have anticipated, the clear winner was *The Three Musketeers*, an adaptation of the classic novel already done to death in the provincial theatre of that time. Undeterred, Planchon scanned the existing adaptations, and, finding them uninspiring, turned up for rehearsals on the first day with a copy of the original novel in his hands. Tearing pages out of the book, he handed them out to the company, and told them to go away and work out a way of staging their particular section. In this way, supposedly, the production was born.

Again, the process described here is not dissimilar to the one we used in rehearsing the second part of *The Mysteries* in 1980. In the absence of Tony Harrison (who as 'bard' in residence had coordinated the adaptation of the earlier part), this second instalment was essentially adapted by the company itself, with the director functioning not as a dictator, telling everyone exactly what to do, but as a catalyst, inspiring all those taking part to take the creative initiative.

And just one other thing: in the course of the plays, or so I was told, Madame de Winter fried an omelette on stage. She didn't seem to fry the omelette, she actually did it. People could smell the cooking. This was a deceptively subversive moment, exposing the make-believe of what then passed for naturalism in the theatre. This idea that everyday processes are in themselves interesting and not to be fudged in the interests of providing pace and entertainment, took root at the Royal Court, where for many years it became a kind of unwritten law. The principle was compromised finally in Stephen Daldry's production of Arnold Wesker's play *The Kitchen* in which, even though the stage was fitted up with fully functioning gas-fired ovens, the preparation of the food was *mimed*, giving the cooks the aspect of mental patients let loose in the kitchen of an asylum.

Planchon wasn't the only influence, of course. Innovatory ideas from the Continent had been coming into Britain since the turn of the century, but had never taken a firm root in mainstream theatre.

Epic theatre had been explored by Brecht in Germany before the Second World War and by André Obey in France. Obey created plays without language, but the kind of mime he developed was a long way from the mime of the street entertainer, with his gloved hands and whitened face. There were no objects on stage. Everything had to be created by the precise movements of the actors. Obey took on large themes like 'The Fire' and 'The Flood', moving as far as he could from the Boulevard theatre of the time.

These ideas arrived in Britain in the late 1930s at the school run by Michel Saint-Denis and George Devine in Islington, and were revived when the same duo ran what became known as the Old Vic School in the 1950s. Here actors were taught about the physical and the 'expressive' side of their craft, through strategies developed on the Continent. Although the Old Vic School didn't last for long, its beliefs and practices were to continue at the Royal Court Studio, under the influence of George Devine, and at the Central School of Speech and Drama.

I first became aware of what was happening at the Central School through a television documentary made in 1961. What was on offer at 'The Central' looked challenging and radical; glamorous, too, in the sense that it offered classes in the 'Method'. It was the 'Method', after all, that had inspired both Marlon Brando and James Dean, the two undisputed icons of my adolescence.

Harold Lang taught the basics of 'Method' acting. Yat Malmgren and Christopher Fettes taught the Laban theory of movement. And the Principal, John Blatchley, together with his wife Catherine Clouzot, trained the students in the *physical* side of acting, techniques which had been taught at the Old Vic School and which they'd both learned through their experiences in French theatre over the previous two decades. At that time the focus of British theatre was very much on the spoken word, the beauty of language. The physical side of acting had been neglected. I think John Blatchley saw it as his duty to try and redress this balance. He had worked with Michel Saint-Denis's company in St Etienne, taking theatre to the workers. He loved Brecht. He taught mime, and how to work with masks, both full masks and half masks, clearly having assimilated the influences of both Obey and Jean Lecoq (whose school in Paris is still the place to go for anyone wishing to learn the skills and the discipline of physical theatre).

In our final year, under John's direction, we created an epic play in the style of André Obey: *Hiroshima*, a mime in four parts, about the devastation wrought by the dropping of the first atomic bomb.

The piece was rehearsed and performed in a church hall in Chalk Farm. By this time, John was co-principal of a new school, the Drama Centre London, which came into being when John, his wife, three of his staff and a good half of the students resigned from the Central.

There was no dialogue in *Hiroshima*. No music. Like dancers, we wore clothes that wouldn't hide the expressiveness of our bodies. The characters we portrayed were not in any sense individualised. I played 'the Father', Sonia Nerdrum played 'the Daughter', and so on.

In the first two scenes, the citizens of Hiroshima were seen going about their everyday lives; lives that were suddenly thrown into the most terrible chaos by the nuclear detonation. In the scene that followed, we revealed the horrors of the ensuing firestorm, ending with a sequence in which a small group of survivors found a temporary sanctuary in the river. The drama was heightened by a violent thunderstorm, which broke overhead during the final act.

It was given one performance.

I can't remember whether Michel Saint-Denis came to the performance or not. He certainly attended a production of the *Medea*, performed by the final year, around the same time. After the performance, the students waited for the great man's opinion with bated breath. When he was finally heard to say that they had, in his opinion, '*transformed the space*', nobody was very sure if this was a compliment.

'*Transform the space.*' This phrase was to haunt me for the next forty years.

2. A Royal Court Actor

The Royal Court Studio: Jack Shepherd

I joined the Royal Court in 1965 (the year that it became a repertory company) straight from drama school. I was to understudy the two Men from the Ministry in N. F. Simpson's *The Cresta Run* and the entire gang of South London youths who stone a baby to death in *Saved* by Edward Bond.

I had got the job largely on account of a letter I had written earlier that year, in which I expressed a desire to be involved in the creation of *new work*, plays that engaged directly with the society we lived in; a position I haven't really veered away from, incidentally, in the intervening years.

The reputation of the Court in those days was very high and it seemed to me to be at the epicentre of what was happening in the theatre. There were formidable directors in Bill Gaskill, Jane Howell and Peter Gill, with Tony Richardson, Tony Page and Lindsay Anderson glittering threateningly in the background. The building had energy and focus, due, I have no doubt, to the uncompromising nature of the theatre's manifesto, '*The right to fail*'. Writing talent abounded, which wasn't surprising given the reputation the Court had at that time for being a writers' theatre.

There was David Storey, whose affable exterior belied a mind as sharp as broken glass, rattling off plays in a few days it seemed, whenever he got bogged down with one of his novels; Christopher Hampton, a student from Oxford University, writing with fluency and maturity at the age of eighteen; and, of course, Edward Bond, whose play *Saved* opened the first repertory season in 1965. I have a lasting image of Edward sitting in at rehearsals, listening to his own work. And I mean *listening*. His eyes lowered, making chessboard patterns on the fabric of his trousers with the blunt end of his gold pen. When I first read *Saved*, I felt as if I'd been punched on the nose. I could taste blood in my mouth for hours afterwards. Another play of his, *Early Morning*, had a similar effect. But as well as blood, this time, I also had a sense of rottenness, like something going off in a kitchen cupboard.

In the main house, the focus was very much on the text, both the writing of it and the speaking of it. In the Royal Court Studio, however, almost as a counterpoint to this, the work begun by Saint-Denis at the Old Vic School, on the physical side of acting, the *craft* of acting, continued to develop.

By 1965 George Devine had become too ill to continue running the theatre and control of artistic policy passed to a triumvirate of Artistic Directors: Bill Gaskill, Keith Johnstone and Iain Cuthbertson. As the year progressed, it became clear that it was Bill who was actually calling the shots. Keith Johnstone's play *The Performing Giant* fell about as flat as a play can possibly fall. And Iain Cuthbertson's hilarious production of Jarry's *Ubu Roi*, with Max Wall in the title role, didn't go down at all well with the Royal Court establishment. And so, in the end, Bill took control. The repertory system was abandoned, and by 1968 the room at the top of the building, which had been both a studio space and a rehearsal room, was transformed into the Theatre Upstairs.

After his resignation, Keith Johnstone went to Canada, to teach drama at Calgary University. His ideas on comic improvisation (developed at the Studio) were set down in *Impro*, a book which has had a significant impact on successive generations of actors and stand-up comedians right up to the present.

During the lifetime of the repertory company (1965–66) all the actors had access to the Studio. Time not spent rehearsing could be spent learning and developing skills, though for a Drama Centre graduate like me the classes had a familiar ring to them. Mime, motivation, full masks, half masks. Much more challengingly, Bill Gaskill was making a determined attempt to explore the world of epic theatre, incorporating not only European ideas, derived mainly from the writings of Brecht, but also from the Noh theatre of Japan. In one particularly demanding studio session he said: 'What I want

10

you to show me is . . . *an old woman comes down to the river.*
That's all you have to act. *An old woman . . . comes down to the*
river. Is there anyone who thinks he can show me that?'

An actor got up and gave it a try, hunching his shoulders
and, in a vaguely feminine sort of way, setting off, as he hoped,
for the river. He was stopped almost before he'd begun.

'No. No. No. What you're showing me is *the* old woman
comes down to the river. What I want is *an* old woman. *An* old
woman comes down to the river. Is there anyone else thinks
they can do it?'

After this, no one was really very keen to give it a try.

What Bill was after, I've always supposed, was the
realisation of a true *alienation effect*, a way of playing a scene
where the actor's ego is not at the centre of the performance.
It's something Brecht was always searching for, in order to put
his political message at the centre of the drama, at the expense
of the actor's sense of personal catharsis. Some hope.

To be honest, I've never experienced or even witnessed such
an effect. What I did discover, however, during the run of *The*
Mysteries at the Cottesloe, a truly epic production in the
promenade style (where the audience were invariably standing
a few inches from your face), was that you couldn't keep
secrets from them. Wherever you were, they were there too.
Everything you said became a public declaration.

A word on the acting: Jack Shepherd

By the late 1960s I was known as a 'Royal Court Actor', and
not just because I had worked there a great deal.

There were layers of meaning attached to that phrase. For
one thing it pinned you down as working class, or at the very
least someone with working-class sympathies. It also implied
that your politics weren't exactly going to be right of centre.
You were 'one of *those* actors', more likely to be in a play about
a deprived childhood on a housing estate than starring in the
West End. It was, I suppose, a back-handed compliment.

There were, of course, many other actors working at the

Royal Court during this period who were labelled in the same way: the very actors who were to form the nucleus of the Cottesloe Company only a few years later. I'm thinking of Derek Newark, Mark McManus, Oliver Cotton, Ken Cranham, Bob Hoskins. They all played leading roles at the Court in the late 1960s and the early 1970s.

And there was Dave Hill, who arrived at the Court via the *Road Show*, Brian Glover from the film *Kes* and the world of wrestling, and Tony Trent (a late addition to the company) who'd learned his craft at the Royal Court Studio and had been a key player in Keith Johnstone's improvisation group, Theatre Machine.

Although we were all labelled 'Royal Court Actors', it didn't necessarily define the kind of actors we actually were. Not everyone, for example, was on the Left. Derek Newark was an army man down to his very boots and Brian Glover was a kind of a Tory – a radical Tory, in the Victorian sense, but a Tory none the less. What distinguished us, in the main, was not so much our politics as our class backgrounds. Looking back now it seems clear that we were fairly representative of the class that had been drawn into the theatre (and into the films) in the mid-1950s, when authentic working-class issues became an acceptable subject for both the dramatist and the film-maker.

If we had to have a label, then I suppose 'Royal Court Actors' was as good as any. There were of course other labels. 'Rep Actors' for example, grinding away in weekly rep, in venues such as the Theatre Royal Leeds, where the posters outside the building declared that Harry Hanson's Players would perform 'A different West End Play every week. Twice nightly!'

In contrast, 'West End Actors' were supposedly middle class in the same way as we at the Royal Court were all working class. Charming and skilful, 'West End Actors' were always on the look-out to solicit a knowing response from the audience, as though the performance were a kind of game played between the actors and the people watching: 'We all know it's rubbish,' they seemed to insinuate, 'but if you laugh, I promise you, you'll have a good time.'

'RSC Actors', on the other hand, always spoke very 'beautifully' in the Oxford accent of the 1930s, with a tendency to turn the verse inside out so that the guts of the poetry were displayed, and with a definite weakness for standing downstage and shamelessly thrusting their pelvises in the direction of the young girls in the front row. Or, at least, this is the image many of us had when the phrase 'RSC Actor' cropped up in conversation.

Life at the Royal Court, on the other hand, was a good deal more puritanical. On stage, that is. What was required at the Royal Court, in those days, was a natural way of acting, though not in any sense 'naturalistic'. The actor was required to stand on stage and tell the truth, and to tell it loud enough to be heard. The acting shouldn't be a slave to theory, nor should it be stylised in any sense. The way of playing a scene had to be found out *through the act of doing it*, not through instruction or discussion. This approach was encapsulated in Bill Gaskill's much quoted phrase: 'Don't *talk* about it, *do* it.'

There was an unwritten rule at the Royal Court in these early years that every action performed on stage was in itself *interesting*, and that it must be performed properly, taking whatever time was necessary in order to complete it. If you're making a cup of tea, for example, actually make it. Don't pretend to make it. Don't *cheat*, in other words. Boil the water. Pour it into the pot. Wait for it to brew. Let it take as long as it's going to take. The process is always going to be interesting.

As in life . . . so on stage . . . might well have been the Royal Court mantra at that time. It was a sound principle. And it still is, for all plays rooted in the process of day-to-day existence. Though there were occasions at the Court when the idea was taken a little far. In the first production of *Saved*, for example, when this principle was applied to the scene changes, twenty minutes were added to the running time of the play.

Another of the Court's guiding principles in those days was a 'respect for the text'. It's something I suspect that actors and directors take pretty much for granted these days, but at that time, at the Royal Court, it was an idea pursued with evangelical zeal. The text had to be respected. The punctuation had to be obeyed, words phrased and not mumbled, not choked to death in the motivational mincer of the Stanislavski Method. The text had to be spoken beautifully, in other words, and unself-consciously, even if the sentiments being expressed were ugly and crude. This also was taken a little too far on occasions, but again the principle is a sound one. And it's been around for a long time.

'Speak the speech, I pray you . . .', Hamlet tells the players, 'as I pronounced it to you, trippingly on the tongue; but if you mouth it, as many of your players do, I had as lief the town-crier spoke my lines.'

The line was the line. You just said it. Comfortably. Easily. You didn't try and 'do things with it', or draw attention to it. It was simply an expression of the need to communicate something and as natural as breathing.

If, after the rehearsal of a particular scene, a watching member of the cast was seen shaking his head and muttering ruefully, 'There's an awful lot of "acting" going on', this was a sure sign that things were not right. In other words, if the people watching are aware of 'the acting', then you clearly aren't doing it properly, because your *performance* is demanding more attention than the play. When this happens, naturally enough, the audience ceases to believe in what's being said and becomes much more involved in the virtuosity of the individual performer.

It's a kind of alienation effect, but not one I'm sure Brecht would have approved of.

All the people who worked at the Royal Court at this time were, to differing degrees, influenced by this principle. And, in a rather grudging sort of way, it lay at the heart of the acting style of what was to become the Cottesloe Company. It wasn't followed through with anything like the same purity and fervour that Peter Gill applied at the Riverside Studio, Hammersmith, during the same period, but it was there all the same.

The problem with the 'Cottesloe style' of acting is that often it can look so effortless and everyday that the audience don't realise the skill involved, or that there's any technique employed at all. 'Anyone could do that,' they think. 'Even I could do that.' And I'm pretty sure critics think like this on occasions too.

The actor who invented the phrase 'There's an awful lot of "acting" going on' was Trevor Ray. In football parlance, Trevor was a left full-back, one of the deadliest tacklers in the game; but more inclined, as he got older, to sit on the sidelines and run on every so often with the cold sponge.

Transforming the space: Jack Shepherd

There are two distinct approaches to creating a set for an epic play. There's what you might call the Bill Dudley approach, constructing a complex series of tilting planes and sheer walls, dizzying heights and vast depths, all powered by hydraulics. This is very effective, but expensive.

The alternative is to strip the stage to its essentials, revealing the back wall and the hanging ropes, the conduits and the gantries in the wings. This approach is cheaper and often equally effective. The space thus created can have the grandeur of a Piranesi prison engraving and yet be flexible enough to become any location the play may require, through the use of lighting and the power of imagination. It's also possible to transform this kind of space through the way an actor uses his body. The technique belongs more to the world of dance than it does to drama, and it's not easy to understand. But here's an inkling of how it works.

If an actor stands on stage, facing the audience, the area *behind* him can be said to represent his *past*, and the area in *front* of him is his *future*. Any movement from the back of the stage towards the front can therefore be perceived as a movement from the past into the future. If the actor looks upwards towards the 'Gods', he will then express optimism about his future. (Just think of all those workers in the Stalinist posters, gazing expectantly towards the millennium, and you start to get the idea.) But if the actor looks up *on the diagonal*, high up on his right, he will be expressing a *thought* about something in his future. And if he then looks downwards *on the diagonal*, towards the ground behind him on the left, he will then be *thinking* about something in his past.

And if you are completely baffled by this theory, don't worry, there have been many before you. You'll just have to take my word for it, that it is possible for an actor to open up the stage space in this 'expressive' kind of way.

In epic plays, the most accessible, the most effective way of transforming the space is through the actor's imagination. This was certainly true of Keith's play, *Pirates*, performed at the Royal Court in 1970. How else could all the disparate elements of a swashbuckling yarn like this one be realised, on an open stage, stripped of all illusion? For Keith's play was truly epic in its scale. A worldwide panoply of events, ships at sea, harbourside taverns, tropical islands, a slave mutiny, a public hanging. And at its heart a parable about a Utopian society, founded by pirates on a remote island in the eighteenth century, that went disastrously wrong. In the absence of any kind of a set, all these different locations were going to have to be created through the power of imagination.

It's a challenge I've faced up to more recently at Shakespeare's Globe. It's a problem every director faces when confronted by the architecture of that particular stage. Whatever you do on it, it's always going to look like a neo-classical street, painted in the most garish of colours. The only way to transform this space, in my view, is through the intensity and the precision of the actor's imagination. Get them to *believe* they're in a living room for example, then with the aid of a few props – a teapot, maybe, or an armchair – *transmit* this belief to the people watching, hoping that they will be able to see in their mind's eye what the actor believes to be true.

An epic play doesn't need a lavish set. It doesn't need complexity. It needs a space that the power of imagination can transform into whatever is required, in the twinkling of an eye. The sets and the costumes are there to aid this act of imagination, not dominate it.

3. Bill Bryden

The Greenock dreamer: Keith Dewhurst

Greenock, whence came both the pirate Captain Kidd and James Watt the inventor of the steam engine, is an ex-shipbuilding town on the Clyde estuary. Bill Bryden was born there in 1942, the son of a bus inspector who at the time was a rear-gunner in Bomber Command. Bill had an older half-brother, and went to the local secondary school, where he captained a football team that included the future international and ball-juggler Charlie Cooke. Bill did a lot of amateur theatre but, more crucially, perhaps, had a friend whose mother was a cinema usherette who would sneak the boys in after school. That it somehow resembles Hollywood movies is one of Glasgow's more puzzling beliefs about itself, and Bill was smitten by an overwhelming, and in the end near-fatal, passion for the world of the studios; and, in fairness, he was inspired to dream, not least by the Westerns of John Ford.

After a job in the Corporation Sanitation Department, where he was told by an official that 'with your looks you could become Chief of Glasgow', he became a researcher on an STV local news show, booking the Beatles to appear on one programme, and, via an Arts Council bursary, assisted Anthony Richardson at the Belgrade Theatre, Coventry. He moved to the Royal Court in 1967 but did not stay long because he thought that he had the money to make a movie, and went to South America to reconnoitre. 'What happened to Bill Bryden?' Tony Richardson is supposed to have enquired at this juncture, and one can see now that it was a forewarning of mishaps to come; but this time he was lucky and was soon re-engaged by the Court.

To be there was one thing. To hack through the thickets of competing egos was quite another, and Bill's romantic rhetoric sounded incoherent to many. He taught at RADA, directed a

Sunday-night show in which Jack Shepherd acted, and showed entrepreneurial flair when he assisted Bill Gaskill on the 'Come Together' Festival. Then he was offered my play *Pirates* for another Sunday-night show, and together we had lucky breaks. Bill capitalised on this and, to look into the future for a moment, after 1970 his career dazzled. He revitalised the theatre in Scotland and the National Theatre deployed his extraordinary company. In 1978 he was nominated Best Director for *Lark Rise*, arguably the production of the decade, never mind the year, but he failed to win. Then in 1985 his production of *The Mysteries* achieved mainstream success when it moved from the Cottesloe Theatre to the Lyceum, the scene of Henry Irving's triumphs a century earlier. Bill took both the *Evening Standard* and Olivier Awards in a recognition of his genius that was as belated as it was ironic.

It was ironic because the Cottesloe had been shut for six months, Bill's power base there was long gone, and his company was dispersed. His co-director Sebastian Graham-Jones had gone into television and I, his co-thinker and chief literary collaborator, had deserted him. Between one awards ceremony and another his marriage foundered, and he took a desk job at BBC Scotland, a thing he had sworn never to do. For a time he had no home, and rented a houseboat, from which his awards statuettes were stolen, although the police recovered them. He had a minor breakdown, another spell in the desk job, at which he was actually very successful, and in the following twenty years has been hampered by money troubles, and directed as many stage shows as he would in twenty months at the Cottesloe.

This personal trajectory I never imagined, as I never imagined the change in society, on the crisp autumn day I first met Bill, in the foyer of the Royal Court Theatre. The fact is that we hit it off at once, and within minutes were ignited by each other's ideas. I was the older by ten years, the son of a cotton mill manager, and after Cambridge I had been a sports journalist and a TV playwright and presenter. In 1967 my first stage play, *Rafferty's Chant*, about a Manchester conman, had been performed at the Mermaid without much success. I also wrote a column for the *Guardian*, the newspaper read by an old acquaintance from Granada days, Bill Gaskill.

This journalism must have jogged his memory. He was directing a short play at the Theatre Upstairs, wanted a companion-piece, and asked me if I still had a play I had written earlier called *The Greatest Team in the World*. I said that it was too short and what if I wrote something else? 'What?' he said. I sent him *Pirates*. He read it and said that he would find a director for a Sunday-night performance.

Gaskill was a brilliant matchmaker who had already put together Christopher Hampton and Robert Kidd, and he must have guessed how much both Bill Bryden and I needed a collaborator. Could Bill's uncoordinated energy and rhetoric be brought into focus by contact with a like and articulate mind, to produce something solid? Could I find someone able to stage what I could imagine, and help me to take my writing to another level? Yes, was the answer to both questions. Bill wanted plays to have the frontal immediacy of a rock concert, and I wanted them to have the sweep and vitality of the Elizabethans, to break the prison of the proscenium, and convey more information than naturalism can. Concerts, films and football had excitement. Why couldn't theatre?

At the first mention of film director John Ford – a hero of both of us – we were away, and walked at an excited pace from the theatre in Sloane Square to have lunch at the Antelope, a pub in Eaton Terrace. Bill's charisma, the madcap passion that swept people along and made them think that their dreams would come true, was immediately apparent. He waved his arms, his eyes flared and shot glances, his laughter was wild, his long hair swung above the straps of his Walker Evans sharecropper-style boiler suit. He was nervous, he stuttered, he had a Greenock accent, he talked over me and slang fizzed off him. It's an Antelope job with them paying. Elbow. Sussed. Bottle job. Tony Richardson's arrival at a design meeting was an instance, he said. Of what, I wondered. What he said was not always coherent, but it was an enchanting torrent that made sense to him, though it was a style that decades later could seem impenetrable. On the day he knew that I took him seriously, which to that point not everybody had. And, of course, I picked up at once on what had confused so many: his football metaphors. Indeed, as a friend and disciple of the great Manchester United coach Jimmy Murphy, I had always used them myself.

'You're wearing the blue shirts tonight!' Bill raved once at his actors in Edinburgh. Celtic supporters among them were aghast at the notion of being forced into a Rangers strip, but someone had the presence of mind to cry, 'He means Scotland, you fools!' These team talks, as we called them, sharing his Stein-cum-Busby fantasy, became legendary, and 'What's the score?' was from the first our question to each other, to judge the quality of a performance and its effect upon the audience.

A time was to come, in the Green Room at the National Theatre, when he sought my opinion on whether we should apply for the vacant managership of Stoke City, and I said he didn't have time to do two jobs at once. But that was in the future.

'What this play needs', he said now, before we had even reached the Antelope, 'is high-energy ball-winners in the middle of the park,' which was my introduction to a way of acting and its effect upon the audience that I had not before defined for myself, but which blew open my mind in the ensuing rehearsals and pub discussions. The pub, we always reckoned, was where the most telling notes could be given. It is worth noting that the ball-winners he selected for *Pirates* were Jack Shepherd, Brian Glover and Derek Newark who, with Mark McManus, made up the midfield in many later productions, and became the heartbeat of the Cottesloe Company. 'And wee Victor,' added Bill. 'I see wee Victor in the lead!'

Wee Victor turned out to be the reprobate Victor Henry, small, ginger-haired and irascible, and at that time in the Court's bad books for, among other things, a rehearsal-room brawl with Jack Shepherd. Bill reckoned that Victor could be rehabilitated in a suitable environment, which is to say, the company of the same old bar-room sparring partners. This might have worked, because what wound Victor up was usually what he imagined to be bourgeois condescension. Unfortunately, Bill went and bragged about his idea, and the little terror was snapped up by the director Peter Gill for a main house production, and could not be released for our rehearsals. This was, of course, a classic Royal Court situation: one director doing the dirty on another, and plunged me within a week or so into the paradoxical reality of the place.

To be asked to work at the Court was an accolade. From the outside it was a self-appointed elite, criticised, envied and resented. It seemed austere, high-minded to the verge of being killjoy, arrogant, contemptuous of its rivals, and impossible to join. From the inside it was a comic whirlpool of treacheries, egos, irreverence and eccentrics. Many key people were homosexual, both openly and suppressed, but their opposition to the theatre of campery and display was virulent. Standards were high, and people larger than life.

Lindsay Anderson, the Duke of Wellington of show-business, might curl his lip as he accused others of a 'lack of integrity', but would not hesitate to bend the opinions of the reviewer Harold Hobson over a gentlemanly lunch. Anthony Page would send his assistant to pick up his laundry. Bill Gaskill once refused to lend someone his office on the grounds that 'he's a very bad writer'. On first nights the general manager Helen Montague would stand in a corridor and whack a radiator with a piece of wood, so that the final applause seemed to reverberate like the San Siro stadium.

The theatre's situation at this time is described in Gaskill's book *A Sense of Direction*, written in 1988. In the Court's first phase, that of Devine and Richardson, the leading writers were Osborne, Wesker and Arden; after Devine's illness and death, Gaskill was in charge and later shared the power with Anderson and Page; the leading writers were Osborne again, perhaps under some sufferance, Bond and David Storey. Gaskill's book describes how by 1970 he was wearied by the theatre's financial problems, and barely hidden differences with the board; he felt that the Court's original impetus was spent, and that it no longer empathised with younger people who wanted to work there.

Gaskill was to resign in 1972, which did mark the end of an era, and this uneasy late period is the context of the opportunity he showed me and Bill Bryden, while not agreeing entirely with our ideas. I was Gaskill's friend, a slow-starter, and Bryden the most gifted of his assistants, who would carry much of the old Court's spirit, and many of its actors, into other arenas.

It is typical of Royal Court shenanigans that Victor Henry did rehearse with us on Saturday mornings, adding gleeful venom to scenes of life among the pirates, and on the day of the show he appointed himself my minder. Alas, he had far too much to drink and was so angry at being out of our play and in another that he threw a chair at me in someone's dressing-room. Some years later my obituary of him appeared in the *Guardian* before he had actually died, but that wasn't my fault, either.

The Journey of the Fifth Horse: Jack Shepherd

I first met Bill Bryden at the Criterion Theatre in 1967, while playing the lead in David Storey's *The Restoration of Arnold Middleton*, which had transferred from the Royal Court in September of that year. He stumbled into my dressing-room in a state of high excitement, a young RADA student in tow (David Bradley as I learned some thirty years later) and set about persuading me into being in his Sunday-night production of *The Journey of the Fifth Horse*, a play by Ronald Ribman, based on Turgenev's novel.

Bill was irresistible. A force of nature. I remember drinking with him till late into the night at my flat in Tufnell Park with a wide-eyed and rather drunken David Bradley still in tow, thinking, as he told me later: 'So this is how *real* actors carry on, is it?'

I can't remember much about *The Journey of the Fifth Horse* other than the fact that it was a play about a nobody, someone surplus to society's requirements, as the title implies, so I looked it up on the internet and was very surprised to discover it is in fact the play that made a name for Dustin Hoffman. But if Bill was trying to repeat the play's Broadway success in London, he was to be disappointed. The production didn't get past first base. The teeth of the Royal Court intelligentsia were very sharp at that time.

Bill always had an eye to what was happening in New York and Los Angeles, and went out of his way to work with its stars whenever an opportunity occurred. There's a contradiction here, in the sense that a man who created one of the few viable theatre companies since the Second World War should be so fascinated by celebrity and the lure of Hollywood. A contradiction, by the way, he's never had any difficulty in resolving. He once said to me: 'If only more of you went away and became stars, you'd make my job so much easier.'

In 1967, though, we knew little about each other, and, did we but know it, we were both at the beginning of a very long learning curve. Two things, however, have stayed in my mind from this production: the mounting chaos of the final performance and the energy, the group commitment, Bill was able to generate in rehearsals. With Bill there was always a sense that the scene was being created *collectively*, not through the authority of the person in charge.

For example, the second scene was about a coach journey, and it seemed to me, as we struggled to find a way of staging it, that we could either create a static sort of scene, set in the courtyard of a coaching inn, or we could attempt to stage it in a much more epic style, creating the whole journey, the galloping horses, the wheels of the cart, the road and the night sky. I realised that if we took the second option, here was my chance to put into practice some of the epic skills I'd learned at the Drama Centre and the Royal Court Studio. I put the idea to Bill and he agreed. The result would almost certainly seem a bit old hat now, but at the time we felt as if we were breaking new ground. It was a lesson for both of us, I think, that imagination can, in the immortal words of Michel Saint-Denis, *transform the space*.

My other memory concerns the fact that we were still trying to finish the technical rehearsal on the Sunday evening, as the audience were coming in. We toiled away behind the theatre curtain, driven by Bill's inexorable will, until only seconds remained before we were due to start. I think we'd reached the scene where the amorous landlady, gleefully played by Moira Redmond, attempts to seduce the hero over a butcher's block, wielding a castrating butcher's knife. The remaining twenty minutes had to be improvised in an explosion of adrenalin and a series of wild guesses by technicians and actors alike. This was not only 'dangerous' acting, it was what Mark McManus used to call 'kamikaze' acting. Not that anyone came down in flames on the night.

Andy Phillips lit the play, trying to guess in those final hectic minutes where the actors might end up, and then confidently bringing the lights up, hoping we could adjust. Andy had a lot of nerve. He drank too much. He was opinionated, acerbic, highly critical of our work, and yet intensely loyal, and sensitive to a fault. He lit nearly every production we put on.

A vision of the future: Jack Shepherd

In the 1960s Bill had will and energy to spare, as well as irresistible powers of persuasion. He was thin and rangy, with a mass of dark hair flopping into his eyes. And he was always very stylishly dressed. He usually looked askance at the clothes I wore and once asked me in genuine bewilderment, 'Why do you always dress like you're going on a ten-mile hike?'

Bill has never been one of those directors who treats actors as the mere chess pieces of the genius in charge. For him, rehearsal is an act of collaboration between people of equal talent. His vision of the play might not be coherent, but he always has the basic colours of the thing in his head, the building blocks. He puts himself at the centre of the rehearsal storm, channelling all suggestions through his own imagination, before putting them into practice.

In the early years, Bill was unceasingly optimistic, positive and confident of success. He was totally committed during the hours of rehearsal, and never a bully. He respected the actor's

24

process and for the most part he left us to get on with it, reckoning that if he'd cast the parts correctly, we were all good enough and experienced enough to get the result he wanted. He was reluctant to give detailed notes to an individual actor, fearing that a misplaced note might well make the performance worse. Frantically over-sensitive on occasions, he preferred to avoid confrontation and to deflect criticism, if he possibly could.

His stammer often made him seem incoherent. In my view this stemmed from the fact that whenever he was nervous and found that he couldn't say a certain word, he'd immediately find an alternative that he *could* say instead. Sometimes it was a word like 'dipstick', for example, which he was always able to pronounce and which could mean whatever he wanted it to mean. At other times he'd use a similar-sounding word to the one he was unable to say, but crucially different in meaning, pushing him further and further away from the point he was trying to make.

It soon became clear that Bill was beginning to imagine a form of theatre that was entirely his own. Only vaguely conceived at first, little more than a pattern in the clouds, but a real vision nevertheless.

What he was trying to do, it now seems to me, was to bring together all the things he loved in popular culture – folk music, films, Glasgow Celtic, Jock Stein, Bob Dylan, John Ford – and fuse them into a theatrical event, though it was going to be a good few years yet before this vision came into focus.

The next production I worked on with Bill was Keith's play *Pirates*; another Sunday-night production at the Royal Court.

4. Pirate Black

Staging *Pirates*: Keith Dewhurst

Pirates was a massive, and probably over-ambitious, epic contrasting the lives of two pirates: John Avery, who captured a Mogul treasure fleet but died impoverished in Bristol, and Captain Misson, who took a slave ship, liberated his victims, and established a communistic colony on Madagascar. Some say that Misson is a fiction invented by Daniel Defoe, but Avery, the part originally intended for Victor Henry, was real. It was played by Patrick O'Connell, a somewhat shattered force after health problems, and Misson by Robert Powell, at that time a rising TV star but not really a Royal Court Actor.

The cast received a fiver each, I think, for a month's rehearsal and the one performance, and the writer got a tenner. We were lucky to get as many good people as we did. Apart from the half-back line they included Celia Bannerman, who had trained at the Drama Centre with Jack Shepherd, David Leland and Oliver Cotton, and the marvellous Norman Beaton.

Bill had hoped that Jocelyn Rickards would design some clothes for us but in the end she couldn't, although she attended the reading, where the lighting designer, Andy Phillips, paid me a compliment that at the time I did not fully grasp. 'This play', he said, 'doesn't need lighting.'

Bill, at that time, was not very experienced, but his energy was amazing and he had the confidence to let loose the discussions in which ideas in common were forged, so that for me it was the most intense working time in all my life. After ten years as a writer I had found my soulmates. There was a lot to learn, and a bit I could give in return.

One character in the play was written as a fat man but for some reason Bill cast a thin person. I refused to change anything, which was humiliating for the actor. But we were at the Royal Court, where the essence of serious theatre was that the text is sacred until proved in its acting out to be wrong. Or so I argued at the time; and although I was a good rewriter when I saw that things were wrong, I was always ferocious in defence of my ideas. My gesture of emphasis became known in the Cottesloe as 'The Claw'.

Actually, a thin actor should never have accepted the part of a man who hates his own ugly fatness, hoping to have it re-written; nor should a casting department have pushed him. It was personal, I suspect, to help a friend. A casting department's power is negative, of course, and includes chances to stop mistakes being made, but it will often try its luck against a new director. Bill asserted himself thereafter, and I do not recall another blatantly wrong person being foisted on him. As for me, I protected my text and showed where I stood, and would not have been respected by the Royal Court Actors if I hadn't, even though the performance was weakened by a thin man talking about being fat.

That was our only hiccup, apart from when Bill let go a black actor who did not want to play a slave, not even one given freedom and weapons. People were so enthusiastic that they wanted to cram in more rehearsals, but there were no rooms booked. Luckily, Robert Powell wangled us an illicit Saturday in the BBC rehearsal complex known as the Acton Hilton.

Hitherto I had thought about problems of writing, but in isolation. What I realised on *Pirates* was that they are linked to problems of staging and acting. Theatre, I was made to see, is a spatial art, which takes place in a location shared by the actors and the audience; and that it is the nature of the location that determines the nature of the suspension of disbelief: that is to say, what for the purposes of the event the audience will accept as 'real'. It is by thinking through these issues of staging, I realised, that one tackles the problems of putting into a play more than strict naturalism allows. What naturalism *does* allow is leaving things out, in the manner of Harold Pinter.

Jack Shepherd believes in the ability of the actor's imagination to transform the space, and that must happen; but I am not sure that it can, always, if the space itself is incapable of transformation, or if the actor's part is not properly written, so that his efforts go into cobbling his character together. This was the second fact that I was forced to confront: the absolute necessity for each character's narrative line to be logical, both on and off the stage.

Apropos of this, one of the subtlest comments about playwriting was made to me by Bill Gaskill after he had seen a play set in a hotel room. I asked him what it was like. 'Dreadful,' he said. 'The wrong people kept meeting in the corridors off stage.' Meaning that they would have mentioned it on stage, but didn't.

Another lesson from these rehearsals was the importance of the 'resistance', Stanislavski's word for the push and pull of the characters' emotions, aims and actions. This arose from the scenes in which Misson exhorts his crew. Too many dramatic expositions and scenes of ideas contain long speeches without any comeback. The speakers are not influenced by their listeners, because the writer has preached and not dramatised. A masterly display of the ebb and flow of the resistance occurs in Shakespeare's *Julius Caesar*, when Brutus and Mark Antony address the crowd.

Pirates was written using an orthodox, shambling sub-Elizabethan structure with some speeches to the audience, and because the production had no money for décor the usual problems of scene changes and spatial integrity did not occur, even when they existed in the text. The actors still had to imagine, of course, but we did not have to worry about the length of time it would have taken to change scenes, or what sort of single set might have worked for every location. On the contrary, it was the slickness of the unencumbered flow, particularly in the airy spaciousness of the Acton Hilton, that set us thinking.

This flow owed a great deal to Jack Shepherd's rehearsal demonstrations of how an actor's position and body outline could define emotions and our sense of the space itself. Bill was quick to pick up on this. 'The diagonal of passion', when the actors face each other across the top-to-bottom diagonal and the space between them seems alive with feeling, became one of his deadliest weapons; and, of course, if the angles of the actor's stances change, so does the emotion. It was here, and in rehearsing *Corunna!* in 1971, that Jack had his greatest influence on the future work of our group.

Another aspect of acting that *Pirates* forced me to consider, one considered fundamental by Stanislavski and his followers, was the nature of a performer's energy. A heinous crime, in the eyes of Bill and our actors who worked at the Court, was what they called 'laying down beside it'.

What this means is that, a great deal of the time, actors take it upon themselves to depict the emotions that the scene, speech or action is intended to arouse in the spectator. They act what the audience is supposed to feel or think, instead of what their character feels or thinks; or, more importantly, what their character simply *is*. They indulge themselves, instead of looking for their character's identity. They lay themselves down beside it, instead of being in it. Royal Court acting, in classic productions by Gaskill, Peter Gill and Jane Howell, could be simple to the point of almost seeming to lack colour; but it had intense concentration, and the product of concentration is energy.

As Jack Shepherd said recently, Bill Gaskill's 2005 production of *Carver* at the Arcola Theatre in East London was a perfect demonstration of this 'house style' of around 1967. What reviewers treated with caution in 1967, of course, they hailed as revelatory in 2005.

'Emotion in excess of the facts' was how F. R. Leavis defined sentimentality and, unlike 'laying down beside it', and that other fault where the actor is moved more than the audience, true energy is never sentimental. Of course, audiences like sentimentality, a fact which Bill Bryden, a working-class man raised on Scots football dreams, TV, popular music and Hollywood movies, knew only too well: when he referred to Hamlet's death scene as 'the proper show-business', he was implying that it is the basic task of popular theatre to get the audience to like the show without it being sentimental. Ways of doing so were to become our pre-occupation.

One major thing came out of *Pirates*. For the previous six months Bill had worked with Bill Gaskill to set up 'Come Together', a festival of Alternative Theatre at the Royal Court, with an emphasis on performance groups such as the People Show. As part of this festival Bill organised a Sunday-afternoon folk-rock concert that featured Sandy Denny and her band, Fotheringay, and the re-formed and fully electric Steeleye Span.

One of Steeleye's recruits was the great singer Martin Carthy, with whom I had worked when he and his then partner Dave Swarbrick recorded music for a television play I had written called *Men of Iron*, about railway navvies in the 1840s (Jack Shepherd was a co-lead); and the band's female vocalist, Maddy Prior, was the daughter of my old *Z Cars* writing colleague, Allan Prior. So when we all met up at the concert there were warm personal links, which began to give substance to a dream.

Bill had wanted to do a play like a concert and I had a long-cherished notion to do a ballad-opera about the Peninsular War retreat from Corunna. Here were the people with whom we could work. For the time being Bill asked Martin to play in the foyer as the audience arrived for *Pirates*. In the end Martin had a gig and couldn't do it – a foretaste of the difficulties of adapting musical life to theatre – but Maddy, Tim Hart and Peter Knight were vivid stand-ins, and Mark Long of the People Show improvised an interval display of a pedlar selling broadsheets and oranges, which he tossed up into the circle, at a pirate's execution.

The show itself went brightly. I sat between Bill Gaskill and Bryden's father-in-law Michael Killanin, who had produced John Ford's *The Quiet Man* and was soon to be President of the International Olympic Association. Bill's wife, Deborah, was backstage, doing costumes and props. I remember very little except a classic Brian Glover moment.

Bill had been obsessed with the idea that the sightlines of the Royal Court were not very good, and because we had no time on the stage itself to adjust groupings, he had a white line painted on the floor. Inside it you could be seen by everyone, outside it you were marginal. The line had the shape of a ship's deck-plan, which some people thought symbolic, but was in fact a coincidence. Glover, coming to confide in the audience, made use of it. He looked this way and that. Was he observed? No. So he stepped over the line, as though it was a low fence, and into the audience's space. Brilliant, and a one-step demonstration of what Bill Bryden wanted above and beyond the classic Court acting: he wanted human colour.

In his press release Bill had described the play as an allegory, which it wasn't, but the reviews all called it one, and this alerted us to future spin-doctoring possibilities. The reviews weren't breathless but they were friendly, and at the Court, where so much new work was greeted with abuse and incomprehension, this was acceptable. So far as it went, we were OK.

The actors: Jack Shepherd

As Keith has intimated, I had a midfield role in this production playing the 'common man', as it were, caught up in the wild sweep of events and somehow surviving to tell the tale. I still have a vivid memory of sitting on a barrel at the front of the stage and, as if to affirm my credentials as a man of the world, informing the audience that I'd seen a sea serpent, '*Twice*'.

Apart from Brian Glover and myself, few of the actors in this production graduated into the full-blown Cottesloe Company of ten years or so later. Hugh Armstrong was definitely a candidate but, for whatever reason, he never made it into the team. John Dearth was another such contender. At that time John was well into middle age, but he still had the energy and the reflexes to give a good account of himself in a sword fight with the young Bob Powell, his body-builder's frame ravaged by years of alcohol addiction. There was Alfred Fagin, actor, writer and fantasist, who was to be an inspiration to the up-and-coming generation of black actors. And there was Norman Beaton who, over the next twenty years, was to become the most successful black actor in the country. As I remember it,

Norman had no problem with the idea of playing a slave – he was first and foremost an actor.

And, finally, and for one brief moment, there was an actor who deserves a chapter all to himself: Alexander Victor Henry.

5. Victor Henry: The Company Member Who Never was

Jack Shepherd

Victor, I know, desperately wanted to be in *Pirates*. He was spiritually drawn to the idea of being a pirate. In a sense he was a pirate – freebooting around the theatres and the television studios, terrorising producers and directors and holding to ransom every other actor, male or female, who didn't for one reason or another come up to scratch. Victor was dangerous, competitive and pitiless. If he sensed the other actors weren't up to much, he would eat them alive. '*OK kid . . .*' he would seem to be saying. '*If you can't live with this, get off the fucking stage.*'

He was small – his parents were even smaller – short-sighted, red-faced and thin, with a frizzy mop of red hair and a terrible wiry strength. Nor was he good-looking, boasting that he had 'a mouth like a dog's arse'. Victor's power to attract lay in his personality and, above all, his energy. He once told me that he saw himself as the reincarnation of Eric Bloodaxe, the Viking war leader and 'first king of Yorkshire'. He was only half-joking.

I remember a Saturday-morning rehearsal for *Pirates* which one of the cast couldn't attend and Victor was only too keen to stand in for him. In the scene we were rehearsing, he had just the one line. Standing on deck with the rest of the crew, myself included, he was asked by the captain what colour the ship's flag should be. 'Black,' he replied, with the cruellest of smiles. '*Pirate black.*' And he said it with such unholy glee that I laughed out loud. The thing was, though, he took his glasses off before he said it and then tucked them away in his top pocket. Horrible wiry things they were, which he'd got years before on the National Health and broken so many times, they'd become twisted out of shape. This instinctive gesture with his glasses, with its sense of public-bar menace, made the pirate's suggestion even more threatening.

I came from an estate in Leeds, built in the late 1930s, and inhabited by working-class people, intent on working their way up the social ladder. Victor was from an altogether tougher neighbourhood, not so very far away: the Gipton Wood estate. In fact, whenever our gang from the Gledhow Park estate met a gang from the Gipton Wood estate in the Gledhow Valley woods we both shared, we'd say, 'Ey, look, *the slums* are coming,' and start throwing stones at them. A running battle would invariably ensue. These tough-looking kids wore their dads' trousers cut off at the knees, no shirts but braces and sleeveless pullovers, usually green; plimsolls in the summer, wellingtons in the winter, and no socks. Plus the customary trickle of snot running from nose to upper lip.

Somehow or other (I think he failed his Eleven Plus) Victor found his way to RADA in the early 1960s. He chose RADA, he told me, not because of the quality of its drama education, but because it was close to the pubs of Fitzrovia (a small enclave in Soho), where he dreamt of talking and drinking with the likes of Dylan Thomas, Augustus John and Frank Harris. He was deeply disappointed to discover that by the time of his arrival in London, the heady days of bohemian Fitzrovia were well past their prime.

People who knew him at this time tended to call him Alex, but people like me, who got to know him later, always called him Victor. He was romantic, creative and very self-destructive, living his brief life in the spirit of Baudelaire or Rimbaud – a part he played, incidentally, in Christopher Hampton's play *Total Eclipse* – determined to experience everything before he died, in a blaze of alcohol and a kind of streetwise existentialism.

We first met, at the Royal Court, in the spring of 1966. He was playing Sparky in John Arden's *Sergeant Musgrave's Dance* and, in those early days, not drinking to excess. We were both in Middleton's *A Chaste Maid in Cheapside*, Victor with by far the larger part, followed by Christopher Hampton's *When Did You Last See My Mother?* in which he was astonishing. A little later, he was in the revival of *Look Back in Anger*.

It was not until later that the drinking began to overshadow everything else. I was rehearsing a play called *Bloomers* at the Gardiner Centre, about six months or so after the production of *Pirates* at the Court. Out of the blue one morning, a very worried company manager burst into the rehearsal room. 'There's someone wants to see you in the bar,' he said. 'He says he won't go until he's spoken to you.' The man was obviously rattled.

When I got to the bar, I found Victor waiting for me, drinking his second or maybe his third pint. It was about 11.30 in the morning. As it turned out, he was on the run from rehearsals of *The Friends*, and 'not getting on too well', he said, with Arnold Wesker. He produced a knife from his pocket and laid it on the bar top. 'See this knife . . .' he said, his Leeds accent thick and sluggish with drink. 'I'm going to scrape his face off with this.' And he picked up the knife again and made nasty little skinning movements with his right hand. He also told me he was carrying a gun, but I didn't really believe that. It wasn't just that he wasn't getting on with Arnold Wesker; he was clearly becoming paranoid.

The paranoia intensified and reached a peak in the period just before he set off for New York, to play the lead in David Halliwell's *Little Malcolm and His Struggle Against the Eunuchs*. Years later, the director of the production, Alan Arkin, told me that the reason for the play's failure on Broadway was that Victor lost his nerve. I still find this hard to believe. He did, however, seem quite mad in the days before his departure.

On his return he took to living in an abandoned car at the bottom of Dartmouth Park Hill in London, where I had a flat. I think this was the lowest point he reached. But once he'd moved into a room in Mike Wearing's house (just over the road as it happened) and once the pair of them had started planning a production of *The Diary of a Madman*, he began to get his drinking under control and, with his demons at arm's length, he set about rebuilding his shattered reputation. When he shaved his head to play the part, his appearance finally began to reflect the terrifying things that went on inside his head; even lorry drivers would cross the road to avoid a possible confrontation.

I last talked to him at the Edinburgh Festival in 1971, not long before the accident that killed him. That afternoon I'd seen him scintillating in a performance of John McGrath's *Trees in the Wind* in which he'd played a young revolutionary. He seemed to be a true embodiment of William Blake's archetypal creation *Orc*, the flame-headed demon of energy, the spirit of ungovernableness. Himself, in other words.

At the bar in the Festival Club that night he was very passionate, manic, desperate to talk about something that he never actually got round to talking about. He even ate a glass; at least, he certainly bit into it and seemed to swallow the fragments. I wanted to leave the Festival Club with a woman and he didn't think I should. He almost seemed jealous and, after failing to persuade me to break off the relationship, he kissed me goodbye in the taxi, full on the mouth, something he'd never done before. A kiss that reeked of alcohol and blood. That was the last I saw of the Alexander Victor Henry I knew. The following year he was involved in a road accident. His body lived on in Pindersfield hospital near Wakefield until 1986, but what was left of the man himself is very hard to say.

What happened, supposedly, is that he'd been buying cans of lager in an off-licence in West London and was taking them back to the flat that he shared with a group of people living on the dole. A car mounted the pavement and crashed into a bus stop, which snapped off at the base and smashed into the back of Victor's head. This caused a lesion of the middle brain, fatally disrupting all his functions other than those governed by the autonomic system. In other words, he could breathe, swallow, defecate and all the rest of it, but, in the view of most of the doctors who treated him, his brain could do very little else.

No one had expected him to wither and finally die in such a

horrible way. It wasn't the 'romantic' death we'd all envisioned. For one thing, Victor had a real love of violence. He'd been known, after all, to seek out middle-class men, rugby-playing men, in pubs round the King's Road and, in front of their sneeringly erotic girlfriends, provoke them verbally to such an extent that the unfortunate men would have no alternative but to insist that they 'go outside and sort this out'.

He would always use long words when provoking people. 'I find your verbosity rather . . . offensive . . . and bereft of any coherent content,' is an accurate enough example, uttered, of course, with a wilfully exaggerated Leeds accent. Once the middle-class male had, as he thought, beaten the living daylights out of him on the pavement outside, a blood-boltered Victor would take off his glasses and place them carefully in his top pocket, saying, 'Is that the best you can do?' and then proceed to take his revenge in the dirtiest way imaginable.

People who knew him were surprised by the circumstances of the accident, many of them disbelieving it altogether. In fact, a conspiracy theory began to develop: Victor had been fatally struck over the back of the head and the accident had been staged in some way to cover the attack.

Admittedly, there were suspicious circumstances. When John McGrath had gone to the flat to collect Victor's things, he found the place deserted. The occupants had all disappeared and nothing belonging to Victor remained, not even his phone book or his diary. As far as I remember, all that McGrath actually found was an abandoned pair of Victor's National Health spectacles. But when John and Victor's estranged wife Rosemary went to the police with their suspicions, they found no one willing to take the matter any further; which of course served only to intensify the convictions of those believing in a conspiracy.

As it so happens, I talked to the man who had been with Victor at the time of the accident. I met him at Mike Wearing's flat a few days later. It was late in the afternoon and the sun was setting through the kitchen window. He described the accident in the most intense detail: how Victor had been thrown up in the air by the impact, ripping away the clothing from the lower part of his body; how the doctors at the hospital had initially failed to notice the injury to the back of his head and that at first the prognosis had been encouraging. All his other injuries, though severe, were remediable through orthopaedic surgery and confined to the lower half of the body.

The strangest thing about the telling of this story, in Mike Wearing's ever-darkening kitchen, was that the longer he went on, the more like Victor he started to sound: the accent, the rhythms, even the expressions on his face. It was as if he had become possessed by the man.

This was, I have to say, a not uncommon phenomenon. Victor had a spellbinding personality. People close to him not only drank like him and thought like him, they started to talk like him as well. Both Denis Waterman and Martin Shaw had at different times come under his dark and strangely hypnotic influence.

I went to see Victor on two separate occasions at the severe head injuries unit at Pindersfield hospital, in the mid-1970s; several years after the injury to his brain. On the first occasion I went with the writer Trevor Griffiths. We were both of us shocked by Victor's appearance. Muscle wastage had brought about profound changes in his body shape and he looked like Humpty Dumpty.

There were very broad differences of opinion as to how much he was able to understand. His parents, of course, were convinced that he could understand everything; they were in fact teaching him to speak again, and his father, a teetotaller, was spoon-feeding him with neat whisky. But the doctors were much more sceptical.

On the occasion of the first visit, however, he was clearly very excited to see us both, sweating profusely, his eyes flicking diagonally upwards as he tried to focus his attention. I quickly made the assumption that he *was* able to understand me. And so I talked to him for a while, telling him things that had happened to me and to other people that we both knew in the intervening years. Trevor was less convinced than I was, unsure that all this news was actually being taken in. And after a while we decided on a test: 'If you understand what we're saying, Victor, turn over in bed.' It took him twenty minutes, but he did it. And yet Trevor was still unconvinced. 'He might be like a plant moving towards the sunlight,' he said. 'And he'd've done that anyway whether we'd've been here or not.' I didn't agree. I found the experience very distressing. I became convinced he was trying to communicate something to me. Something very dark. 'Of all people . . .' he seemed to be saying. 'You must know . . . that this is hell . . . And there's got to be an end to it. Do you understand? An end to it all.'

The next time I went to see him, he looked up from his bed, saw that it was me, and then apparently fell fast asleep. I didn't go again.

He lived on for another ten years, learning how to speak again – or so his parents believed. But his parents died before he did.

One day he was left unattended, watching a tape of his performance in *Diary of a Madman*. He fell forward and jammed a finger in his eye, which he was quite unable to remove. According to the nurses, he didn't learn any more after that.

He died in 1986.

6. *The Baby Elephant*

Keith Dewhurst

An opportunity for Bill Bryden and me to work together again fell into our laps almost as soon as we had finished *Pirates*. Early in 1971 Bill Gaskill directed a main-house production of *Man is Man*, Brecht's play about the British army in India. For the original 1926 production Brecht wrote a curtain-raiser called *The Baby Elephant*, which was performed in the theatre foyer. Gaskill proposed that Bryden should borrow the small-part players from the *Man is Man* company and stage *The Baby Elephant* in the Theatre Upstairs for the week preceding the main opening. Because Brecht's playlet was too short for a full evening, I was asked to devise a first half.

The meagre studio royalties had to go to the Brecht estate so I was never paid, but received instead a book of Cartier-Bresson photographs that was signed by everyone who worked on the show; one of the things that happens when we are hungry for work and success. Fortunately, I had just had a good financial run in television, which subsidised me through *Pirates*, *The Baby Elephant* and *Corunna!*, from late autumn 1970 to early summer 1971. That would probably not happen today, and decisions to mount plays would not be made in such an off-the-cuff manner. The writing life is much less viable than it was, another sign that a great epoch of drama is effectively closed.

Long before Bryden, Brecht compared the theatre to sports events, and *The Baby Elephant* concludes with a boxing match whose patrons are invited into the theatre to see if it is as exciting and illuminating as the fight; so it is appropriate that it was the first production on which Bill showed some characteristic magic. He remembered that the Theatre Upstairs, having been a restaurant run by Clement Freud, still had a liquor licence. Drinks could be served before, during and after the show. He turned the theatre into a café, with the audience at tables, and the cast became waiters, and what they performed was the cabaret.

And a hell of a cast they were, those small-part players who could leave their own rehearsals to be with us. They were two of the midfield, Derek Newark and Mark McManus, Dave Hill from the Ken Campbell *Road Show*, Tony Milner and two men who later became world famous: Bob Hoskins and Tim Curry. In the interval Georgia Brown sang, accompanied by Stanley Myers (who later wrote the music for the film *The Deerhunter*). There was a splendid moment when Lindsay Anderson complimented Georgia on her performance, and suggested that it might be even better if she turned it down a bit because she was in the Theatre Upstairs and not her usual haunt, the London Palladium.

My contribution to the cabaret was called *Brecht in '26* and was a mixture of full-frontal documentary information about Brecht, songs, and sketches around the theme of the British army in India, one of which involved the construction of the boxing ring. At the end of *The Baby Elephant* itself, a farce on the *Man is Man* theme of identity, a member of the audience was invited into the ring to go a round with our fairground bruiser, Derek Newark; a Health and Safety nightmare today, I imagine, but in 1971 there was always a volunteer, of whom the most celebrated was Roland Miller.

Roland was a performance artist (I once saw him strip off and masturbate at a lunchtime show at the old Angela Flowers Gallery in Poland Mews; nobody, he said, had been taking a blind bit of notice) whom Bill Gaskill had used to run acting exercises. Some of these took place in Sloane Square itself, observed by Gaskill and Roland from the roof of the theatre, and there were many silly stories: one actor was supposed to have been sent into the Square to kiss the first person he saw, only to be told to 'piss off' because he had happened upon another actor in another exercise.

Roland was cheeky and amusing, boppy on his feet, with a thin moustache and a lot of talk, and the actors never really liked him; so when it was realised that he was in the audience (how, really, could he have resisted it?), there was much excitement. Newark, a former professional soldier, growled like a dog on a chain. He'd knock Roland's head off. He'd finally nail the bastard. But will he get into the ring? wondered Dave Hill. If he won't we'll shame him, vowed Hoskins, in Cockney gangster mode.

When the time came the actors rushed at Roland and grabbed his arms. He resisted, in a token sort of a way, and then got up, serious but with smirking asides. When the bell rang they stormed out and for a second it seemed that Newark might indeed knock his head off. But they were both so nervy that neither landed a proper punch. Apart from the subtext, it was the dullest fight of the week. Newark later averred that he held back, and Roland claimed that his defence had been too nimble. What a pity that Brecht could not see it, we thought.

All in all, the week was a triumph, the most perfect promenade show, we realised years later, that we could ever have thought of. Michael Killanin was there again on the first night, at a table with Milton Shulman, who excelled himself in the *Evening Standard*. 'This may be all very well for the dwindling band of Bertolt Brecht supporters but for the rest of us it's pretty thin gruel.' But Helen Dawson of the *Observer*, later married to John Osborne, enjoyed the event so much that she is reputed to have spent the night asleep on the floor of the gents' lavatory. Other reviews were favourable, and Harold Hobson's was the best seat-selling notice that Bill or I ever received. The evening, it proclaimed, was crammed full of talent. Unfortunately, the review appeared after the show had closed, and a queue down the stairs and into Sloane Square had to be sent away. With the aid of the bar, it had been popular theatre *in excelsis*. It greatly advanced Bill Bryden's status, and made it easier for him to persuade the directors and the Literary Committee to commission *Corunna!*.

7. *Corunna!*

Writing for a company: Keith Dewhurst

My inspiration for *Corunna!* was a performance of Robert Burns's cantata *The Jolly Beggars* that I saw on TV in about 1954. I was interested in the Peninsular War against Napoleon and thought that it would suit a similar sort of play. About ten years later, Stella Richman, then the Head of Drama at ATV, asked me to think of an idea for a Christmas play and I wrote a synopsis of *Corunna!* which contained an outline story, some of the characters, and the words of a lullaby. Stella thought the idea 'too hard to sell upstairs', as she put it, and it lapsed. But it stayed with me, and Bill thought it ideal for our purpose. Early in 1971 I was commissioned to write it.

Corunna! (the exclamation mark was inserted by Bill Bryden) is set in Spain in 1808, when a British expeditionary force under Sir John Moore was sent to harass the invading French, but was forced to retreat in appalling weather to its transports at Corunna. Discipline breaks down, and the characters are a group of stragglers who fall behind, get drunk and rape a dead officer's widow. To mock her they clothe her in his uniform jacket, but as soon as she wears it she has the aura of command and leads them to safety. Years later the war is over and Lomax (Jack Shepherd) returns to Manchester, to find it transformed by the Industrial Revolution. He cannot remember the England he fought for. 'What was it like?' he cries out. 'It was all green, wasn't it?' The band answer him with 'The Lark in the Morning', a haunting evocation of a lost countryside.

Roger Croucher, who had taken over from Nicky Wright as director of the Theatre Upstairs, negotiated with Sandy Roberton of September Management, who handled the band, Steeleye Span. The five members of the band would be balanced by five actors. There would be a week at the Theatre

Upstairs followed by a tour, arranged by Sandy, of the kind of venues played by the band. So far as Bill and I were aware, it was plain sailing, and everyone liked the idea that the musicians would act and the actors sing. Ashley Hutchings, the band's bassist and front-man, would be our Narrator and embody our frontal energy. Shepherd, McManus and Glover would be in it, and we added Dave Hill and Juliet Aykroyd, whom Bill had taught at RADA, as we went along. For the first time I was writing for specific performers, which raises the questions: how does one go about that, and what sort of performers did we favour?

'Acting from your centre' was a phrase as important as 'laying down beside it', and what it means is that actors are most truthful when playing closest to their own character, social background and experience of life; 'type-casting' is the more familiar way to describe it. The number of actors who, like Alec Guinness, can truly make themselves different is very small indeed. What actors can do, if they are good, is exploit the facets and further reaches of their personalities and experience. If they had energy and bottle and their personalities displayed what Lindsay Anderson referred to as 'the grandeur of generality', they were what Bill Bryden wanted: the ball-winners in the middle of the park.

The trick of writing for a company is to read the actors' personalities, what lies beneath as well as on the surface. It is a curious fact that writers can often do this, and perceive the undercurrents in situations, without it making them any better at dealing with people in real life. Why writers, women as well as men, are like this I don't know, but they are. They see it and write it down, but it is in the other, made-up world.

It goes without saying that a cleverly assembled acting company will have a spectrum of human types, and the members of Steeleye certainly gave us more range, although we had to gauge their acting abilities as we went along. Ashley Hutchings, a hugely important figure in the history of modern folk music, was well nicknamed 'Tyger', and was a dangerous, bright-eyed and confident front-man. Using him as a Narrator enabled me to extend the convention and give other actors direct frontal speeches and contact with the audience. Martin Carthy had begun his career as an actor in musicals, which we knew, and is always effective down his centre. Maddy Prior was direct and spirited and Peter Knight a gangly amusing persona for whom I wrote the part of a fiddler who has his tongue cut out in an atrocity, so that when people speak to him he makes his instrument talk back. Tim Hart, alas, was not very sure of himself as an actor, and we had to do some cutting and rejigging.

The main hazard of writing a play with music soon revealed itself: until we heard the music in context we had no absolute idea of its effect. We knew that certain emotional things would occur, but not their effect upon the tempo and construction of the evening. Sometimes a song will stop everything stone dead, so it has to go. More frequently it will push awareness forwards, so that the dialogue scenes are superfluous or need alteration.

In *Corunna!*, as in the later plays, we knew some of the music from which we could select songs because the band had released their record *Please to See the King*, but often numbers would have to be decided upon in rehearsal and tunes put to lyrics I had written. Inevitably, the script was a bit loose, and we knew that we would have to fine-tune it in rehearsal, and this was a major factor in what became the unique collaborative nature of the plays, though the reality was never as collaborative as many of the participants imagined. When an optimum was reached Bill wanted suggestions to stop, and he was very clever at making people think that they had decided this moment for themselves, and at bouncing a decision off me or, later, his co-director Sebastian Graham-Jones. Unfortunately, as the years passed, success inflated both egos and petty niggles, and the work could be harder rather than easier. Sebastian left to find his own way, and eventually Bill's concentration wavered: the very process that had made our group extraordinary hastened its demise.

All that was in the future. In *Corunna!* we were dealing not with tediously known routines but with our inexperience of things like the politics within a band, the contrasting temperaments of actors and musicians, and the differences between musical and theatrical cultures. Music is so easy of access and yet so much bigger than its individual participants. The theatre is so difficult to make meaningful, and so dependent on individual choices and integrity. In our innocence we thought that the band was marvellous and were flattered that they had joined us. It was huge fun, and the idea of a play doing one-night-stand band gigs seemed to be a perfect definition of popular theatre.

A question that I always asked Bill before a new project was: 'What do the audience see when they first come into the theatre?' 'A concert,' he replied on this occasion, and our designer Di Seymour did him proud. At one end of the Theatre Upstairs was the bandstand with a map of Spain behind it. A narrow ramp (or traverse stage) jutted into the audience like a catwalk. The bar served drinks at one side. The costumes were excellent but there was no scenery and no props that could not be taken on and off by the actors themselves. It was very pure, stripped down for the tour, and contained early on a classic illustration of the sort of alienation effect that could be obtained by such use of the space.

'If I was you,' said Brian Glover's blustering Blacker-me-Boy to another soldier, 'I'd get the Sergeant off my back and crank that wind-machine.'

Which Peter Knight did, stepping up to the machine and turning the handle, whereupon Glover shivered, stamped his feet and said, 'Cold, isn't it?'

Rehearsals were in the Irish Club off Eaton Square, and Ashley missed many of them with tonsilitis: but, really, it was a big cat's sniffing out, I think. I wrote him a new long speech to cover the band retuning, and we chopped and changed various scenes and songs. One incident of the actual retreat saw soldiers throw casks of money containing their pay over a cliff, so that they could travel unencumbered, and the casks of money scene became a joke at which Dave Hill will break up to this day. We placed it here and placed it there, but it added nothing to the narrative and Tim Hart couldn't act it, so we threw it out.

Tim made up for his acting by coming up with ideas for

tunes, and Bill Gaskill watched a run and gave us excellent advice about cuts. What we ended up with was streamlined and effective. And it was in these days, of course, that Jack Shepherd stopped and cried out, 'Oh! I see! What we're doing is Impossible Plays!'

Why 'Impossible'?: Jack Shepherd

Pirates may have been the prototype of the Impossible Play but *Corunna!* was very definitely the thing itself. Impossible, in this instance, because the scope, the *vision* of the piece far exceeded the means at our disposal. Our task was to dramatise the circumstances of the British army's retreat, on a very limited budget, with the aid of a text, an electric folk band, five actors and a wind machine. It seemed an impossible sort of venture at the time and in its way as impossibly heroic as the retreat itself.

It was to be the first of many such endeavours, as it turned out, though none of us was aware of this at the time. I think we all – actors and musicians alike – regarded *Corunna!* as a one-off: an inspired venture into our history and our musical heritage, not a way of working with drama and with music, that was going to keep us occupied for another fifteen years.

A Comment: Keith Dewhurst

Bill Bryden and I never thought that *Corunna!* was a one-off. On the contrary. We realised even in rehearsals that we were on to a red-hot idea. The question was where and how would we be able to try it out again? Yet Jack's conviction that it was a one-off underlines my personal definition: an Impossible Play is one for which no one has been trained, and for which the conventions of the day make no provision. Bill Bryden's definition is that an Impossible Play is an idea that has no basis as a drama: no evident narrative; no dialogue. On that score I guess that *Lark Rise* would be impossible but not, perhaps, *Corunna!* itself, because it is based on a historical story.

The flower path: Jack Shepherd

It seems to me now that one of the most original aspects of the Impossible Plays was the way they used the space of the entire auditorium and not just the stage, in order to create the world of the play. It was a process that began with *Corunna!*.

A few years earlier, just after Bill's wedding to Deborah, I spent the day at their house. Lying on the coffee table was a book of photographs taken at a recording studio during the making of a Beatles LP (I forget which one). Late in the afternoon, when most of the guests had gone, Bill picked up the book and dropped it into my lap, already opened at a certain page: a black-and-white photograph of a deserted recording studio, the musicians having departed seconds before, only there by implication. What I saw were amps, a tangle of cables, microphones, bottles of Coke, cartons of coffee, smoke curling up from a cigarette abandoned in an ashtray. 'This . . .' Bill told me, without quite explaining how or why, 'this is the next production. This is the future. This is it.'

I could see in the photograph a *latent* energy, an excitement, an expectancy . . . but what I couldn't see then was a way in which this was going to relate to the creation of a play. At the time it seemed to be an expression of his love of popular culture and the stars of the day, and in a sense this was true. But what was at the heart of it, I now realise, was a desire to fuse popular music – the music of the people – folk music – with the spinning of a great yarn.

Corunna! became the production where Bill's vision, expressed in that glossy photograph, began to be realised. He made it clear from the beginning that one end of the theatre was going to be a bandstand, replete with all the para-phernalia of a rock concert: amps, leads, mikes, even ashtrays with smoke rising up from abandoned cigarettes. But as rehearsals progressed it became clear that if songs were going to be sung *and* scenes acted in this same space, it was going to get unbelievably cluttered. In no way was this space ever going to be transformed into the Spanish landscape of the Peninsular War.

The problem was finally solved when I remembered reading about the 'hanamichi' or the 'flower path', a device used in Japanese Kabuki theatre. The flower path is a walkway which connects the back of the auditorium to the stage, down which the protagonists make their entrances at key moments in the drama.

And so what we ended up with finally was a 'T'-shaped stage, with the bandstand at the top end. It formed a kind of roadway jutting out into the audience, along which the British army could retreat. All we needed was a few trestle tables and this arrangement could be constructed in virtually all the venues we were due to play in during our tour.

The alienation effect: Jack Shepherd

Corunna! was a very irreverent piece of writing, covering a wide sweep of history, with no respect for the 'unities' of time and space. It was drawn with a broad brush and in bright colours: a collage of songs, dramatic scenes, poetry and the most surprising 'alienation' effects designed to shake the audience out of their *belief*, their *involvement* in the narrative of the play and to nudge them towards an objective understanding, a *revelation* of the play's message.

Brecht used this device to make the politics of his plays more important than the human drama that was being acted out in his narratives, but I've never believed it possible for an actor to create an alienation effect within the framework of his or her performance. All you can ever do is use your imagination, believe in what you're doing and try to tell the truth. Anything else looks like bad acting. If there's any kind of gap between what the actor is saying and what they are feeling inside, they're usually said to be 'phoning it in'. Or 'laying down beside it', as Bill used to say. Or worse, they become a cipher, a caricature, a propagandist's mouthpiece.

Alienation effects *within the text*, however, are a different thing altogether. Keith's play was littered with them, placed like booby traps every few miles or so on our journey down the road to Corunna, designed to remind the audience that they were watching a play, and to discourage them from taking a romantic view of our history. When the French Cavalry galloped into action, they were played by actors in huge plumed three-cornered hats, riding hobby horses, shouting nonsensical French and singing the Marseillaise: 'Nous sommes nous sommes the Lords of Life . . .' About halfway through, Martin Carthy and I suddenly broke away from the traditional version and started out on a 'scat' version of the tune, snapping our fingers and singing in syncopated style, '*Shap n' doo shap-shap n'dooyah . . . oooh!*', instead of the inspiring words of the anthem of revolutionary France.

It was a silly idea really and not consciously xenophobic. Its intention was to debunk the notion of glory in war, a device to pull the audience out of their involvement in the narrative, to entertain them and make them think.

The alienation effect I have always found the most effective is when the actor suddenly breaks out of the convention of the scene and addresses the audience directly. I had such a moment in *Corunna!* very near the end of the play, when my character, having survived the war, returns to his home town in Lancashire, only to find that the houses in the street where he once lived have been pulled down and a large warehouse constructed in their place.

What followed was an angry confrontation with the warehouse owner, played by Dave Hill. I can't remember much of what I said to him. All that remains in my memory is the character's bitterness, his rage and his sense of injustice at the social changes that had taken place in his absence. 'It was all green, wasn't it, this England that we fought for?' The last part of the speech was delivered directly to the audience. (In Manchester – the author's birthplace – it was more of a harangue.)

This was to stop the audience from losing themselves in the pathos of the event, and to make them realise that this was the moment when the Industrial Revolution began in earnest, and that the changes it wrought would reach far into the future.

And to remind them finally that, in 1970, we as a country were still suffering, socially and politically, from the effects of this revolution.

A Comment: Keith Dewhurst

What seems to me to be important from a writing point of view, here, is that Jack's entire closing speech could be said to be directed at the owner of the warehouse or at imagined passers-by in the street. It was realistic. He was able to address the audience, and the band and their front-man who could reply, because of our deployment of the energy of a band concert. The trick, I suppose, was to give him dialogue that was heightened but not so much as to weaken belief.

Be that as it may, my best memories of the acting in *Corunna!*, apart from full exposure to Brian Glover's serio-comic personality, and the sheer heroism of Mark McManus as Sir John Moore, concern Jack himself. There was an old upright piano in the Theatre Upstairs on which he would give tea-break bursts of a mock blues: 'I got wanker's doom! Yeah! yeah!' And there were his ad libs. At the last performance of all he interrupted his closing speech to shout 'Bastard!' at a man creeping out to the loo, and at one performance he memorably responded to Dave Hill. As the French General Colbert, Dave had to explain his revolutionary principles to the audience, and at the same time be unable to resist attempting to make love to various female spectators. He had to be called back to the play by the Narrator. Alienation indeed! One night Dave wobbled, and as he struggled for his lines he banged his despairing fists against his tricorn hat. 'Pourquoi frappez-vous votre chapeau, mon Général?' cried Jack, ever ready, which did little to restore Dave's morale. Actors in Bill's companies were competitive and could be comically savage where mistakes were concerned. To lose your bottle was the biggest sin of all.

Corunna! on tour: Keith Dewhurst

The *Corunna!* tour was exhausting but extraordinary. We travelled in a bus with the costumes on a rail and minimum staff: Di Seymour, Bill's wife Deborah, who did the costumes, stage manager Sally Crocker, the band's roadie Dennis Jordan and their sound man Gordon Grahame. Gordon was hirsute, and often to be discovered in a yoga posture or standing on his head. At Kent University and Harrogate we played theatres, one with an apron stage and the other a proscenium. The Hampstead Country Club was a dingy rock venue where we toiled to make an acting space, and in the Student Unions at Southampton and Manchester we dragged refectory tables to make our bandstand and traverse. At the Fairfield Hall, Croydon, we played on the orchestra stand, and the Concert Room at the St George's Hall, Liverpool, was in effect a theatre in the round, a marbled Victorian gem, with statues on which Di Seymour placed sans-culottes hats and rosettes. Bill's energy in restaging the show for each venue was indefatigable.

On the way to Canterbury, Jack Shepherd and I were diverted to a local radio station where the interviewer asked if the band had learned how to be actors. 'No,' said Jack, 'but they've begun to learn how to rehearse.' At the universities audiences were huge. Elsewhere there had been little or no publicity and they were small, except that we played two nights in Liverpool and on the second word-of-mouth filled the place.

At Manchester University, the last show and I think the most powerful, I split my trousers clambering over a bench and went backstage. Deborah Bryden said, 'Take them off and I'll mend them,' so I stood there in half a dark suit and the cast dashed around me. Afterwards none of them could remember me trouserless, which speaks little for my legs but a lot for their concentration.

The mysteries of the wrestlers' hotel: Jack Shepherd

The tour of *Corunna!* didn't fit the usual pattern; it was little more than a succession of gigs at a series of different venues throughout the country: familiar territory to the musicians in the company and a little less so to the actors. We stayed overnight in Harrogate and Liverpool, but most of the gigs were one-night stands. At the Fairfield Hall, Croydon, we had to speak into microphones to be heard at all. It was a shambles. Only the music survived. Looked at in football terms, we rated most of these gigs as a win away from home: 3–1 or even 4–0. But Croydon was a home defeat. We blamed the pitch, but there were far too many goals conceded.

We'd set off early in the morning, put up the stage when we arrived, do the sound-check, rehearse whatever needed rehearsing, perform the play in the evening and be back in London in the early hours.

The coach journeys home have stayed in my mind: long conversations with Martin Carthy, learning about the history of our music, Pete Knight's impromptu fiddle playing, and the band's a cappella singing, always bang in tune and singing for the sheer joy of it. One of their sea shanties still lives in my memory. A slow chant with deep discordant harmonies. 'Ranzo!' sings the leader. 'Go down you blood-red roses!' comes the groaning response, as the sailors haul on heavy ropes. 'Go down you pinks and posies!' Almost certainly it was an allusion to the lash marks on their backs. When I first heard this music, my hair stood up on end. I knew it was for me. Dave Hill and I would invariably find ourselves drawn into it, Dave singing lustily in a basso profundo. The only one of us, in fact, whom I don't remember joining in was Mark McManus. Mark would invariably be sitting happily on his own, smiling, his face shining like a boxing glove – a red boxing glove – with all the whisky he'd been drinking.

Mark's gift was for reading poetry. Near the end of the play, he would recite 'The Burial of Sir John Moore'. It was something he was really good at. He didn't emote or in any sense act it out. Nor was it 'sung' in that curious way that poets adopt – Liverpool poets particularly – when they declaim their own verse. He just said it, pure and simple.

> Not a drum was heard. Not a funeral note,
> As his corse to the ramparts we carried.

The lines came from so deep within, you couldn't even guess at what was motivating him.

Bill was always exhausted after the performances, fast asleep next to his wife Deborah, his face pressed against the window of the coach, crushed with fatigue, looking for all the world like 'Tollund man' – the Iron Age man sacrificed in a Danish peat bog, at least a thousand years ago.

Keith would be talking football as often as not; Dave Hill would be at the back, always with a supply of beer; Brian would be chatting up Sally Crocker, the stage manager; I'd be talking to Maddy Prior; and Tim Hart would be deep in conversation with Juliet Aykroyd. Juliet was the romantic lead, playing the part of an abandoned officer's wife, raped by British soldiers. Juliet was very beautiful, but she didn't later become a member of the Company. (Very few women did.) And then of course there was the sound guy, Gordon Grahame, who had a cracked larynx and could sing in harmony with himself.

Brian Glover was always first off the bus when we arrived back in London in the early hours. He spent the night at 'Martinos', as often as not, the legendary wrestlers' hotel. All we ever saw of the place was the half-open door, but if Brian's wrestling stories were anything to go by, he was entering another dimension, through a magic door that would take him into a world where the rules all the rest us lived by no longer applied.

There was a moment in *Corunna!* when I very briefly wrestled with Brian, during a fight between my character, Lomax, and Brian's character, the magnificently named Blacker-me-Boy. It was merely a squabble in the ranks. In the course of the rehearsals, Brian was persuaded to add a few wrestling moves so he suggested I attempt a 'Monkey Climb'.

Now, in a 'Monkey Climb' the aggressor leaps feet first into the air, wraps his ankles around his opponent's throat and hurls him to the canvas. I swallowed hard and said I would give it a try. But no sooner had I launched myself into the air, feet first, in the general direction of Brian's chin, than he seized me powerfully by the ankles and held me upside-down for the rest of the scene.

Brian was justly celebrated for his wrestling stories. They were funny usually, sometimes frightening and very, very rude. He could have written the most scabrous and hilarious play about the wrestling game but, to his everlasting credit, he wasn't prepared to betray any of his friends. Or maybe it was simply that he feared reprisals; ancient wrestlers who'd heard he'd written a play about them, queueing up at his doorway, armed with monkey wrenches and baseball bats.

A *Corunna!* summary: Keith Dewhurst

During *The Baby Elephant*, Bill and I had come up with the idea of the float, a notional sum of money held by one or the other of us that would enable us to buy lots of drinks without feeling guilty. During *Corunna!* it came into its own, notably when we took a bottle of whisky and two paper cups into a box at the Theatre Royal, Harrogate, and it was to carry us through many subsequent adventures. (It also came in handy when our Theatre Upstairs ASM Michael Coveney ran out of cash, and I lent him ten shillings until the end of the week. Michael later became a major theatre critic, and hardly if ever gave us an unenthusiastic review. If there is a connection here, the reader must dare to make it.)

Corunna! was reviewed in both the musical and national press. Thirty years later, the clippings confirm that there was a clear age division: younger reviewers were friendly if not very analytical, older ones not so much hostile as puzzled. To us the electric folk music spoke poetically of England's past and traditions; to them it meant little. Harold Hobson, the old doyen of theatre critics, came from a more lively angle, and challenged the play's central argument that the Industrial Revolution was as powerful an agent of change as the French Revolution, and that the war against Napoleon, presented as a stand against tyranny, was also a class struggle in which English aristocrats preserved their status. To us these were important points of reference. The war against Napoleon had been widely compared by popular historians to that against Hitler, and to re-examine it was to respond to the social changes begun during the Second World War: a redefinition of England. Was that not what the new intellectual classes attempted? Harold Hobson was on one side and we were on another, but at least he saw where we were coming from. All too often critics made the easy decision to regard our work as entertaining and well-acted nostalgia, and missed the subtext.

Soon after the tour it emerged that the producer, Michael White, wanted to transfer the show, and had secured the Young Vic, which Bill Gaskill thought the best place for it. Then there was a delay, and then it became evident that there was trouble with the band. Roger Croucher invited them to tea and cakes and they all appeared except Ashley. Sandy Roberton was not invited and was furious with us; but it showed the limits of his power, and the murkiness of band politics, because the transfer never happened. They all wanted to do it except Ashley. A rift had appeared, and in October the band broke up.

How a three-month transfer, which could have accommodated the band's other commitments, would have affected future awareness of our work it is difficult to say, but it could not have done us any harm. *Corunna!* has never been performed since, and was not published until twenty-odd years later.

8. The Royal Court: Publicity and Personalities

Keith Dewhurst

Our run of luck at the Court, and the fact that we had turned three different opportunities to our advantage, moved Bill up the ladder, and in the summer of 1971 he returned to Scotland as an associate director of the Royal Lyceum Theatre, Edinburgh, where everything blossomed and we were able to make our next stab at popular theatre. I was in London, meanwhile, and until Gaskill left the Court in 1972 attended the weekly publicity meetings, which was like having a bit-part in a sitcom. I remember one meeting that turned into a discussion of whether or not *The Winter's Tale* was a good play, opinion being divided. And there was always textbook catty dialogue:

GASKILL: Oh, I thought your assistant was coming!
PAGE: No. He sent me instead.

Helen Montague would guffaw, Gaskill thought the whole thing vainglorious, the publicist Gloria Taylor could be a straight-faced provocateuse, Roger Croucher would wear an anarchic grin, and Lindsay Anderson, exasperated at the lot of us, had his work cut out to keep the class in order. He was a brilliant lateral thinker where publicity was concerned, and at the Cottesloe Bill and I pinched his ideas.

I wrote a long rehearsal piece about Lindsay's production of David Storey's *The Changing Room* for the *Guardian*. The cast did rugby training and as Storey drove me and Brian Glover to the playing field the following conversation ensued:

STOREY: Been doing anything, Brian?
GLOVER: Wrestling tour.
STOREY: Where?
GLOVER: Persia.
STOREY: Oh.
GLOVER: We saw one thing that not many have.
STOREY: What's that?
GLOVER: Public execution.

As a quid pro quo, or a piece of lateral casting, Lindsay asked me to record the voice on the play's dressing-room tannoy, although I don't think he liked my performance. On the other hand, he didn't dump me, not even for the West End transfer.

That autumn I went to Paris and saw Ariane Mnouchkine's *1789* at the Cartoucherie de Vincennes, which was a splendid experience. It is a measure of the English theatre's isolation that it was the first show of this kind that I saw, although Bill had seen Ronconi's *Orlando Furioso* at an Edinburgh Festival. Ronconi had used platforms, although he tried many other innovations in his factory space at Prato, and *1789* was partly on platforms and partly promenade. It contained a unique promenade moment when an Equerry cried 'Laissez passer!' and the audience parted to allow Louis and Marie Antoinette to return from Varennes.

Naturally I was on the phone to Bill about this, as I was about *The Speakers*, the promenade production Gaskill directed with Max Stafford-Clark after Bill left the Court. This was a small show created for studio spaces, and I wrote another rehearsal piece for the *Guardian*. Its promenade rationale was that it was set at Speakers' Corner, and we were the crowd, although some scenes were set with minimal furniture in the characters' homes. It had evolved out of rehearsal and what was great about it was the impact of the acting in the promenade, the nearness of the energy. At *1789* I had been on the bleacher-type seats, although actors did come up the aisles, to rally us for the storming of the Bastille. So the other great lesson of *The Speakers* was that, although the piece was not very long, one could stand and wander around very happily.

It was Lindsay Anderson's idea around this time that I should be commissioned by the Court to write an official history, and Helen Montague urged me at once to take a large advance and not worry about a contract. I pushed for neither, although I did some preliminary interviews and conversations, because in my heart of hearts I don't think I was ever convinced that one could give the feel of the place so close to the events. There they were, ambitious, vain, conniving and altruistic, each bad-mouthing the others in private and defending them in public, setting traps by asking one's opinions about such and such a writer, who was supposed to be a hero but was regarded by the questioner with contempt. Each was convinced that he alone was the true heir of George Devine. The Court was trumpeted as a writers' theatre yet all the decisions were made by directors from entirely personal points of view, and more than once productions that everyone hated were brought in from outside because of a desire to stymie one close colleague or another. All big subsidised houses are the same, of course; what made the Court unique was that politicking was enmeshed with enormous integrity and talent.

My tentative solution was a book of interviews in the manner of Truffaut's about Hitchcock. I floated this idea with Lindsay and a cloud passed across his face. He realised that other views would have to be expressed, and remembered that I was a Bill Gaskill man after all. Pretty soon he arranged for Anthony Page to take me to lunch and dustbin the whole idea. For years afterwards Helen Montague would say, 'What did I tell you? You should have taken the advance.'

A subtextual irony is that it was a speech Lindsay made at George Devine's memorial service that inspired Bill Gaskill to set aside thoughts of a return to the National, and apply for the directorship of the Court. There was this ludicrous side to many of Lindsay's experiences, I suspect. He once sent me a stinging 'Be Fair!' postcard after something I wrote in the

Guardian, but when I deployed my arguments in reply sent another postcard that said, 'Sorry to turn tail in this controversy!' He was a magnificent personality but how fine an artist he was I am not sure.

Bill Bryden has often said to me that, in a way, the Royal Court's critical faculty outweighed its creativity, and Lindsay exemplified that tendency. He was meticulous, but his portraits of working men were not as convincing as those by Peter Gill or Bill Bryden, and that is not a slur upon David Storey who wrote the scripts. Neither was Lindsay's comedy as glorious as Gaskill's, nor his presentation of emotion as unswerving. Lindsay was always present, somehow, as he is in the films, telling you how you weren't looking hard enough to see the truth. As the director Michael Rudman is supposed to have said when peering through the train window at Wakefield: 'The North of England – directed by Lindsay Anderson.' Lindsay was still, of course, twice as good as most of his detractors.

One of his arguments was very true: that a theatre doing original work must, when it can, get its productions into the mainstream, because if the mainstream is not stiffened in this way it will get worse and not better, and risky work will be pushed further to the margins. Bill Gaskill did not care about what he would call commercial success. He never trimmed a production to make its transfer more likely, even when that might have brought a political benefit: Edward Bond's *The Sea*, the most accessible play by the Court's most extreme writer, being a case in point. A tide turned after that, I always thought.

Gaskill's scene changes could be a source of hilarity among the Court assistants, and Bill Bryden has always claimed that there was one in *Man is Man* during which he and Nicky Wright repaired to the bar for a couple of drinks; but that is the sort of apocryphal tale that was told at the time, and my only experience of actually working with Gaskill, when we were elderly and did *Black Snow* at the Cottesloe, is that what he did was seamless and brought joy to the audience. I call him 'The Admiral', half in amused memory of when he and Paul

Freeman and Ken Cranham sank their holiday narrow boat in Shipley Lock (sitting gloomily in the pub afterwards, Gaskill looked at the local inhabitants surrounding them; 'You have to love people very much to be a socialist, don't you?' he said), and half because, despite everything, there he has always been on the quarter-deck, half austere and half chuckling, disdainful of the sharpshooters, and steering the fleet at the heart of its philistine foes.

Tony Richardson: 'Can No One Clear the Peacock Shit off this Terrace?': Keith Dewhurst

Tony Richardson and Bill Gaskill knew each other from school-days. When Richardson broke away from the wartime subsidised Bradford Civic Theatre to start what he called Young Theatre, Gaskill needed a role and the modern theatre's system of the director and his promising assistant was invented there and then. When the time came for the assistant to direct his own show, the money ran short. Richardson said that his uncle was putting up for the council, and that if they distributed his leaflets he might help them out.

'Wait a minute,' said Gaskill. 'Your uncle's Conservative and we're Labour.'

Back came the pattern-setting reply: 'Do you want the show to go on or not?'

Early in 1973, in the trough of his career, Richardson asked me to work with him on the script of the movie *Dead Cert*, and although I was fired by the American studio along the way, I had a vivid time at his house in the South of France. To the Court generation of Bryden and Robert Kidd, Richardson was a hero because he had triumphed commercially, and won an Oscar, by doing the proper work. He had shown that popular theatre's faith in the audience could be justified. Not that by the time I met him he cared, particularly. He was more into life. Richardson knew that you could do what you wanted, and that God would not say a word. He was fatalistic, elusive (which is what he accused me of being), unsentimental, untrustworthy and very kind. He lived in the moment, a gift of which the flip-side was his boredom. For example, we spent one evening combing his record collection. 'Is Mozart boring?' asked Tony. He was. We threw him on the open fire.

After lunch one day we had coffee on what had been an olive-drying floor and he called up to his assistant Will Chandleigh: 'Will, Will, can no one clear the peacock shit off this terrace?'

Once he asked me: 'Have you ever been to Los Angeles?'
   'No,' I said.
   'You'll love it,' he said. 'It's very like Bradford.'
   Which, of course, when we consider the provincial, smug, energetic, money-equals-respectability city of Tony's youth, it is; although it takes someone like him to notice it.

Part Two:

Scotland

9. *Willie Rough*

Keith Dewhurst

While I was in London and the South of France, Bill Bryden
forged ahead in Scotland. Throughout his time at the Royal
Court he had been writing a play, *Willie Rough*, and Sean
Connery had expressed strong interest in doing it as a Sunday-
night performance. But the script was extremely long and
nothing came of it. A copy had been sent to the Scottish
Actors' Company, a subsidised group formed to tour modern
classics such as Ibsen in what their founder Andrew
Cruickshank called 'educated Scots'. Cruickshank's associate
Roddy McMillan liked the play, and as a result of Bill's rise in
status and some smart negotiating by Clive Perry, the artistic
director of the Edinburgh Theatres Trust, a deal was done
whereby Bill would have an associate's job at the Lyceum,
where interested members of the Scottish Actors would form
the nucleus of a company. The incumbent associate, Richard
Eyre, was about to leave to take over Nottingham Rep. The
company would do an October-to-March season, there would
be a summer show and a few incoming tours, and, it was
hoped, a show at the Edinburgh Festival. Clive Perry,
ingenious, genial and generous, oversaw both this and a more
showbusiness-orientated programme at the King's Theatre,
with the lightest of sure touches.

In the first autumn season in 1971, Bill directed Jack
Shepherd in *The Misanthrope*, a play about Vietnam in the
studio, and *The Burning*, a big costume piece by Stewart Conn,
a poet who ran BBC Radio Drama in Scotland. This contained
what was, I believe, Scotland's first nude appearance by an
actress.

To understand the impact made by *Willie Rough* when it was

staged in early 1972, we must remember that Scotland, like other countries that were part of the British Empire, suffered from what Australians call the 'cultural cringe'. That is to say, the artistic forms and subjects of the English rulers were considered to be superior to indigenous material. Scotland had some radio plays, it is true, and there were local TV sitcoms. There was a tradition of revue-type summer entertainment and excellent pantomimes, but even James Bridie, when he founded the Glasgow Citizens' Theatre in the 1930s, had not really written about Scotland, and new plays tended to be nostalgic accounts of Bonnie Prince Charlie or Mary, Queen of Scots.

By 1972 the Glasgow Citizens was run by the most design-led management of recent times, and did many European plays. The King's in Edinburgh was a general touring house, the Traverse what might be called international fringe, and the Lyceum a good rep. *Willie Rough* burst upon this scene like a tornado.

Set on the Red Clyde in 1915, and profoundly working-class realist, *Willie Rough* loosely dramatised the story of Bill's grandfather and the opposing sides, represented by the protagonists, of Bill's own nature: the dreamer and the selfish opportunist. It was serious and funny and about ordinary Scots, it was the first time that modern notions of high-energy, down-the-centre ensemble acting hit the Scottish stage, and it was Scotland's first Royal Court-style production with white light, meticulous costumes and absolute attention to the text. It triumphed in Edinburgh and Glasgow, was kept in the repertoire, visited London, and led Peter Hall to ask Bill what play he would like to direct at the National Theatre. Without *Willie Rough* the Traverse would not have become a theatre for indigenous writing as soon as it did, and many horizons would have been narrower. Virtually overnight, Bill had invented the modern Scottish theatre.

10. *The Misanthrope*

Jack Shepherd

A few weeks after *Corunna!* ended, I went to the Lyceum Edinburgh to be in Richard Eyre's Festival production of James Hogg's *The Justified Sinner*. Not for the last time, I was playing the devil. I then stayed on to play the protagonist in Bill Bryden's ill-fated production of *The Misanthrope*, during the autumn; ill-fated because Marianne Faithfull had to be replaced about three days before the opening night. Ann Balfour took over the part, knew every line by the time we opened and gave an astonishingly good account of herself as Célimène, the archetypal flirt.

My own performance was somewhat controversial. Bill had loaned me a book called 'From Poquelin to Chaplin' and we decided to try and make the part really funny.

I'd learned from John Blatchley at the Drama Centre that there had been a decision taken at some point, by the French, who are inclined to systematise everything, that there are only seven ways of making people laugh. The list is as follows:

1. Mistaken identity (*Twelfth Night*)
2. Mimicry (Rory Bremner)
3. Physical impediments (Feydeau)
4. Knavery (Sergeant Bilko)
5. Wit (Oscar Wilde)
6. Falls and blows (Chaplin)
7. Buffoonery (Tommy Cooper)

Categories 3 and 7 are a little politically incorrect for this present day and age.

It was the category of 'Falls and blows' that I decided to incorporate into my performance as Alceste. He was, after all, in a fury about everything, pretty much all of the time. So whenever I had a scene with my long-suffering servant, I didn't waste an opportunity of releasing my frustration by kicking him up the backside, in a succession of increasingly unsuspected ways.

It *was* very funny, I have to say, but it didn't really win me any friends. Richard Eyre clearly didn't approve. I tried to explain my reasons for behaving with such quirky violence, but he wasn't convinced. 'But there's *another* side to the play,' he countered. 'There's a sense in which it's like a Dresden ornament. Didn't you ever consider that?' I shook my head. I truly hadn't.

Christopher Hampton, on the other hand, did at least find it very funny. I think the academic in him was probably quite shocked, but the rest of him found it hilarious. He didn't say anything, when he came backstage afterwards, he just looked at me and laughed.

11. Life at the Lyceum

The acting company: Keith Dewhurst

Bill's dream of a permanent theatre company that would establish a style was inspired by what he had read about the Moscow Art Theatre and New York's Theatre Guild, by seeing John Ford's actors on the screen, and by direct experience of Gaskill's 1967 Royal Court ensemble. His notion of the acting midfield as the bedrock of a company, he told me in 2004, came at the onset of his career, when he was an observer on Peter Hall's *Wars of the Roses* at the RSC. He realised, he said, that 'all the barons were played by these strong forty-year-old actors'. At the Royal Lyceum he was able to put his ideas to the test, and his Scottish company, with which I was lucky to work, had a midfield of Fulton Mackay, famous on TV, John Grieve, Joe Brady of *Z Cars* and Roddy McMillan. A compelling, troubled, rugged personality, McMillan was a marvellous actor, a competent playwright and a rock of integrity. He was the guarantor, somehow, from the 1940s to the 1970s, of the dream that Scots theatre would find a voice, and in *Willie Rough* it did.

One could argue that when such a midfield was fronted by genuine leads like John Cairney, Rikki Fulton and Ian Bannen, and had in James Grant an elusive but fascinating fourth striker, Bill's Scottish team was better than the one he assembled in England. To make ends meet, actors in Scotland did more varied work than those in England, and it was easier for them to be actors but not middle class. The result was that there was a wide range of types and skills. There were attractive juvenile men in Paul Young and David Rintoul, talented girls like Morag Hood and Vivien Heilbron, and solid character women; and eventually Bill strengthened the squad with Irish imports, character men like Godfrey Quigley, Niall

Toibin and Jimmy Devlin, who were as good as anyone in Britain.

In 1973 he directed *The Aquarium*, another play by Stewart Conn, Roddy McMillan's *The Bevellers*, an interesting play about the workplace, which had a London season, and the classic *Three Estaites* in an arena production at the Edinburgh Festival. In 1974 came his own play *Benny Lynch*, about the boxer, at the first night of which Lynch's widow hit him over the head with her handbag, and at the Edinburgh Festival John Morris's *How Mad Tulloch was Taken Away*. Punctuating this work I wrote two summer projects in which we continued our partnership.

Kidnapped: Keith Dewhurst

Robert Louis Stevenson's *Kidnapped* and its sequel *Catriona* together make the best political narrative in our fiction. They present profound moral choices and a clash of civilisations, as tribal society's Jacobite Rebellion is crushed by England's capitalistic modern state. The characters are vivid, Stevenson's dialogue sparkles, and the adventures are famous: ideal material for a popular theatre summer show, for which the re-formed Steeleye Span agreed to do the music. They were managed now by Joe Lustig, and all business went through him, so that there were no unexpected pitfalls.

Joe was a friend of Mel Brooks and John Cassavetes, a glorious Brooklyn Jewish Norman Mailer lookalike who had been a New York theatre press agent. British bands that he managed included Jethro Tull and the Chieftains, and at the end of his days he made TV documentaries, most notably, if improbably, a piece which dramatised the attack by Dr Leavis upon C. P. Snow. Decades after *Kidnapped*, Joe distributed a Cassavetes film and invited me to a screening. We stood in the foyer of the Curzon, Mayfair, and I asked him what was the difference between distributing a film and managing a band. 'A film', he replied, 'doesn't call you in the middle of the night to complain about the hotel room.' That was our man, and very supportive he was. He brought singer Loudon Wainwright III to the first night of *Kidnapped* and they sat in a box like Staten Island Ferry royalty.

The band had Maddy singing, Rick Kemp on bass, Peter Knight, his friend Bob Johnston on guitars, and Tim Hart. They played sailors and soldiers and so on but did not act roles as such. They had no suitable ready-made repertoire, so most of their rehearsal time was spent assembling the music. There were various Jacobite songs, which can be heard on the album *Parcel of Rogues*, and Tim came up with excellent tunes. They had comical arguments among themselves, kicking their instrument cases and storming out of rehearsal. Their sound was less haunting but more commercial, perhaps, than that of the old band, and later Joe guided them to US tours, the hit parade, and financial success. (I hear Maddy's voice deprecating this last as I write it.)

Clive Perry knew how to look after people, and the theatre rented me a flat in Edinburgh's Dean Village. Bill and Deborah lived just up the hill and one morning, a week or so into rehearsals, I walked up for breakfast with them and there at the table was Rikki Fulton, a presence both comical and commanding. He was a huge star in Scotland, and had agreed to take over two smallish roles from an actor who had gone into hospital with alcohol poisoning. (We were in Scotland, after all.) Rikki's world was comedy and pantomime but he was a splendid straight actor. As James More Macgregor, Catriona's impoverished and treacherous father, he made his entrance as a prisoner under escort, on the top to bottom corner diagonal. His rapid, skulking walk, and his shame when he passed Catriona, will stay in my mind for ever; one of those moments from a master of the space.

Before beginning the writing I asked Bill what the audience should see when they came in and he said the Battle of Culloden, which is what we did, with smoke, a mound of corpses and a survivor engaging the audience in Gaelic (written phonetically on the inside of his shield). Then Colin Campbell of Glenure appeared, saying that the whole thing was a sham, the bodies mere stage-dummies and the

Highlanders whining barbarians. This was very effective alienation and historical explanation. It was also unwieldy, because we had to start the play again, with our hero David Balfour.

Bill contrived great showbiz moments, such as at the end of the first half when David arrives in Edinburgh. The dock doors opened at the back of the stage to show the real Edinburgh Castle in all its floodlit glory (round of applause). During a game of golf at the start of the second half, the stage trap opened for the actors to putt into (another round of applause). To condense the action I had a character announce that the evening would conclude in the form of a concert by Steeleye Span, and the actors sat on a row of chairs and played snippets of plot and music out front. This was a delightful alienation effect, though an experiment earlier in the play – an attempt to have sections of the narrative told in song – failed.

The story encompassed many locations and the set comprised scaffolding, amplifiers and instrument stands. The Lyceum is a beautiful proscenium theatre but, despite many bold and effective scenes, I think both Bill and I realised that *Kidnapped* did not sit easily therein. The reasons for this went to the heart of what we were trying to do and gave us much food for thought and discussion. Could the sort of effect we wanted be created at all within the proscenium, and if not, why not? What sort of space did we need, and how would we have to employ it?

The integrity of the space: Keith Dewhurst

Once, during my marginal career as a presenter of TV arts programmes, I interviewed the classical harpsichordist Gustav Leonhart, and asked him why, in his opinion, the harpsichord had been superseded by the piano. 'Because', he replied, 'people wanted a different sound.'

Bill Bryden showing Jack Shepherd a photo of an empty recording studio, and saying that he wanted a play to be like that, is a classic expression of a similar desire; so was Bertolt

Brecht's attempt in the 1920s to write a play about the workings of the Chicago wheat market, which he abandoned because he could not dramatise the impersonal. One could, of course, write a play about a person who worked in the wheat market, and that is how in effect a lot of trendy-left writers in British theatre and television operated: naturalistically, with characters who delivered chunks of moralising. But Brecht would say that this missed his point.

Brecht's point was that the impersonal sum total of things was precisely what he knew to be important. He wanted to convey the *zeitgeist* and the hidden reasons that naturalism finds hard to encompass. History, politics and economics were to him part of someone's life and identity, whether they knew it or not. His insight was Marxist, but could just as well have been Freudian or Darwinian, because the same awareness of buried information applies, and the same desire to extend the suspension of disbelief.

The covenant with the audience that underpins the suspension of disbelief has always involved spatial and scenic integrity. In the Elizabethan theatre, for example, the scenery was the structure of the theatre itself, and a change of location was indicated when one group of actors went off and another came on. The stage jutted into the audience and there were conventions of frontal energy: a chorus, soliloquies and asides.

In the theatre of the nineteenth century, when the Edinburgh Lyceum was built, the proscenium made a fourth wall, through which the audience watched actors supposedly unaware of their presence. Plays and productions reproduced the surface of life, even when in the work of the masters Ibsen and Chekhov it was highly manipulated. When the location had to change the curtain came down and the scenery was changed. Spatial and scenic integrity were preserved.

There were many attempts in the early twentieth century to go beyond naturalism. Diaghilev borrowed the styles of modern painting, and although expressionist theatre might have begun as a design concept, people soon applied its ideas to writing, with violently exaggerated characterisations, situations and juxtapositions. In much of his Berlin work, Brecht is an expressionist, and Eugene O'Neill's early plays attempted a fusion of expressionism and realism which, however powerful the ideas, has proved difficult to stage. England fell back upon Shakespeare and verse: think of Auden, Isherwood, Eliot and Fry at the highbrow end, and a prose romance like Gordon Daviot's *Richard of Bordeaux*, in which Gielgud had such a success, at the middlebrow. But the problems persisted. How do you keep changing the scenery? And if you don't, what sort of setting will represent different locations? This is the background to Michel Saint-Denis and his 'transformation of the space'. If the scenery couldn't do it, maybe the actors could.

The action in *Kidnapped* took place on ships, mountains, glens, prisons, elaborately furnished rooms and the sand dunes of Holland. What proscenium setting could possibly encompass all of these?

The Lyceum's designer, Geoffrey Scott, was very good, and the scaffolding was as practical an idea as anyone could have come up with at the time. But it was neither a fixture which, like the Elizabethan stage, could work for all plays, nor a representation of any location. It was like those devices employed by men more famous than we were: the ramps that John Bury built for Joan Littlewood and Peter Hall, or the box set in which Gaskill staged classics at the Royal Court. It was an attempt to fit a play written for one set of conventions into a theatre built for another. Of course, *Kidnapped was* written for the Lyceum, except that in my head it was looking for an empty space.

Bill's idea of the recording studio implied a notion that space equals function, and, like a photograph, that it should freeze a moment in time. It is no accident that Bill arranged for me to be given a book of photographs by Henri Cartier-Bresson for *The Baby Elephant*. The influence of what for convenience's sake we might call the Magnum school of photo-journalism, although its greatest days occurred before Magnum was formed, was huge. Photographs by Cartier-Bresson, Robert Capa, Alvarez Bravo, Walker Evans and the people who worked for Stefan Lorant on *Picture Post* and *Life*, which is where we saw them, of course, were images that showed what the popular epic theatre should look like: ordinary people as anonymous but monumental figures in history; actions caught in their most significant moments; the typical and its background; the rest of the world proceeding unawares. There is a lack of melodrama because the protagonists in even the highest dramas were feeling only what they felt, and were not aware of the photographer.

These things are why, when we came to do *Lark Rise*, images by the nineteenth-century rural photographer Peter Henry Emerson were used in promotional material, why Vietnam War photos influenced *Dispatches*, and why the photographer Nobby Clark was so important to our work.

In the 1930s and 1940s, theatre photographs were there to glamorise and glorify the actors. In his later work, Angus McBean sought to convey the flavour of a performance, an idea taken further when photos were not posed but taken on the hoof during the playing of a scene. Tony Armstrong-Jones, as he was then, was the early exponent of this phase, working for Anderson and Gaskill at the Royal Court, where John Haynes later also snapped excellent rehearsal photos. Nobby Clark took the idea further by photographing plays as though they were actual events: he catches the essence of something in exactly the way of the Magnum photographer. He shows not only the public, but also the creatives, what is going on. Michael Mayhew, who photographed the Cottesloe as a National Theatre staffman, was somewhere between Haynes and Nobby. And there was Brian Windsor, a friend of someone on the Cottesloe front-of-house team, and an amateur photographer who fell in love with *Lark Rise* and used an old Hasselblad with plates to make extraordinary sepia-tinted classical images. If what Nobby did was like Capa on a battlefield, Windsor was like a sculptor recollecting in great calm.

From a writing point of view, the photography reinforces what Stevenson learned from Sir Walter Scott, and was taken up by the French and Russian realists: the presentation of social structure through typical individuals. The world did not look like Hollywood films or a West End set: it looked more like a Walker Evans photograph.

The Miser: Keith Dewhurst

Bill proposed that our 1973 summer show at the Lyceum should be a Scots version of Molière's *The Miser* with Rikki Fulton in the lead. I paid a bilingual friend to do a literal translation and then transposed it into a Stevensonian idiom – not as difficult as it sounds. In all cases I kept the same number of lines as Molière, and as far as possible the same length of line and number of syllables. Molière's build-up is very deliberate, and a lot of his lines are not meant to be funny, but to lead you at the desired tempo to what is. We experimented with various notions, in particular a mirror at the back of the stage to reflect both cast and audience, but decided to play safe and respect the proscenium.

Bill did a graceful production, set in one room in Edinburgh's New Town in about 1790, and Rikki's performance was outstanding. The show was popular and in the autumn it was revamped by the assistant Peter Farago and sent out on tour.

Bill was rehearsing the *Three Estaites*, so Clive Perry flew me to the first night of *The Miser* in Aberdeen. His Majesty's Theatre is a marble and granite classic and as people poured in, I thought: if the rest of the tour's like this I'll be able to pay the school fees. Then Clive bounced up and the evening commenced. It was soporific. Laughs that have been foolproof for three hundred years did not happen. 'Come along!' said Clive at the interval. 'Drinks are ordered!' In the bar I said: 'Clive, what's happening?' 'For Aberdeen,' he replied, 'this is a riot.'

12. *The Magic Island*

Keith Dewhurst

Nineteen seventy-three was also the year in which I went to Australia to research a TV drama series, and met and fell in love with Alexandra Cann, who became my second wife. I went back and forth to Australia until early in 1974, just before Bill directed Wedekind's *Spring Awakening* for the National Theatre at the Old Vic, and a touring *Romeo and Juliet*, I was asked by Michael Simpson at the Birmingham Rep to do a Christmas show, and we came up with *The Magic Island*, a play with music about King Arthur.

We negotiated with Ashley Hutchings to provide a band, but he was put off by a meeting in a Hampstead pub to which I took my then agent Sheila Pickles. I think that what she most wanted was to satisfy her curiosity and meet Ashley, but he did not want to be pinned down and backed off. I asked Karl Dallas, the folk-rock expert at the *Melody Maker*, if he could suggest another band and he proposed Hedgehog Pie. They were delightful people with a strong Irish beat to the band, and an extremely talented singer-composer named Martin Jenkins. Their only album, *Hedgehog Pie*, contains two or three of the show's tunes.

The Birmingham Rep is a strange place. When you climb its auditorium's steep face you reach a point where you look down on the tops of the actors' heads, and during one performance I saw a nun, attempting to restrain the excitement among her charges, miss her step and tumble about fifteen feet down the escarpment. The huge stage is not exactly a proscenium but not an apron either, although it is open enough to have suited the play's frontal energy and changes of location. The set by Chris Dyer was a clever raked floor in the form of two Celtic circles – one for the band – and had a curved curtain at the back. It showed that even a small forestage could make the space non-specific and transformable.

Unfortunately, the casting was too provincial rep and underpowered, with the exception of Robert Peck who played Merlin but was nervous about the genre. In one way the script was a bit skimpy, but the best thing about it was the integration of the narrative and the music. I had absorbed a lot of lessons, and Birmingham was a good testing ground.

On all the shows we did, together or separately, Bill and I used music in the same way. We believed, as did Michael Simpson, that language is the hallmark of freedom, democracy and open debate. We had no faith in that moment when characters burst into song because they feel more than the words or the actions can express. Balderdash, we thought, language can express anything. So we used music not to take over from dialogue, but as a comment upon it: to add an emotional element that the characters could not themselves envisage. Songs about the characters were hardly ever sung by the characters themselves. When a character sang it was always what he or she would do as part of the action.

As for Hedgehog Pie, I met them here and there over the next few years, but like almost all folk bands they were swept away by punk, and never really had their due.

Late in the Birmingham rehearsals Alexandra and I went to Edinburgh for a night to see Bill's production of Eugene O'Neill's *The Iceman Cometh*, in which Ian Bannen headed an astounding cast. It was the best of all Bill's proscenium productions, and the first time, I think, that his work had the absolute assurance, the restrained power and sense of the rightness of everything that only a great director can command. By the time we returned again from Australia, in the spring of 1975, he was back living in London and an NT Associate.

Part Three:

The National Theatre

13. The Early Days of the NT

Watch It Come Down: Keith Dewhurst

No sooner had Bill Bryden and a lot of other people been engaged to work in the three theatres that made up the National than it was admitted that the building work on the South Bank was behind schedule. Almost two years passed before anything was staged there. In two years at Edinburgh, Bill had directed some fifteen productions and revivals. In his first two years as an NT Associate, he directed three. John Osborne's *Watch It Come Down* and J. M. Synge's *The Playboy of the Western World* (a very good account of the play fronted by Stephen Rea and Susan Fleetwood), premièred at the Old Vic. The ill-fated *Il Campiello* opened the Olivier Theatre.

Bill had the time to write *Old Movies*, a play about a Hollywood producer, and *Jesse James*, an epic film script about the western outlaw. In the same period I wrote *The Bomb in Brewery Street*, a play, researched on the ground, about the British army in Belfast, directed at the Sheffield Crucible by David Leland, and a children's TV series called *Boy Dominic*. I also went to Rome and Morocco to be the rewrite man on Franco Zeffirelli's television epic *Jesus of Nazareth*.

The Bomb in Brewery Street is a strong and amusing piece but it was damned with faint praise because it is not overtly political, although I always thought that when the soldiers (as they did) call the Irish 'wogs in houses', a number of points had been made. Bill came to Sheffield to see it and like me admired David's casting, and the élan of his scene changes on the Crucible's epic stage.

Later in 1975 Bill's production of *Watch It Come Down* made an interesting contrast to Osborne's other recent plays that had been directed at the Court by Anthony Page. Page,

81

with whom I worked on *Z Cars*, was the best of the TV studio-drama directors. Unlike virtually everyone else, he never tried to make TV look like cinema: he knew that it was a medium for talking heads, and his style of rapid cutting between close-ups created intense concentration and emotions. In the theatre he was more orthodox. He cast stars and had the assurance to handle them. As often as not they were centre-stage with the other actors fanned out in descending order of importance – an old West End tradition.

Bryden was unimpressed by English traditions of any kind. His notions of acting derived more from the performances in movie versions of the American stage hits of the 1940s and 1950s, which he had seen as a boy. Later he admired Al Pacino and character leads like Harvey Keitel and David Carradine. They were men, they were macho, they had high energy and when the focus of the action was on them they took it. The ability to take the focus is crucial in the promenade, but Bill exploited it in the proscenium to an unusual degree, so that he seemed to be cutting away from the rest while one actor held focus. This had been very effective in *The Iceman Cometh*, where so many people are static on stage for so long, and it was a technique that was always heightened when the lighting was by Andy Phillips, who could sculpt the actors wherever they were. The fact that Osborne wrote *Watch It Come Down* in a traditional style while Bill's approach was different gave the production its energy and edginess.

They seem to have been a good duo in rehearsal. Bill told me that Osborne's words to the actors were never critical but always encouraging. When he had a criticism, he would make it to Bill, sotto voce, as they stood watching. Osborne smiled as he spoke and his eyes never strayed from the cast, so that they had no idea of his disapproval. Later Bill would deliver the note.

The play itself was the last of that group in which Osborne, although he could not explain how it would happen or quite why, foresaw that the world would become a more dangerous place, and England nastier and shallower. It was near the bone, and did not flatter the audience like a play by Shaffer or

Stoppard. Its end was as unexplained as that of *West of Suez*, the first in this group of plays, had been shocking. In *West of Suez* the leading character was subjected to a tirade of foul language, to symbolise the decay of rational communication, and then shot by freedom-fighters. In *Watch It Come Down* the converted railway station in which the media-world characters lived was inexplicably machine-gunned. The consensus by which you have lived for thirty years is coming to an end, it said; who is to blame, and who will win or lose?

The effect of this upon the audience was to puzzle and enrage. On some nights there were protesters, men in suits and striped shirts who stood up and shouted, 'Money back! Money back!' Eventually the audience dipped below a certain percentage and the play was taken off. Osborne objected, but to no avail. It was the beginning of his exile from the theatre, and no one since has written about our country with the same tragic force and clairvoyance.

Social life: Keith Dewhurst

If the fact that Bond's *The Sea* did not transfer left a tidemark, the rejection of *Watch It Come Down* was an early warning of the change in society and the audience. It was a play about something new that the audience decided from Osborne's tone was old hat. It had a sense of unease about their way of living which did not interest them. They liked what they were becoming. The mainstream taste and the radical were coming apart. Osborne sussed this at the time, I think, but to our shame we did not. We were too fussed about reviewers, who had far more influence than they do today when many newspapers are indifferent to the theatre and reviews can appear days after an opening. At that time we laughed at the men who shouted 'Money back!' and their girls who egged them on. Yet we did not stop to think about them. We were having too amusing a time, and felt that our own moment was about to come.

What made our lives fun was the fact that in 1976 parts of

the South Bank NT were opened: rehearsal rooms, offices and the bar in the Green Room. It was pleasant to drift down, talk, drink and make plans. When there was an acoustics test in the semi-completed Lyttelton Theatre, Bill restaged parts of *The Baby Elephant* and I wrote some new material. At some point for a benefit concert I wrote a sketch in which Albert Finney did a mind-boggling impersonation of Tony Richardson. Bill was also writing and made additions to his eventual team: the stage manager John Caulfield and Frank Nealon, who came down from Edinburgh to be Caulfield's deputy. It was Nealon who, behind the scenes at the *Iceman*, realised that Ian Bannen was about to make his entrance an hour and a half too soon, and rugby-tackled him to the floor. Caulfield, ex-Coldstream Guards, ex-taxi driver, ex-many things and known always as 'the Captain', was a vital pillar of the eventual Cottesloe Company; and in that powerhouse of people who could behave very badly lost neither dignity nor control.

The most important new chum at this time was Sebastian Graham-Jones. Unlike the rest of us he was an Old Harrovian and a gentleman, from minor landed gentry and public service on one side, and high-minded Edwardian trading wealth on the other. He had broken the pattern by becoming an actor, musician and director, had caught Peter Hall's eye, and been offered a staff directorship. He was good-looking and person-able and believed in having a good time, and because there was nothing much to do at the National, Hall let him go for a while to be John Schlesinger's assistant on the movie *Marathon Man*. It was understood that when the time came he and Bill would direct together, though why someone as personally ambitious as Bill would want a co-director is a fair question. Some of the answer lies in the fact that Bill detested day-to-day bureau-cratic politicking, and Sebastian became both interpreter and ally (just as, years later, when Bill was Head of BBC Drama Scotland he had the stout-hearted Norman McCandlish at his side). For most people, the buzz comes from their little bit of fame or power or money, but for Bill these things merely gave access to the buzz: the buzz itself was having achieved the work, and its impact on the audience. Bill was an innocent and half the fun of him was that the preposterous could seem real. To him his career *was* like football. It was obvious that George Best was brilliant, and people said so, so why didn't people say the same about us? But in football there is an actual score. In theatre the score is a metaphor, and you can never prove that your men are the best.

Il Campiello: Keith Dewhurst

In the late summer of 1976 I went to Australia and, apart from a brief visit when I stayed as usual with Bill and Deborah, did not return to England until the following spring. While I was away, Bill was lured into directing Goldoni's *Il Campiello*, in the Olivier Theatre, for the official opening of the new National, and in the presence of the Queen. 'A set-up', is how some still describe it, and, indeed, it was always an axiom that one tried never to direct the first production in a new theatre. And what a theatre, one might say of the Olivier.

The architect's brief had been that the three NT theatres should comprise a flexible space, a proscenium and a Greek auditorium. As everybody knows, the essence of a Greek theatre is that it is an unbroken fan, but somehow, at some committee meeting or other, the great and the good allowed the Olivier's fan to be broken by an aisle and a row of production boxes. Split in two, the Olivier has no single point of command (the place on the stage from which the actor best dominates the audience) and no true emotional unity. It is to this day, despite various alterations to the stage, the most difficult major theatre in Britain, and the main reason why everyone wants to direct in the Cottesloe. If the Olivier were a real Greek fan, or like the Sheffield Crucible, say, that would not be the case.

Hayden Griffin, who designed *Il Campiello*, realised the drawbacks as soon as he set foot in the theatre, and had a famous spat with Lord Olivier himself. 'Why are you building the stage up?' asked Olivier. 'Because you can't play comedy on a flat floor,' said Hayden. 'Nobody's tried yet,' responded the noble Lord, to win the skirmish but not the actual debate.

Goldoni is notoriously difficult to make work in English because his high and low characters speak the same Venetian dialect. This problem was not resolved, and although Bill hurled event-type effects at the piece, including a sort of Venetian carnival in the foyer, it did not succeed. Helen Montague told me that on the first night she was sitting in front of a semi-famous writer who tapped her on the shoulder and said, 'It's every bit as bad as we hoped it would be.' This is typical of the silly envy that was directed at Peter Hall's NT, and of the way in which the new intellectuals thought that their subsidised playgrounds would stay open for ever. Reviews were poor, and Hall had to resist board members who wanted Bill sacked.

On the phone Bill said that things were very bad and I might as well stay in Australia, but I needed to see my children and to meet my colleague John Davies, with whom I was in the middle of doing twenty-six episodes of Richmal Crompton's *Just William* for Stella Richman at LWT. On the second night of my flying visit I went to the Olivier. The first person I met in the foyer was Derek Newark, the most valiant of all our actors, who was dressed like a figure from the Commedia and had a live monkey on his wrist. He was hurt and puzzled by the show's reception, and even the monkey seemed downcast. There was more to it than artistic taste, they implied; and to this day the memory of *Il Campaniello* is uneasy, like that of a defeat in a major cup final.

Socially, the presence of Bill and his comrades in the Green Room, and the adherence to them of amusing characters like the director Richard Mangan and the graphics designer Michael Mayhew, set a tone which at the time was a sort of boisterous, heterosexual version of the old Royal Court irreverence. Classic manifestations of this are the Apologies Slip (see illustration), the legendary barring of the actor Pitt Wilkinson from the Green Room and the committee meetings of the Cunt of the Month Club. Amazingly, these were held at lunchtime in the NT boardroom, and attended by directors,

NT Apologies slip

To:

From: Date:

* Sorry if I was: busy/pissed/stoned/unconscious/unkind/absent

Please answer the following questions: (Tick where appropriate)

1. Was it a good evening? (yes/no)

2. Was it expensive? (yes/no)

3. If the answer to question 2. is yes: who paid?
    (a) You
    (b) Me
    (c) Someone else

4. If the answer to question 3.   is (a) How much do I owe you?
                                    If (b) How much do you owe me?
                                    If (c) Forget it

5. Was it   (a) Your place
              (b) My place
              (c) Somewhere else

6. Who else was present? (Answer on a separate sheet please – you
    don't HAVE to answer)

7. See Question 1. How good?

8. Did I   (a) stay
             (b) go
             (c) don't *you* even know

9. Do I see you again?
             (a) tonight
             (b) some time
             (c) never

10. Do I owe apologies to anyone else?
    If so, are they   (a) Important
                       (b) Unimportant
                       (c) Pitt Wilkinson

11. Any suggestions on how to:
                       (a) Get it better
                       (b) Get it right
                       (c) Call it off

*Delete as appropriate

stage staff and miscellaneous actors and actresses. The Cunt of the Month Award was a chunk of amethyst quartz on a chain, and the winner was the person deemed to have broken the Green Room's social code in the most obnoxious fashion. The first winner is still alive and he was succeeded by the late Mark McManus (for peeing outside Buckingham Palace, recalls Bill, although how anybody knew he had done it I don't know), and Derek Newark, who won twice and was given the trophy outright, which brought the solemnities to an end.

Somehow, I can't imagine this happening today.

14. Medieval Mysteries

The Passion: Keith Dewhurst

On a wettish day in March 1977 I returned to London, settled into my rented flat, and phoned my agent. There was a message to go at once to Rehearsal Room 3 at the NT, which after lunch I did. The legendary stage-doorkeeper Jimmy recognised me and waved me in. (Nowadays this formality can take minutes, although, needless to say, the only systematic thefts from the NT have been by security staff.) In the rehearsal room the actors were processing around what was clearly a promenade space, and the Albion Band was at full blast. By a stroke of luck, Bill had got *The Passion* up and into rehearsal in little more than a month.

Bill had long talked about the medieval mystery plays, and had been encouraged by Peter Hall who gave him the Festival of Britain version by Canon Purvis, but it was the failure of John Schlesinger's production of *Julius Caesar* to reach its attendance targets that provided him with the opportunity to stage them. A Schlesinger *Heartbreak House* had been widely admired, but *Caesar* did not work. Sebastian assisted Schlesinger, and always maintained that on the first night one of the actors changed his performance and threw the rest into confusion. Be that as it may, Seb had influenced Schlesinger in the casting, much of which was of Bryden-cum-Royal Court actors, who were contracted beyond the curtailed run of the play.

There was a meeting at which Peter Hall asked, 'What are we going to do with these actors?' Bill pounced like a hawk and offered a medieval crucifixion play. Tony Harrison was available to adapt, and Bill proposed to import the odd extra person like Brian Glover and to have music, as he put it to me recently, 'to make the plays less dry'. Ashley Hutchings and his Albion Band were the obvious choice.

In the five years since he left Steeleye Span, Ashley's circumstances, like those of folk-rock in general, had deteriorated. He had pursued purer strains of English folk, made some fascinating but esoteric albums and, as he sought his ideal sound, gone through changes of personnel in the Albion Country Band. The final line-up included Martin Carthy, and they recorded the album *The Battle of the Field* in the summer of 1974. The band then split up, having spent a large advance from their record company, Island, and were not available to promote the album.

Island retaliated. They said that they would never again have anything to do with folk bands because they were 'too much bother', and refused to release the album. Ashley himself had met the singer Shirley Collins and was living with her in Etchingham in Sussex where, disillusioned with the music business, as his biography puts it, he became the village postman. This was about the time at which Michael Simpson and I tried to lure him to the Birmingham Rep.

Then the Sex Pistols and punk hit the world. At the Malcolm McLaren level, punk was an attempt to create something unbourgeois, outrageous and untainted by tradition; as such, it inevitably became another category of middle-class fashion chic. On the street it was a scream, a change in the masses, a disillusionment with what the consensual society had to offer. It ended that golden period in which rock music was both popular and profound, and indicated a future in which the market would fragment and dumb down. Very few folk artists, who relied on melody, survived it, and the university audiences that had been the mainstay of their record sales and touring gigs were lost.

But Ashley has always had his hard core of support, and after two years of people lobbying and writing letters to the music press, Island succumbed and released *The Battle of the Field* in April 1976. Bill and I thought that it was marvellous, with a defiant energy, and as soon as I heard the haunting tune 'The Battle of the Somme' I knew it was the music for the end of a play, but not as yet which one.

The album cover was by William Dudley, who had designed

Man is Man and its notorious two-drinks scene change. Dudley played squeeze-box, most movingly, years later at Brian Glover's funeral, and was in touch with Ashley through Morris dancing. Since Bill wanted Dudley to design *The Passion*, everything came together. Ashley's new Albion Band was gigging, but not as of yore, and the theatre was not a luxury as it had been before, but a lifeline.

Initially, *The Passion* played for one open-air Easter performance of the Crucifixion play on the NT terraces, and a week in the Cottesloe. I missed the Easter show because I had to go to Italy, but it was a turning-point, and showed that Bill could achieve something remarkable. The traffic stopped on Waterloo Bridge, and the sun came out at the right moment. In the theatre the rationale was that since the medieval play had moved around on carts, the actors would represent Craft Guildsmen and move around the space. The energy, the acting, the music, Harrison's crisp dialogue and the impact of seven years' worth of ideas and experiments were, in the promenade, explosive. The promenade was the logical next step and Bill had taken it. It was rough but it was mythic, and when Richard Johnson walked away in the middle of a scene and said, 'Frank, I think my bottle's gone,' Nealon turned him, said, 'No, it hasn't,' and shoved him back on.

Seeing *The Passion*: Jack Shepherd

I first saw *The Passion*, at the Cottesloe Theatre, in October 1977. At that time I was just another member of the audience, and I hadn't worked with Bill for about five years. And although I was familiar with his style, I was unprepared for what I witnessed. For a start there were no lines of seats in the auditorium, nothing to pull us all into line, discipline us, if you like, into a civilised response. We weren't an audience in the modern sense at all, we were a crowd, a mob, vaguely milling around, still wrapped up in our winter clothes, very self-consciously waiting for the performance to start, in the dimly lit and distinctly smoky atmosphere of the auditorium.

It was like going into a shrine in the corner of a cold cathedral, full of the smoke from burning candles. And yet none of the objects one could see was in the least bit devotional. The trade union *chapel* had returned to its roots. Banners in the William Morris style decorated the upper levels. There were display cases secured to the walls, with samples of tools revealed inside, and boards exhibiting the different kinds of bread that could be baked. What's more, a myriad little lights had been suspended from the ceiling of the auditorium; oil-lamps with a dim and flickering electric radiance, suspended cheese graters with torch bulbs hardly even glowing from within, and oil drums crudely punctured, emitting a dull red glare. The auditorium was charged with a dark medieval magic and yet everything in it came from the modern world. *The space had* (most definitely) *been transformed.*

At one end of the auditorium there was a bandstand on a raised platform, with microphones, leads, amps . . . Something at least that I recognised.

As the time approached for the performance to start, I began to notice that the cast, dressed in working clothes, boiler suits and overalls, were drifting in from the sides and mingling with the ever-growing crowd. Then, after a brief and informal speech of welcome from the band, the proceedings got under way with a country dance.

Everything that followed was acted out in the public arena, the audience swirling around making patterns discernible from the galleries above, as they jostled with each other to get a better view.

I still remember Oliver Cotton's entrance as Judas, dressed in a simple black robe, swinging down on a rope from the gantry above, getting stuck into the obsessional alliteration of the text in a spray of spittle, haranguing us all like a man selling plates in Leeds market:

What waste wailed I then that woman hath wrought.
Seeing spikenard so slopped sir, seers my soul sore!

I'd never heard anything like it.

Impact: Keith Dewhurst

Promenade theatre's impact on the audience was equalled by the sense of liberation, and of crossing a frontier, that it gave the performers. 'Oh, I get it,' said Warren Clarke in an early rehearsal of *Lark Rise*, 'it's a whole new bottle job.' It was, although I am not sure that there have been many since. Exponents of shock-and-awe-type violence have added little to Edward Bond, and the one true technical innovation is the computer-projected scenery pioneered by William Dudley. Too often today's theatre hypes frontiers when there is none to cross.

Judas: Jack Shepherd

When I took over the part of Judas in the autumn of 1978, I had some intriguing and unusual choices to make. I soon learned that the part I was playing was not Judas, in fact, but a man, a *working* man, who was *playing the part* of Judas. It's an interesting idea, a built-in alienation effect, which stops the actor from identifying too closely with the character.

As I watched the company rehearse, I could see this idea working most clearly in Mark McManus's performance as Jesus. What Mark was actually *playing* was a Glasgow shipyard worker, dressed in a boiler suit and speaking the lines with such seriousness, such unaffected simplicity, that he hardly seemed to be acting at all. Any sense of him being Jesus was coming from somewhere deep inside him, unsought for, his unconscious if you like, his soul.

And so I had a lot of decisions to make: What did the man who was playing Judas do for a living? What kind of clothes would he wear? And more to the point, was he even a good actor? After a while I began to sense that the piece needed a sense of darkness emanating from the character, to contrast with Christ's halo. And that it might help if he seemed to be a kind of pariah: hidden, unpopular, socially inept, tainted in some way. And so I quickly decided that this man earned his living unblocking drains and that he was as good an actor as I could show him to be. In the end I was given a faded red boiler suit to wear – like the kind worn at the time by the men from Dyno-Rod – a dark robe to go over the top and an ancient pair of black boots.

Coming from Leeds was a big advantage in speaking the text, because I could use the accent I'd grown up with, the back-street accent of my native Chapeltown, with its blocked nose, back a' t' throat, adenoidal twang; an accent that reflected the pollution that had been endemic in Leeds since the earliest days of the Industrial Revolution. Even in the 1950s, the River Aire ran a sulphurous yellow and the public buildings were an inch thick in encrusted soot. I still have no sense of smell, a result of the corrosive air I breathed as a child. The lines

> All hail, master, in faith, and fellows all here,
> Wi' great gracious greeting on t'ground be arrayed

with those Leeds intonations, could sound like snot running down a slum kid's nose.

The problem with rehearsing something that's been done before is the absence of any kind of energy from the people who've done it already. They have no *fear*, they drift around in a complacent haze, vaguely trying to remember what they'd once said, while the newcomers sweat and stammer their way through the lines as they desperately struggle to catch up. For the actor taking over a part, the first day of rehearsal is like drowning at the bottom of a pool, watching everyone else swimming happily on the surface.

I remember when I first tried Judas's opening speech without the book, Trevor Ray came up to me and stood within inches of my nose, smiling insolently up at me. I sensed this was a kind of test. Did I have the nerve, the 'bottle' for this kind of venture? The audience, after all, could well come within inches of the performance.

I passed the test, I'm pleased to say; I might well have laughed nervously, my eyes might've rolled like those of a cow in an abattoir, but I kept going right to the end.

The poet's revenge: Jack Shepherd

Tony Harrison was responsible for the text. His role was to make the language of the plays accessible to modern ears, finding an equivalent for a word that had fallen out of common usage; replacing it with a dialect word as often as not; altering the rhymes, where necessary, but keeping the rhythms intact. And wherever a scene was missing in the original, he would set about reconstructing it.

I was surprised to learn that Judas's speech to the crowd, which had impressed me so much when I first saw the play, was in fact a Harrison original; Judas's speech was missing from the text, so he'd simply written one of his own.

The poor's plight pricked me not to play no pretence,
What pricked me and pined me was the loss of my pence.

What Tony had realised was that all this rhythmic alliteration wasn't merely a formal device. It was there so that the actor's lines might be heard above the din of the crowds milling about on Corpus Christi day; rising above the braying of animals, the crying of babies. And distinct from the yelling of street traders and all the other sounds competing for the audience's attention.

His advice was to keep the rhythm of the verse, to make the speaking *natural*, not *naturalistic*, and hit the consonants hard. He also insisted that the plays should be performed in the accent of his native Yorkshire. They had been written for the city of York after all, in a form of early English that needed a degree of translation to make it comprehensible to modern ears, so why, he argued, perform these plays in the accents of the educated middle class? In his opinion, the Yorkshire accent was the most appropriate, the most well suited to the demands of constant alliteration as the emphasis is always on the *consonants*, unlike a London accent, say, which lays stress on the *vowels*.

There was another, more personal reason for the Yorkshire accent. Tony was angry at the way the educated classes had appropriated the poetic voice, not taking seriously those who didn't speak as they did and effectively excluding the working class, his class, from the world of poetry and the finer sensibilities. It delighted him to hear the poetry of these plays declaimed in the raw accent of his native tongue. It was almost as if he was getting his own back.

The Crucifixion play: Jack Shepherd

Of all the plays in the York Mystery cycle, it's the Crucifixion play that stands out. As a piece of writing it holds you spell-bound. It's probably the longest play in the cycle, self-contained and beautifully structured, with its own beginning, middle and horrifying end. In simple terms it shows Christ being nailed to the cross by a gang of workmen. They're referred to as Knights in the text, but they talk like builders putting up scaffolding.

Their callous, almost farcical disregard for Christ's suffering is common to the art of the time. In German paintings, a witness to the scourging, for example, might well be depicted pulling his eyes downwards with both forefingers, stretching his mouth sideways with his little fingers and sticking his tongue out in Christ's direction as far as it will go. It's a gesture that's funny, horrible and utterly irreverent; a gesture common to children the world over.

As a piece of writing, the Crucifixion play is as cruel and as funny and as morally serious as any play by Edward Bond. Now, it so happens that Bill Bryden had directed Bond's own *Passion* in 1971 at a CND Easter rally, in the grounds of Alexandra Palace in North London.

In Bond's play, Norman Beaton played Christ, and Bob Hoskins played Buddha. The event was dominated, however, by the revelation of a crucified pig whose carcass, fresh from the slaughter-house, had been spreadeagled on a wooden cross, nailed into place and then hoisted into an upright position. The genes of pigs and humans are just about similar enough to make the image very disturbing. It looked like a sculpture created by Francis Bacon.

At that time the WRP was trying to structure a party that would lead the revolution, when the objective conditions for a revolution were judged to be right. There were a number of other events that day besides the performance of *The Passion*, all of them overwhelmed by an apocalyptic speech by their leader Gerry Healy.

In the 1980s Bill made a film called *The Holy City*, in which Christ comes to modern Glasgow. Like other writers, directors and artists, among whom Stanley Spencer springs to mind, the story of Christ is deep inside him.

15. *Lark Rise*

Luggage: Keith Dewhurst

When we were talking at his house one day Bill came up with
the idea of staging Flora Thompson's *Lark Rise*, but he was not
then the actual director of the Cottesloe, and knew that for me
to be commissioned to write it I would have to audition for the
Literary Department run by John Russell Brown. This was the
era of platform plays and events run by Michael Kustow,
which from the TV documentaries *The Undersea World of
Jacques Cousteau* were known as 'The Under-rehearsed World
of Michael Kustow', a slander, really, because there was always
something interesting going on.

I wrote a fifty-five-minute play called *Luggage*, which was
directed as a platform performance on the Lyttelton stage by
Nik Simmonds, and acted by Brian Blessed and June Watson.
In it a Northern couple put suitcases in their car before going
on holiday. They bicker and reveal gulfs in their lives. Then
they remove the suitcases because this is a rehearsal to see if
their luggage will fit. Such pieces would fill the Lyttelton stalls
at about 6 p.m. and be reviewed, and their abandonment
because of cost was a loss. In this case I passed the audition,
got a nice mention in the *Sunday Times* and was commissioned
to write *Lark Rise*.

Lark Rise: Keith Dewhurst

Flora Thompson was born Flora Timms in the Oxfordshire
hamlet of Juniper Hill in 1876. Her father was a stonemason
and a misfit, her mother had been a lady's maid. In her early
teens Flora was sent to Mrs Whitton, a remarkable woman

relative who kept the post office and smithy in nearby Fringford. Later she took postal work in Grayshott and Bournemouth. There she met and made an unhappy marriage to a clerk named John Thompson, who discouraged her efforts to be a writer. Eventually they ran the post office in Brixham, in Devon, and their son Peter was killed in the Second World War as Flora's brother Edmund had been in the First. In her old age her trilogy *Lark Rise to Candleford* was recognised as a masterpiece for its portrayal of England's vanished agrarian world. *Lark Rise* is the first and best-known of the books and describes Juniper Hill in the 1880s. Its adaptation seemed an ideal project for ourselves and the musicians.

The Passion was forged in a burst of creative heat and it ran for a week. There was no real time to draw lessons until it returned months later. Its staging was simple: the actors moved around the space as the pageant-wagons had moved around a medieval town, and at about eighty minutes it was, like *The Speakers*, relatively short. *Lark Rise* would be a full-length play and we did not know how audiences would react to being in the promenade for what turned out to be two hours and forty minutes. We realised that we would have to make them turn and walk, from end to end of the theatre and from side to side, and that as often as possible they would have to give way to actors coming through them: the scene in which a line of mowers go down the space was placed as early as possible, to get people used to the idea, and in production the changing patterns of spectators were even more a part of the spectacle than they had been in *The Passion*.

Sebastian Graham-Jones and I would watch the same scenes in *The Passion* from different positions, and we learned a lot from one interesting change in acting personnel. Pitt Wilkinson had been a much-loved member of Bill's early NT casts, a person with an interesting mind and tales to tell, and in the original *Passion* he played the man whom Christ cures of his blindness. Pitt played it on the floor, like an Oriental beggar, and with great emotion. By the time the show was revived he was terminally ill, and was replaced by Albert Finney. Finney played it like the blind people he had seen on the streets of Salford, upright but leaning away, with a worn, pressed suit, and a gabardine raincoat that his mother had folded over his arm before sending him out. To stand behind him and read on the faces of other spectators the moment at which his sight returned, was as powerful a theatrical experience as I have known. Finney is a great actor, and what he did in no way disparaged Pitt, but it did illuminate the promenade; and not least did it suggest that if someone is on the floor, as Pitt had been, then some of the audience must be persuaded to join him. Bill achieved this very smoothly in the big 'Men Afield' scene in *Lark Rise.*

It is always said that you do not have to see actors in the promenade so long as you can hear them, and this is true, with the proviso that if you can't see the actor he must be visible in theory. That is to say, you could see him if you were in the right place or willing to move. If someone is on the floor, few of those standing can see him, unless a space is created. When too many people cannot see, or have no possibility of moving, the audience's concentration sags.

This may seem like nit-picking but the fact is that just as there are what I would call hidden wrongnesses, like the scaffold in *Kidnapped*, so there are also hidden rightnesses, and in the promenade the essential hidden rightness is that all the audience have access to all areas of the space. Even people who remained seated in the Cottesloe galleries could in theory have moved, and others taken their places. As it was, people could stand behind them. If these conditions are not met, people will feel an unexplained unease and find it hard to concentrate.

It follows that acting in the promenade, when there may be spectators between you and the other people in the scene, is about focus. It is about being positive, so that people will move for you, and about acting with your whole body so that people behind you can read its language. Brian Glover was habituated to this by his career in wrestling, and Trevor Ray always made good body shapes. What they did was simple, but readable from all parts of the arena. Also important is the taking of the focus when it is your turn.

Bill's team-talk metaphor here was the relay: the focus, and with it the energy, is the baton that is passed from runner to runner, the audience's attention being seized, frequently at the other end of the space, by distinctness of voice and gesture. No one was better at this than Dinah Stabb in *Lark Rise*.

One autumn Sunday we went in a convoy of cars to reconnoitre Juniper Hill. Ashley Hutchings and Bill Dudley were in our car and the others carried Bill, Deborah, Sebastian, Susan Fleetwood, Caulfield, John Tams, Derek Newark and Trevor Ray. It was a sunshiny day that turned grey, and we knocked on the door of the End House where the Timms family had lived and were shown around. We were astounded by the physicality of the place: the flat fields, the huddle of houses, the vast sky, which was rent by the din of American warplanes, whose base blocked the western horizon. At that time the Fox and Hounds, the hamlet pub described by Flora, was still there, and we had a drink. The pub was low-ceilinged and dark and had a game machine. We went to Cottisford Church, where I wrote down the wording and the names on the Great War memorial. The last name is that of E.Timms, Flora's brother.

We drove to Marlborough for lunch and I sat with William Dudley to discuss the set. It needed three ingredients, we agreed, the cottage, the fields and the sky, and the fact that Dudley had seen the place for himself inspired his simplest and least cluttered design, and I believe a truly great one. His over-reaching sky cloth, through which the sun beat and the stars shone, gave the essence of the place in an extraordinary way.

After lunch we saw where the Squire had lived, and looked at the fields where the harvest had been gathered, and in the early evening went to the Harvest Home service in Cottisford Church, where to the Vicar's puzzlement we filled the front pew and Derek Newark bellowed the hymns in the style of his Coldstream Guards church parade days.

After the service we went to the Fox and Hounds again, and a few days later Alexandra and I flew to Sydney, where her father was dying, and to the sound of the surf on Palm Beach I wrote the play.

Writing *Lark Rise*: Keith Dewhurst

Lark Rise is a book without a narrative. Each chapter describes a different aspect of hamlet life, and although there is a profound sense of everything having changed between the time described and the time of writing, there is also a photographic quality of things fixed in a moment. This is what Bill picked up on when he began and ended the production so memorably with a 'still photograph' of the assembled cast.

Another aspect of the book's genius is that it does not betray the child's eye. In fact, Albert Timms drank and was dissatisfied, and his wife, although a native of Juniper Hill, felt at odds with the community, and to be living beneath herself, which is why she sent her daughter to the relative who in *Candleford* is re-created as the postmistress Dorcas Lane. But in *Lark Rise* Flora Thompson described her parents as she had seen them as a child. The facts are there for the observant reader, but they lie beneath innocence and belief.

To present this situation without betraying it was the most difficult task of the adaptation. The most basic task was to decide upon a narrative structure. I thought at first that I would construct four acts to correspond, as it were, to the four seasons of the year, but it soon seemed wiser to concentrate upon a single day, and to make it the day that was the most important in the hamlet year: the first day of harvest. But I was still obsessed by four acts, and my delivered script and the published versions of the play have act and scene divisions. The idea was that the audience might not last out and would need an interval. But fairly soon into rehearsal, and when we had logistical discussions about ushers and bar staff and so on, we realised that we must risk it and play straight through. After all, people could walk in and out if they wanted, and there were always a few who did (not least us, going to the bar).

Although the book has no narrative, it describes many events and individuals, and because Flora Thompson wanted to give the flavour of a past time, she included many remembered scraps of conversation, figures of speech, proverbs, phrases, old names and notions, and accounts of people's opinions. All these I copied on to several sheets of paper, to cross them out as I used them to make dialogue. What is interesting about Flora Thompson's people and events is that when they are dramatised they assume without strain an epic shape; they are particular but representative. They define a society, and catch history as it changes. Some critics have said that *Lark Rise* is sentimental and reliant upon nostalgia, but to me the essence of the play is that it restates the bleakness behind Flora Thompson's warmth: time destroys everything, she says, although we would do well to remember that the forgotten people had the same humanity as ourselves.

This notion had particular resonance for me because I lived much of my early life in the countryside around a northern mill town. My friends were for a time the sons of a farm labourer, and I worked with them on the field gangs of the local farmer, a fat, foul-mouthed, bucolic man named Tom Fiddler. Then I would go to the cotton mill managed by my father, and see the steam engine, and an industrial process and social structure that had not changed since the late 1790s. This had vanished by the time I reached the NT, just as the shipyards that Bill Bryden knew were dying. My father had gone over the top on the first day of the Battle of the Somme, and survived, which is another reason I was moved by the Albion Band's song; when I saw the Cottisford war memorial I knew that somehow the two together would make the end of the show.

Because *Lark Rise* was planned months in advance, many of the actors, as well as the band, were known to be committed to the NT, so that the parts played by Newark, Glover, Trevor Ray, Edna Doré and James Grant were written for them. Some we hoped would be free turned out not to be, but others were, including Michael Gough, whom we had fancied for the Vicar's key moment at the end. I wrote a few lyrics and indicated where the other music should go, but only had specific ideas for the hymn and 'The Battle of the Somme'. Bill proposed the overture, 'The Girl I Left Behind Me' from the John Ford cavalry films, and Ashley, Shirley Collins and John Tams came up with the rest, although I believe that Martin Carthy suggested he sing 'The Fair at Athy' in the Men Afield scene. A couple of the pub songs had actually been sung there in the 1880s.

At the end of December I airmailed the script to London, and arrived myself in the middle of January 1978, in plenty of time to be involved in the tortuous process of casting what is effectively the play's leading part, Mrs Timms, the mother of Flora Thompson's alter ego Laura.

Casting 'Mrs Timms': Keith Dewhurst

Susan Fleetwood, with whom Sebastian lived at the time, had been a great success when she played Pegeen Mike in Bill's production of *Playboy*. She was a big, brave lead and had worked extensively at the RSC, whose bourgeois rhetoric had influenced her style. But if she had thrown herself into it, and sacrificed personal moments for the narrative line, which she was well capable of doing when she chose, she could have been the natural female lead of Bill's company, and added depth to both it and herself. Yet for whatever reasons she was elusive. Maybe it was an understandable suspicion of a lot of macho idiots, or a fear that the parts might not always do her justice, or her private closeness to Sebastian, or a desire to be an orthodox sort of star. Whatever it was she let events take their course. Although she had come with us to Juniper Hill and we had assumed that she would act Mrs Timms, while the play was being written she became involved in another NT production and was not free. She did work with Bill's company, four years later, in one of the two Shakespeare plays he did, and some time after Sebastian had left.

Our second choice was Anna Massey and we wooed her as ardently as we could in the Green Room, but both she and her agent, the ever-amiable Jeremy Conway, seem to have had qualms about the very nature of the promenade and she declined. This threw us. We saw various people but dithered. Meanwhile we were using Mary Miller to read the part in sessions to cast other actors. She was, I suspect, the Casting Department's secret choice from the start, and when both she and they said that we had to either offer her the part or stop messing her about we offered her the part, and she accepted.

Mary was never in tune with the company's social style, and probably not with its acting either, but just as in my mind I always hear Glover say the lines I wrote for him, so I always hear Mary as Mrs Timms, even when I wonder what it would be like with a different kind of actress. I suspect that it was the fact that the character has to cope with her troubles that made it mean so much to her. She fussed about props in a way that drove some other actors crazy, but even that vulnerability was a part of the character, and the fact is that her performance was a human statement, and lived for the audience in an unusual and powerful way.

We prepared *Lark Rise* in a mood of easy anticipation that matched the atmosphere around the building. Panic was gone. The regime was in full swing. People lived and let live. Things were fun, and Warren Clarke even acted in all three theatres on the same night – a record unlikely to be broken.

Peter Hall had given Chris Morahan charge of the Lyttelton Theatre and Bill the Cottesloe – *Lark Rise* would be the start of his term. On 23 January Bill and I had lunch with Chris Morahan, whom I had long known in the television world, and punted our idea to do *Cinderella* in the Lyttelton as an old-fashioned Victorian pantomime. Bill liked the showbiz, the scenes flying in and out, and the memories of Rikki Fulton, and I liked the idea of reclaiming the popular entertainment drama, which had split off from the 'educated' audience some time in the seventeenth century. Chris agreed to mount the show at Christmas, but then he left to do *The Jewel in the Crown* for TV. Michael Rudman, erstwhile of the Traverse, took his place. Bill was unable to return to *Cinderella* until years later, when the group was in terminal decline.

We thought hard about the *Lark Rise* poster and programme, to mould the image of the show, and took a break with two works outings. One was to see the boxer John Conteh in a comeback fight. We had always followed the boxing and oft-remembered evenings were Joe Bugner versus Joe Frazier at Earls Court, and Richard Dunne versus Muhammad Ali on the cinema screen. We liked Conteh for his classy movement, were disappointed by his troubles, and feared for his future. Bill in particular was very vocal. When we saw the TV replay his voice rang out on the soundtrack: 'Oh, come on, John, this is serious!' On our second outing, to the Hammersmith Odeon, we saw a Steeleye Span farewell concert (yes, they have indeed been farewelling for almost thirty years) at the end of which Simon Nicol and Martin Carthy went on as guests and Martin, already secured for *Lark Rise*, gave an amazing staccato version of 'The False Knight on the Road'. 'There you are,' said Bill with gloomy relish, 'two late goals by our men.' That was a Saturday. Next day I popped into the theatre to see the Albion Band working out, and on Monday we began rehearsals.

Rehearsing *Lark Rise*: Keith Dewhurst

Bill had pinned up group photos of nineteenth-century villagers staring into that strange object, a camera, and thus the future, and as usual did not read the play but began with a team talk, a number or two from the band, and a plunge into the opening scene. Caroline Embling was Laura, and in consequence first up. A small, tough, urchin-sort of person in a grubby raincoat, she was eighteen but could look like a child. That day, her delivery of the opening speech, one shoulder cocked, script ignored and her entire persona pitched at the roomful of high testosterone competitors, was electrifying, a battle cry for the promenade. Bill had gambled the mood on her, and won. We knew that we'd be OK.

Lark Rise was the best rehearsed of the shows I did with Bill, and Sebastian's persistence played a good part in this. There was advice from the Agricultural Museum at Reading University and assistance with accents from the BBC Sound Archive. At one point Brian Glover was in a TV chat show, and when asked what work he was doing said that he was learning an Oxfordshire accent for the theatre. He was pressed to give examples, and did, all in the purest Barnsley. As, give or take the odd vowel, was his performance; since he played incomers, he was forgiven.

By best rehearsed, I mean that everything was so thoroughly explored that the actors were convinced of the essential rightness of what they were doing. Halfway through I went to the Gambia for two weeks to research my slave trade novel, *Captain of the Sands*, and when I returned what was evident in the cast was a deepened conviction. They had not been moulded by the force of directorial personalities, but had been encouraged to think it through as individuals and a team. They had arrived at it. There was no other way to do it. *Lark Rise* was the amplest justification of Bill's rehearsal methods. An old Royal Court ideal had been to do classics like new plays and new plays like classics and *Lark Rise* was a supreme example: it was experimental theatre that had the absolute polish of a great classical revival.

I experienced something similar when Bill Gaskill directed *Black Snow*, except that, if anything, the actors felt that Gaskill had imposed the production on them, and when he went away to America they felt they had improved it in the playing. To me it looked identical throughout. In rehearsal Gaskill had infuriated them by waving them away with remarks like, 'No, no, don't you know the first rule of acting?' But when they all had had time to think about it, they realised that they could not improve upon his template, and so they delivered it with greater confidence. It should be reported, however, that one night I was standing in the Cottesloe gallery, watching the audience roaring with laughter, when Gaskill's magisterial, bearded, back-from-New York presence loomed behind me and he groaned, 'There you are, you see, vulgarisms creeping in!' He had, however, already revealed the first rule of acting. It is: don't look at the floor when you first come on, because all you'll find there is the play.

In Sydney once I saw the RSC in a world tour performance of Peter Brook's *A Midsummer Night's Dream*, hailed as the most inventive production of its time. Not in Sydney it wasn't. The actors were in a line across the footlights, every man jack of them acting out front. How productions by Bryden or Gaskill would have stood up to that sort of exposure on the road I do not know. In Bryden's case the show was always to a huge extent his life and he was present nearly all the time. Even when he was in bad shape he was hands-on, as I think he would have been, or Sebastian in his place, on a world tour. It's unlikely there would have been a deterioration in quality. Attentiveness has its reward, as can be seen in the case of the marathon-running musicals in the West End. Cameron Mackintosh and Andrew Lloyd-Webber spend large sums on repetiteur work, although not everyone has their resources. And there is the old problem that Brook's *Dream* was actually a proscenium format for a non-proscenium play, so that it had more reason to go pear-shaped.

When we got *Lark Rise* into the theatre, our biggest problem was audibility. Even with Dudley's sky cloth, the cubic volume above the Cottesloe floor was large, and it seems to be difficult to make actors understand that you cannot always hear them. Sebastian and I prowled the further reaches and Bill would repeat, 'Consonants!', and, 'Speak the full stop at the end of the sentence!' At the first preview Ashley, who wanted Shirley Collins to have a big singing moment, arbitrarily inserted one at the end, but the next morning's meeting convinced him otherwise. Peter Hall watched and said, 'If you can cut twenty minutes you'll be all right.' There was an obvious chunk, at the end of the afternoon scenes, where the narrative trod water, and so out it went. The result was to give the evening that moment of acceleration which, towards the end of a play, is always a good thing.

A curious thing about the first night of *Lark Rise* is that it occurred during a newspaper distribution strike, so that some notices never appeared at all and others not in London. One or two that did were lukewarm, and some idiot in *Time Out* called the Albion Band's music 'folkzac'. The Milton Keynes Arts Association did, it is true, spend its entire annual budget on taking the show from the Cottesloe to four nights in an unfinished factory, but that was after a mere two-week run, so that although we thought the show was good, and knew that it had held the audience, we didn't realise how successful it was until interest grew around us.

Lessons of *Lark Rise*: Keith Dewhurst

The production itself, and the need to replace people for the visit to Milton Keynes, focused attention on two issues for an acting company of this sort. The first was: how, particularly at point-blank range in the promenade, do actors play several parts in the same evening?

In *The Passion* this was less important because, in the first place, the actors represented members of different Craft Guilds and dressed in corresponding modern clothes, with more or less stylised nods in the direction of the biblical characters they represented. In *Lark Rise* there was a range of different individuals, all of them supposed to be real, as it were. In some cases an actor went off as one person and instantly reappeared as another. Derek Newark wore at least one pair of trousers over another, and an off-stage line at the beginning of the Men Afield scene was written to cover his disrobing.

In the proscenium theatre of the nineteenth century, and the first half of the twentieth, actors made themselves appear different with wigs and elaborate make-up. Such dressing-up became part of the fun of the thing, and in our own time an actor like Laurence Olivier became a master of this sort of illusion. His famous portrayals in the Old Vic season of 1945 of Oedipus, Mr Puff and Justice Shallow involved the creation of totally different, audience-delighting appearances. Oddly enough, such trickery belongs now to the prosthetics and computer wizardry of cinema make-up: the theatre is more pure, a sign of the shift in the suspension of disbelief achieved by the ideas of men like Brecht and Ronconi, and the practicalities of smaller, differently designed theatres and lighting.

'Daylight isn't coloured,' Andy Phillips once said to me, and by focusing his white light on the actors he brought out their natural colouring. Too much make-up would have been cruelly exposed. Even though Bill Dudley was at intellectual odds with Andy, and wanted more light on the set and less on the actors, what he negotiated with the Cottesloe's staff lighting man Lawrence Clayton was pretty pure, and our actors did not wear make-up.

Nor did they alter their performances very much to portray different people. Maybe Glover thought he did, just as he stoutly believed that he changed his accent, but even he allowed his costume to say who he was. After that it was an actor's belief in the character that gave it life. The audience's pleasure changed from appreciating the disguise to relishing the reappearance of the personality. The actors did not invent fictitious personas, but deployed different aspects of their own.

The second issue was that of understudies, and it was more difficult to solve. Only one play in which I was involved with Bill had understudies as such and the reasons for this were financial. What we did at the Court was either too marginal or too specific, and at Edinburgh and in the Cottesloe the price of the theatre paying for a big acting company was that it could not afford understudies. That Peter Hall even allocated the money for the Cottesloe Company in the first place was a huge act of faith.

When someone fell ill during the original run of *Willie Rough*, Bill went on himself with the book, and there is a photograph, which amply reveals his terror, to prove it. In *Kidnapped*, a sick man was fortuitously replaced by Rikki, and when, a few days after it closed in the Cottesloe, *Lark Rise* was re-rehearsed for Milton Keynes, Warren Clarke, Derek Newark and Michael Gough were not free and had to be replaced. Ken Cranham, a special talent from the Royal Court who had been in *The Passion*, was the only ideologically correct incomer, as it were, and this set the pattern: emergency replacements would be drawn from the wider pool.

In the Lyttelton or Olivier there would have been an assistant director to do the repetiteur work, but this could not be afforded either, and the fact is that a lot of these chores fell to Sebastian, and this led some people to regard his input in the wrong way. The designer Hayden Griffin told me that

1. The Bench: Bill Bryden and Keith Dewhurst rehearsing *Corunna*, 1971.

2. *Pirates*: December 1970, Royal Court Sunday night without décor. White line drawn on the floor. Robert Powell (Captain Misson) and Patrice O'Connell (Avery)

3. *The Baby Elephant*: 1971, Royal Court Theatre Upstairs. From left: Bob Hoskins, Dave Hill, Mark McManus, and Tony Milner with his feet up.

4. *Corunna* rehearsal, 1971. Brian Glover and Jack Shepherd perfect the 'monkey climb'. R to l: Maddy Prior, Martin Carthy and Ashley Hutchings.

5. *Corunna*, 1971. Stragglers on the march. L to r: Dave Hill, Peter Knight, Brian Glover, Juliet Aykroyd. The ramp and audience (with drinks) in foreground.

6. *The Passion*, October 1977 in the Cottesloe: the space transformed. Edna Dore as Mary at the foot of the cross.

7. *The Passion*: 1978 revival, Cottesloe Theatre. Brenda Blethyn, Edna Dore, Mark McManus.

8. *Lark Rise*: 1978, Cottesloe Theatre. Floor, wheatfield, sky cloth and audience.

9. Rehearsing *Lark Rise*: 1978, Cottesloe Theatre. Sebastian Graham-Jones and Keith Dewhurst.

10. Rehearsing *Lark Rise*: 1978, Cottesloe Theatre. Bill Bryden paces to deliver a team talk. Listened to, from l to r, by Sebastian Graham-Jones (obscured), designer William Dudley, guitarist Graeme Taylor, Ashley Hutchings, 'The Captain' John Caulfield, John Tams and Shirley Collins.

11. *The World Turned Upside Down*: 1978, Cottesloe Theatre. Mutineers on the ramp. Left rank: John Tams, Mark McManus, Howard Goorney at rear. Centre rank: David Rintoul, Brian Glover, Peter Armitage, June Watson (behind black hat). Right rank: Trevor Ray, Edna Dore, Ashley Hutchings, and Fred Warder at rear.

12. *Dispatches*: 1979, Cottesloe Theatre. The theatre photograph as a real event.

13. One of the last men in the world to smoke Gold Flake: Bill Bryden weighing a rehearsal.

14. O'Neill's *Sea Plays*. 1979, Cottesloe Theatre. Epic realism from the designer Hayden Griffin and lighting designer Andy Phillips. L to r: Bill Owen, Jack Shepherd, Tony Haygarth, Naill Toibim, Howard Goorney, John Salthouse, James Grant.

15. *The Iceman Cometh*: 1980, Cottesloe Theatre. L to r: Oscar James, Geoffrey Chiswick, Gavin Grainger, Frederick Treves, Brian Glover, and Jack Shepherd at rear.

16. *Glengarry Glen Ross*: 1983, Cottesloe Theatre. More American realism by Griffin and Phillips. Jack Shepherd and Derek Newark.

17. *Golden Boy*: 1984, Lyttelton Theatre. Making the theatre look like movies.
L to r: Tony Trent, James Grant, Jack Shepherd, Derek Newark, Trevor Ray,
Christopher Gilbert, Jeremy Flynn and Lisa Eichorn.

18. *The Mysteries*: 1985, Cottesloe Theatre. Coming to an end. Derek Newark,
Robert Stephens and Jack Shepherd.

whenever he had a technical problem he always took it to Sebastian, but the actors never knew that. They saw him as an assistant and not a co-director, and thought his position a false one. In fact, his contribution was being himself, which I can best explain by saying that when Susan Fleetwood was diagnosed with cancer she decided to fight it alone, and asked him to leave her. In the years that followed he never betrayed the secret that could have limited her career, even though he was reputed to have ditched her for drink and girl-chasing. Of course, there were frustrations for him at the Cottesloe, and they were among the reasons why he left, as well as his desire to get out of London. He was a great gentleman who believed in loyalty, as his dignity on his deathbed confirmed, and he made many a situation, and many a decision, much easier.

As for the replacements, the fact is that Bill did not want to rehearse them himself because, although he hailed them as heroes when they showed up, he hated to see the play with them in it. As he once said to me: 'It isn't the real show.' In one way this was true, of course. In another it revealed his fantasy that, somehow, a theatre production was as fixed as a movie (and probably an old movie at that).

The abiding lesson of *Lark Rise*, I suppose, is that an Impossible Play can be realised, and that, as Flora Thompson knew, there is an unfathomable value in the life of every forgotten person.

16. *American Buffalo*

Two questions to ponder: Keith Dewhurst

After *Lark Rise*, Bill launched into David Mamet's *American Buffalo*, a choice of material which prompts two questions that help to define him: Why did he do so many American plays? And: Why did he never do an American musical?

The answer to the second question is that he believed them to be compromised. Musicals may be the passport to popularity and wealth, but they always bend the truth for the entertainment value. They are sentimental. They are not what he believed in.

The answer to the first question is that he is a Scot. Nuances of the English class system passed him by. At a public level Bill saw epic panoramas of history, and at a personal level he was an obsessive interested in the obsessions of others. O'Neill and Mamet were just the ticket, because they wrote about people trapped inside their own behaviour. This seemed to Bill to be more truly contemporary than the work of, say, British trendy-left writers who implied that socialist policies would cure our ills.

Playing *American Buffalo*: Jack Shepherd

I didn't know what to make of *American Buffalo* when I first read it. Admittedly, I read it very quickly, as you do when you're making a first assessment, trying to decide whether to involve yourself in a thing or not. But the language was unlike that of any play I'd ever read before. It was in an unfamiliar idiom and as alien as a play by Webster, say. Or a translation from a foreign language. And at times it didn't seem to make much sense until I read it out loud. What gave it meaning, in other words, was the *flow* of the language, not so much the syntax.

I was also thrown by the fact that the character I was being asked to play was called 'Teach'. I'd played a few teachers on television and come to the conclusion that that was why Bill had approached me about playing the part. As I read on, of course, I discovered that Teach, far from being a teacher, was a kind of psychotic, living in a fantasy world of crime and violence; an overblown little parasite, feeding off the fear and misery of all those around him.

And when I saw that 'Bobby' was described as a 'gopher', I wondered at first if he wasn't some sort of hallucination, maybe even dressed in an animal suit. (There was good reason for this. A few years before I'd seen a short play by an American writer in which two men were dressed as bumble bees. As the drama unfolded, it became clear that this was in fact a spaced-out conversation between two hippie freaks, lying in a pad somewhere in San Francisco, who each saw the other in insect form, flying round the room.) Of course, as I finally realised, 'Bobby' is, in fact, a reformed junkie. So much for first impressions.

Writers, be warned. These are the kind of things that can flit around an actor's brain, as he rushes excitedly through the script for the first time.

On further study, however, I realised that the play was in fact a portrayal of American life, if not at the bottom of the pile, then very close to it. The three characters in Mamet's play are about as low on the social ladder as it's possible to get, without actually dropping out: Bobby is a junkie; Teach a psychopath; and Donny owns a junk shop full of things no one would ever want to buy, and actually looks up to a man who, in any other context, would be a loser and a small-time crook.

We've been conditioned in the UK to think of the Hollywood version of American life as reasonably accurate, as opposed to the fake that it usually is. It's true that through Scorsese, we've learned about the 'glamour' of the New York gangs, and the films of John Cassavetes have provided an altogether tougher, unsentimental alternative to the Hollywood vision of American life. But it took the Cohen brothers and David Lynch to reveal the surreal horror of

Middle America. And it took David Mamet to bring home to us the nature of working-class life in the 'big city' and the percussive poetry of life on the street.

As we worked on the play in rehearsal, we began to realise that nothing really happens. There's the threat of something happening, but it doesn't actually transpire. Teach and Donny plan a 'job', a burglary, but they don't carry it out. Bobby, Teach and Donny float around in a pool of lies and possibilities, living a fantasy, hardly daring to look at who they really are.

Violence simmers just below the surface, erupting at the very end. Bobby sits slumped in a chair, bleeding from an ear, while Teach, bleeding in his turn from a blow to the nose, trashes Donny's store with a pig-sticker. It's arguable, I suppose, that this mindless fit of violence is the only thing that happens, physically happens, in the entire play. As the film director Alan Clarke said after he'd been to see one of the early performances: 'It's a lot of rabbit, Jack.' ('Rabbit' being slang for words or conversation.) I was disappointed.

But Alan was a film director who liked his films to interact with the world he lived in. He wasn't so much involved in the texture of language, the shimmering surface of reality, as in the politics of social change. In 1978, when David Mamet was not so well known, I asked him during rehearsals what he thought about the politics of *American Buffalo*. He looked startled. 'I don't write about "politics",' he replied. 'I'm an artist. What I create is . . . art.'

I hadn't heard a writer use that word to describe his work for a long time. All the writers I knew at that time were on the Left, or at least felt that they ought to be, and all the talk was about changing society. I hadn't heard anyone talk about their 'art' since I'd left art school, fifteen years before.

American Buffalo isn't structured, in the way that a play by, say, Arthur Miller is, where events are manipulated to draw attention to a particular theme or an idea. In *The Crucible*, for example, Miller is not only writing a play about a witch trial in the seventeenth century, he's also looking back over his shoulder at the activities of the House Un-American Activities

Committee in the 1950s and saying how hard it is to stand up for the truth when the state decides to move against you.

Nor does *American Buffalo* possess an underlying formal idea, in the way that *The Iceman Cometh* does. The latter is shaped around the bones of Greek drama, with a tormented protagonist (Hickey) and a chorus of ageing dipsomaniacs. There is no 'message' in the play either, in the sense that Alan Clarke, whose celebrated film *Scum* was a cry of protest about the treatment of young offenders, would have appreciated.

In *American Buffalo*, Mamet simply observes the characters, the day-to-day process of their lives. The narrative is to be found in the meandering pattern of their conversation, their plans, their dreams. He observes the surface. And, like a modern painter with an obsessional eye for detail, he watches their behaviour, leaving the audience to make up their own minds about what it all might possibly mean.

Rehearsals went smoothly enough, right up to the first run-through when it became depressingly evident that we weren't getting to the heart of the play. It was all far too long-drawn-out. It was dull, overblown and not at all funny. So naturally we had to take a step back and reconsider our approach. Dave King was playing Donny, Micky Feast was Bobby, I was Teach and Bill Bryden was directing.

The first thing we realised was that we were playing the text at the wrong speed. We were, in fact, very respectfully taking the same kind of time we'd take if it were a Pinter play, with a slow tempo, full of nuance and long meaningful silences. In consequence the play was threatening to topple over under the sheer weight of the subtext.

Slowly it began to dawn on us that maybe there wasn't a profound subtext, as there would be in a Pinter play. Maybe the characters actually meant what they said. When a Pinter character says, 'Oh, yes?', there's usually something unmentionable lurking just below the surface; but when Teach or Donny says, 'Oh, yeah?', he actually means just that.

Added to that, David had often talked about his interest in the 'Moment by Moment' school of acting, the idea being that you didn't burden the rehearsal with all the 'preparation' you'd been doing at home and all the ideas you had about the 'character', you simply respond to the other actor, truthfully and 'in the moment'. And allow the text to take care of everything else.

So when we resumed our rehearsals, we didn't allude to things lurking just below the surface, we didn't worry so much about 'playing the character' and (remembering the speed at which David himself spoke, spitting out the words with a machine-gun delivery) we upped the tempo quite a bit. The results were breathtaking. The play was now lasting the amount of time it was supposed to, it was becoming very funny, and the speed of the delivery created an intensity of energy that drove the play irresistibly forward.

By the time we opened, we were just about getting up to speed. And from the first night onwards, we ran the lines just before curtain up, saying them about as quickly as it's possible to say them; so by the time we finished the run, we'd just about arrived.

After one of the performances, my old 'Method' teacher, Doreen Cannon, an American, complimented me on my accent. 'You sound just like a friend of mine,' she said. 'He's Armenian New York.' 'Thanks,' I told her. 'I was aiming for working-class Chicago. But at least I'm on the right continent.' Actually, I learned a lot from listening to Henry Winkler, who was playing the Fonz at that time in *Happy Days* on TV. That's where the accent *really* came from.

When we came to put on *Glengarry Glen Ross* five years later, in the summer of 1983, Bill and I both knew exactly what we were in for. We knew that the heart of the play was going to be found in the speed and the precision of the speaking. So this time we all learned the lines straight away and played it fast from the very beginning.

Dave King: Jack Shepherd

Dave had a very interesting way of working on a role. He had never trained as an actor and had evolved his own, very

116

original, way of finding the character. He had a mind like a filing cabinet and over the years he'd stored away the memory of countless performances, leading and supporting, in major films and 'B features' both British and American. So whenever he found himself with a new part to play, he'd flick through these memories until he came to an obscure performance by a little-known actor that most closely resembled the character he was supposed to be playing.

This was his starting point: an impression of some long-forgotten performance. It was this that gave him confidence on the first day, and then triggered his own talent, his own creativity, to get him started in the part.

Dave had started out as an entertainer, a harmonica player, singer and comedian, becoming one of the biggest television stars of the 1950s. Then at the height of his celebrity he went to Hollywood, didn't achieve the success he'd hoped for and lost all his money in a land deal that went wrong.

When he finally came back to England, he was disillusioned to discover that the public had forgotten who he was. Rather than start his career all over again, he hired the 'Talk of the Town' for a Sunday evening, gave a farewell concert to his friends and all those people who'd stayed loyal to him, turned his back on the world of showbusiness, and never sang or told a joke in public again.

Dave was always capable of these kind of gestures. I remember his last football match. We were both playing for the same charity side on a Sunday afternoon. Dave was forty-seven at the time, an old-fashioned half-back. Early in the game, he had a shot at goal from fully thirty-five yards out, he didn't really strike it properly, more with his toe than his instep, but the wind caught it and into the net it went. 'That's it,' Dave said to me as he ran off the pitch, with at least an hour of the match still to go. 'I'm never going to score a better goal than that. Now's the time to call it a day.' And he was as good as his word.

Although he'd turned his back on showbusiness, he eventually made a modest comeback in 'straight' acting roles in the 'legitimate' theatre. I first met him at the Royal Court when he was playing the agent Saraffian in David Hare's play *Teeth 'n' Smiles*. I then worked with him again in *American Buffalo* at the National Theatre. He was to stay with the company for about a year, playing Pilate in *The Passion*, old man Sharman in *Lark Rise* and Yank, the dying American, in *Bound East for Cardiff*, one of O'Neill's four plays of the sea, performed by the company in the spring of 1979.

Despite being born in Twickenham, Dave always talked with a trace of the American accent he had picked up in his days in Hollywood. He always sounded to me like one of those British jazz musicians of the 1950s, so in awe of the music of their black American idols that they tended to talk like them as well. Dave always smiled: smiled when he was happy, when he was unhappy, when he was angry, a smile of enthusiasm, a smile of despair.

He left the company, in rather sad circumstances, well before his contract was up. The truth is, he wasn't really a company man. Dave was used to considering the part as a 'vehicle' for himself, and his ego wasn't easily absorbed into the company identity. His catchphrase, back in the 1950s, had been '*Big 'ead*', and the TV audience would chant it at him whenever he'd done something particularly outrageous. He would encourage them by cupping his hands either side of his grinning face and spreading them sideways, indicating how big that head of his was actually getting.

In his days with the Cottesloe Company, his entertainer's ego lurked just below the surface. But very occasionally, if he felt it was right, he'd allow it out, though only for a very short while. In some performances of *American Buffalo*, for example, if the audience were really laughing at the funny lines, he'd look at me as if to say, 'Are you ready for this?' And I'd nod back with a cagey sort of, 'Go on.' And he'd grin at me like a monkey, as if he was saying, 'Let's have some fun, shall we?'

And from that moment on the audience's laughter would steadily build to the point of hysteria. From where I was it didn't seem as if he was doing anything very different, yet the audience would be laughing so much they'd be threatening to overwhelm the play. At which point he would look at me again, this time signalling, 'I think that's enough. Don't you?' I'd nod. And everyone would slowly begin to quieten down. I've still no idea how he did it.

The circumstances of Dave's departure were unfortunate. He'd never been very popular with the company. He didn't mix at all and hardly drank. He was something of a lone wolf. Bill, though, always stood up for him, having a huge respect for the abilities of people from the world of Variety. But for Dave, it all started to go wrong when he was asked to take over the part of the Cheapjack in *Lark Rise*, a part that, ironically, he was ideally suited to play.

The Cheapjack is a man who comes to the village periodically, selling things from the back of his cart, and like other characters in the play has a song to sing; something that Dave was better qualified to do than any other person in the building. The problem was, of course, that he didn't really perceive it as a song, he saw it more as a 'number', a good 'vehicle' for him (which of course it was), and all his repressed performer's instincts came flooding to the fore.

What he was imagining – as Sebastian Graham-Jones discovered, when he started the rehearsal – was a 'Dave King' *routine*: a song, a little dance, getting kids out of the audience to sit on his knee and all the rest of it. The problem was that routines like this belonged to a Danny Kaye film of the 1950s, a Disney movie, or even a pantomime. When Sebastian tried to point out to him that his ideas weren't really appropriate to Flora Thompson's evocation of village life in the late Victorian age, he was mortally offended, and in a state of terrible rage and confusion stormed out of the building. The Cheapjack scene was cut until a replacement could be found. Dave returned on performance nights to play his other role, but that was effectively the end of his career at the National Theatre.

Most of the company were old enough to remember him from his days as an entertainer on TV. But it was hardly ever mentioned. I don't think he was really trusted. Keith had always considered him a 'pastiche of an American', until his performance in *The Passion* forced him to change his mind. He even considered him for the role of Cromwell in *The World*

119

Turned Upside Down, but his attitude in *Lark Rise*, his unwillingness to come to terms with the style, proved a big disappointment and the offer was never made.

Dave kept on acting. I'd see him from time to time on the television, playing what used to be known as 'character parts'. But I'm not sure his heart was in it. He once told me that the best performance he'd ever seen was a concert given by Frank Sinatra in London. He was clearly fascinated by the man, spellbound by his music and absolutely in awe of the way he could control an audience.

This was the world, I think, in which Dave King's heart truly lay.

16. *The World Turned Upside Down*

Civil war, mutinies and strikes: Keith Dewhurst

In the summer of 1978 I went to Antigua and Virginia to conclude the slave trade research for my novel, and returned to find that *The Passion* and *Lark Rise* were booked for revivals, during which we would rehearse another project: an adaptation of Christopher Hill's book *The World Turned Upside Down*, about the left-wing revolutionaries in the English Civil War. The problem posed by a straight history book was not the *Lark Rise* one of incident and narrative; it was how to explain essential facts that some of the audience may not know. The most important of these was that, in the seventeenth century, politics were expressed in religious terms: King Charles I believed himself to rule by Divine Right and had state policy preached from the pulpits of an authoritarian Church. His opponents among the mercantile classes and the squirearchy thought that their position in society entitled them to a greater say in how it was run, and they worshipped in increasingly independent congregations, who sometimes sought to elect their own preachers. For eleven years the King ruled without Parliament. When a lack of money forced him to call one, it would not vote money without changes. The King refused and there was civil war.

As the fighting progressed, more social barriers were breached. Parliament, backed by the City of London, raised its New Model Army, the core of which was the elite cavalry regiments of Oliver Cromwell and his associates. When it was obvious that they had won the war the men of these regiments, each of which was full of preachers and political activists, wanted to know what they would get out of the victory. The Levellers, as they were called, a movement of some MPs,

London pamphleteers and military agitators, went beyond religion and formulated the first notions of secular democracy. The Putney Debates of 1648 record the discussions about the future of England's political structure between the Levellers and the army high command. In January 1649 the King was executed and a republic declared, and soon after Cromwell prepared to invade Ireland, both to secure a dangerous flank and to pay the soldiers' arrears by giving them conquered land, which would then be bought back from them by their officers and London financiers. It was a sort of privatisation via military force, and several regiments disagreed and mutinied. They were put down at Burford in Oxfordshire, and their ringleaders shot.

The Leveller mutiny was the most extreme political expression of revolution: others were more religious. The Diggers, inspired by an idealist named Gerard Winstanley, set up primitive agrarian communes that inevitably fizzled out, and various fundamentalist cults used the scriptures to justify individual hedonism. The Ranters and their sexual permissiveness are the best known. Hill's book is a treasure trove of this material, with extensive quotations from pamphlets and so forth.

General preparations for the show went well. We screened the films *Cromwell* and *Winstanley* (I had actually been on the BFI committee that voted the money for Kevin Brownlow to make the latter) and through Derek Newark's military contacts we visited the Honourable Artillery Company, who gave the actors tuition in pike and musket drill. Newark himself was not free to act in the play, but gave a rehearsal-room lecture with charts about the organisation of the New Model Army. Christopher Hill paid us a rehearsal visit, and returned to give a remarkable platform lecture in the Lyttelton Theatre.

As for writing the play, I had very little time, but I had lived with the material for years, and had already written various scenes and versions of a play about Oliver Cromwell. I followed chronology and began with the execution of the King, contrasting his actual speech with shouts from the crowd, which I took from old parish register entries about the deaths of poor people. The first half concluded with slightly expanded scenes from the Cromwell drafts that I had written some twelve or fifteen years earlier: the putting down at Burford of the Leveller mutiny. This left the second half to the religious crackpots. The hopeful start and pitiable decline of Winstanley's Diggers ran throughout. As far as possible I adapted dialogue from pamphlets and speeches of the time. My mistake was to introduce a couple of scenes which, although they cast an interesting financial and social light on events, had no real narrative point. As Brian Glover said: 'Too hurriedly written!'

Bill's opening team talk was a classic. He held up a Bible and said, 'We're doing a play about people who lived by this book!' On about the third day Niall Toibin, the Irishman cast as Cromwell, finally joined us and was flung at once into his entrance, which was followed by a soliloquy in which Cromwell seeks God's guidance. His effect upon the macho hordes was that of Caroline Embling raised to the power of five.

A couple of weeks later there occurred one of the silliest and most pointed of Bill's rehearsal-room exchanges. We needed more old men than we could get from the group, and took a Casting Department suggestion named Norman Tyrrel. In the middle of a scene in the Diggers' camp Bill stopped the action and said: 'Why are you acting like that?' 'I'm playing an old man,' said Norman.

'Norman,' came the reply, 'you *are* old.' To Norman's credit, he took it and came back straight and strong.

We cut one of my irrelevant scenes, and rejigged a bit, but the fact is that it was not until I cut two further scenes and built up another, when I was in Sydney some six years later, that the play assumed its proper form, as Sebastian demonstrated when he did an excellent production of it at the Welsh College of Music and Drama in early 2000. I have no doubt that it is the best play I wrote and that, when it settled, the original production contained the best work that Bill and Sebastian and I did together.

I say 'settled' because we were hampered in our work and interrupted by the National Theatre's industrial troubles.

Ironic, one might think, that a play about left-wing agitators should be caught up thus, and to tell the truth we were never sure where our sympathies lay in the dispute. Perhaps the cause, as was said about the Civil War, was too good to be fought for.

Since the South Bank building delays, and the consequent failure of all the stage machinery to work in time for the opening, there had been a muddy situation with the stage-hands. Agreements had been renegotiated to suit a high-tech, low-manpower building. When high-tech did not work, the management wanted to pay old rates for old work and manning levels. As high-tech began to work, the men wanted the new levels of pay but no redundancies. It was irredeemably ambiguous, and juggling with schedules and overtime and so forth kept it going for a limited period. Then the men struck, and on this occasion the management backed off. I remember the stagehands in the Green Room after their victory, raising their pints and chanting, 'We are the Champions!'

What we lost was time for technical rehearsals and previews; in particular, the time to test our rewrites with an audience, or to do more of them. Nor were we helped by the fact that because they had some dates in other plays in the building, a couple of actors had to miss previews and the odd per-formance. Sebastian was a very good deputy, and once Newark appeared and once, late in the run and very effectively, Brian Cox, but the fact was that Bill, who prided himself on delivering the actors in good nick for the first night, was this time not quite able to do so. There were fluffs and early mistakes. Things settled, but the atmosphere was wrong and we did not get good reviews, except from one or two people who were ill and came later.

We had to share the Cottesloe repertoire with Charles Wood's *Has Washington Legs*. Dudley designed both shows for a traverse stage which split the theatre down the middle like our *Corunna!* ramp, and suited us because it made the space resemble the House of Commons. This was equally effective when Sebastian staged the Putney Debates for three nights, the actual speeches being edited by Jack Emery. There were emblematic devices at both ends of the traverse, a Liberty Tree at one end, and a baroque painting that gave way to the Great Seal of the Commonwealth at the other. Nothing went on stage that the actors could not carry as essential props. It was streamlined, and what music there was hurried it along.

We did not have a full band but John Tams and Maddy Prior led the songs and were added acting presences, and there were period-style keyboards, a shawm, and Michael Gregory drove through many of the scene changes with his side-drum. Tams came up with most of the tunes, although I think it was Bill who thought of using 'Bright Morning Star' as a counterpoint to the Burford firing squad. For Ashley, this was a strange time. He fell in love with being in the theatre, somehow, except that of all the productions this was one in which he did the least, and after it his relationship to the company was never quite the same. He was never again the Tyger of whom everyone was a bit nervous, the Tyger of whom Dudley, apropos his *Lark Rise* costume, said, 'I've put him in jackboots but so far he hasn't clocked it.' Slowly but surely thereafter, Tams won more of Bill's confidence.

The acting company for the play was like a Champions League squad: Shepherd, Bob Hoskins, who went on once in his dark glasses, David Rintoul, Oliver Cotton, Howard Goorney, who had been with Joan Littlewood before the war, Gawn Grainger, Trevor Ray, Toibin, Glover, Peter Armitage, McManus inspirational as Winstanley, Marty Cruickshank, Irene Gorst, June Watson, who was outstanding as a woman seeking independence, Tamara Hinchco, Edna Doré. The scene of the Ranters' sex orgy, with naked people fucking a few feet from the audience, was a mind-blow. We never used it for publicity and never received a complaint. But audiences were better pleased than people who wrote about the play, which they did mostly from their own political standpoint.

This latter came as a disappointment. Our intention had not been to promote particular views, but to show how certain ideas came about and were able to exist for a moment before history closed in on them. It took until the nineteenth century for the ideas of the Levellers to become the stock-in-trade of

125

Western democracy, and until the hippie, flower-power, drugs culture of the 1960s for the ideas of the Diggers and the Ranters to bloom again. To me this sense of history and timing was the point. Cromwell understood history's tides, even as he turned them away from extremism, and Winstanley expressed eternal dreams.

On the night after the play closed, some of us went to Wembley to see England beat Northern Ireland 4–0. At the end of the match Toibin stood up and warned the departing crowd: 'Wait for the real Irish, the ones with the power of Rome!'

The postscript to *The World Turned Upside Down* came in March 1980. *The Passion* and *Lark Rise* were in rehearsal for a spring season when the stagehands went on strike again. The National had acquired a general manager from the world of industry, Michael Elliott, who determined to play hardball. The stagehands could not resist a confrontation. There were picket lines, banners and the obligatory bonfires in oil drums, and for four nights we did workshops and question-and-answer sessions for people who had booked Cottesloe tickets. There was also a remarkable incident within the company. One of the current actors was Peter Armitage, a radiantly honest Yorkshireman, who was also a member of the Socialist Workers' Party. During a break in the Green Room, Glover, in politics, I suppose, a bizarre combination of working-class Tory and Ranter, chided Armitage with the thought that if he was true to his socialist principles he would be out on the picket line. What was expected, I think, was a smart-arse reply to a smart-arse provocation. What happened was that Armitage took it to heart, walked out of rehearsals and joined the stagehands on the picket line. But their case was half-good at best, and their bravado misplaced. Their union would not call an official strike because no general principle was at stake, and Michael Elliott won the day. The hard core lost their jobs, and so did Armitage; but whereas the strikers were soon found places at the Royal Opera House, he spent a long time in the twilight. Michael Elliott, after leaving the National Theatre, directed an amateur production of *Lark Rise* in the car park of his local public house.

The epic challenge of the brambles: Jack Shepherd

The Leveller William Thompson, on the run from Cromwell's soldiers, was eventually snagged up in the thorns of a bramble bush, where, after shooting two of his pursuers, he was killed. When working on the casting of *The World Turned Upside Down*, both Bill and Keith decided that I was the man to face the challenge of playing this scene: an actor on a bare stage, first creating the bramble bush, and then dying in it. It's not surprising that they chose me, really. I'd often talked about the training I'd had in the techniques of epic theatre.

I've always suspected that both Keith and Bill had guessed that this might be a challenge too far. And so it proved to be. All my attempts to act the part of a desperate man floundering in a tangle of thorns looked like Marcel Marceau having a fit. In the end I sat with my back to the wall, cradled the musket in my arms and allowed the lines to do the work: 'Damn these brambles.'

The part of Laurence Clarkson, leader of the Ranters, was more accessible. He was a seventeenth-century Timothy Leary, reaching out to God through heightened awareness and sexual ecstasy. I wore a red wig, a full red beard and spoke in an accent midway between Blackburn and the West Country, which felt exactly right.

In the orgy scene, I didn't join the orgy – a writhing organism made up of indiscriminate bits of Tamara Hinchco, Gawn Grainger, June Watson, Bob Hoskins and company – I whirled around in the middle of the stage as if all this sexual energy was spinning out of me. It seemed like a good idea, but most of the company considered it a cop-out, which it probably was.

The World Turned Upside Down was a genuine company play, epic in scale, with a powerful historical narrative: an exhilarating slice of history from our distant revolutionary past. But it wasn't easy to perform. There was no central character. No individual catharsis for the play to drive towards and then fall away from. In the second half the revolutionary flame is slowly extinguished: the Levellers are shot; the Diggers give up; the Ranters are arrested.

It has a sad and fragmented ending: the play's protagonists – heroes and villains – drift back into obscurity and the memory of their struggle is buried at the Restoration.

A Comment: Keith Dewhurst

Thompson's death in the brambles took place near Wellingborough, and when I'm in a train that passes through I always think of him. In Sydney I cut the scene because, after the firing-squad at the end of Act One, the narrative does not need it. But like the casks of money scene in *Corunna!*, it can exercise a perverse fascination.

18. *Dispatches*

Jack Shepherd

The World Turned Upside Down was an Impossible Play that examined English radical history. Our production of *Dispatches*, in the summer of 1979, took us in another direction entirely. It was an account of American history, focused on the war in Vietnam.

I became so involved in the *doing* of the piece that I hadn't paid much attention to its political content until Trevor Griffiths came to see it, a few weeks into the run. I asked him if he'd enjoyed it. 'Yes,' he said, carefully choosing his words. 'As a show it's enjoyable. It's like watching a musical about the siege of Stalingrad, but from the German point of view. Now if that can be said to be "enjoyable" then so is this.' That brought me up a bit short.

This was a Truly Impossible Play. For a start it was taken from a book without any real narrative: *Dispatches* by Michael Herr. It's an account of the Vietnam War through the eyes of a young music journalist, writing initially for *Esquire* magazine, whose view of the war is clouded by the drugs he was taking, the music he was listening to and the extraordinary nature of the time that he was having over there.

The thing that had disturbed Trevor (a committed Marxist) so much was the fact that *Dispatches didn't* have a political perspective. It didn't even declare itself for or against the war; it simply *reported* what had happened. Everything the play revealed led inexorably towards the author's chilling conclusion that, when all was said and done, he had had the *time of his life.* Such a revelation doesn't push people towards a political conclusion, it makes them sit up and *think.*

Michael Herr's catchphrase was: 'It's all information.' This was his take on reality, implying that he didn't really make distinctions between the things that were happening around him, *outside* of him, good or bad, in peace or in war, in joy or in sorrow. It was all *information*, feeding into the brain.

Dispatches, then, was a piece of reportage. In form it was not unlike a film documentary, following the lives of people – combatants and non-combatants alike – caught up in the conflict. My young son watched it in a state of 'bare-knuckle terror'. Looking back, years later, he said it was like being present at a traffic accident and then being invited to take a closer look. The audience were *witnesses* to the events.

This time Bill didn't invite Keith to do the adaptation, he took it on himself. With Trevor Ray as his script editor, they cut and pasted a version that changed little as we worked our way through rehearsals.

Bill was clearly fascinated by the war. He'd directed a play in the Lyceum Studio in Edinburgh, years before, called *Calley Meets Manson*, which linked the massacre at My Lai with the murders of the Manson gang in California. He'd also got actors to learn the written testimonies of troops caught up in the massacre, which were then put on video and shown on a screen, documentary-style, during the action. The idea of a piece about the Vietnam War had evidently been in his mind for some time.

The problem with this adaptation was the absence of a narrative in the Robert McKee sense of the word. The individual scenes were riveting in themselves, weird, funny and at times downright frightening, but they were all part of one man's *experience* of the war as opposed to a story he was telling. The problem was solved through the use of a narrator, called 'The Correspondent' in the script, talking to the audience throughout and binding all the disparate scenes together. Essentially, the Correspondent was Michael Herr and, though I didn't at all resemble him physically, I was given the role to play.

By the summer of 1979 Michael's hair was short. He wore serious-looking spectacles, and there was little trace of the rock'n'roll years apart from his habit of popping marijuana seeds into the ends of his French cigarettes first thing in the morning. His voice floated out in a dreamy New York State accent. This was one thing about him, I thought, that I'd finally be able to nail. His other qualities seemed more elusive.

He would sit at the bar – Armagnac was the only drink he enjoyed – paying attention to almost every conversation that was happening nearby. He'd often break off the exchange he was having with you and burst out laughing as he took in a point being made by someone several yards away, turning to them briefly to say, 'Yeah. Right . . .' And then, still nodding his head in agreement, he'd look right back at you and pick up from where he'd left off.

The main problem I was faced with in playing Michael Herr was that I had no real experience of marijuana. It was a substance that tended to dislocate my sense of reality and all the people I knew who used the drug regularly were slowly turning into blancmange, so I had avoided it. (On second thoughts, it's not blancmange, it's meringue with a crusty exterior and a soft middle.) However, I was playing Michael Herr and, on the evidence of his book, I couldn't do that convincingly without coming to terms with the purple haze of his Vietnam experience.

We simply had to smoke a joint together. I could see it coming. There was no way of avoiding it and it was a question of not losing face. And so a few weeks into the rehearsal period I went round to Michael's Chelsea flat one evening with only one thought in mind. The place seemed very peaceful. Michael's wife was napping on a sofa when we arrived. His child was happily padding about, taking his first few steps.

'You wanna smoke some bullshit?' It was the first time I'd heard him speak with any real authority. Sipping Glenmorangie in the depths of an armchair, I watched him busy himself at a nearby cupboard. After a while he returned with what looked like a very small, very thin cigarette, which he lit up on the sofa opposite, inhaled deeply, and handed to me. I puffed on it nervily a couple of times, holding my breath as I knew you were supposed to do and quickly handed it back. He seemed very pleased to have it returned so quickly and set about it with a will.

What followed was very strange. I found I was watching him

intently. The more he inhaled, the redder his face seemed to get. And then at the point when I though he was surely going to burst . . . A flame erupted from the top of his head and his face started to melt like candle grease.

The hallucination didn't last for very long, but I was not in a good state. When Mike suggested that we go out to eat I felt I was taking giant strides towards the door, like a character drawn by Robert Crumm. Outside, the pavement was stretched rubber and very difficult to navigate. We abandoned the first restaurant we tried, where the 'vibes were bad' and the mineral water went down like broken glass, and finished up in an Algerian restaurant somewhere in Chelsea, where the rocket-ship slowly came in to land and I managed to dock back into some sort of reality. I have no memory of what we ate or what we talked about.

We said goodbye on Battersea Bridge, where my car was parked. I got into the passenger seat, reached for a wheel that wasn't there and bumped my head gently against the glove compartment. My last view of Mike that night was of him leaning against the parapet, near doubled up with laughter. I was fine in the morning, but for the next few weeks, every time I had a glass of Guinness or whatever, I'd get a seismic echo of the event.

The set was designed by Bill Dudley, though, in actual fact, it was less of a set and more of an environment. As in a promenade performance, the audience were made to feel a part of the action, which was played out on a floor of thick wooden boards placed in the middle of the auditorium. The audience surrounded it on three sides and looked down into a kind of bear-pit – at least that's what it felt like from where we, the actors, were standing. Trapdoors had been cut into the floorboards, which could be flipped open to reveal Napalmed bodies. Some of these trapdoors also concealed explosive devices, which were detonated during the course of the action.

The stage end of the auditorium was masked by a giant screen of camouflage netting, behind which the Albion Band were concealed on a raised platform. They were dressed

Jefferson Airplane-style, slewing away from their folk traditions, transforming themselves into a full-blooded rock'n'roll band, with Tams singing leads as usual (this time with an American accent), Mike Gregory laying down the beat and Graeme Taylor featured on electric guitar – at one point blowing all our minds with the Jimi Hendrix version of 'The Star Spangled Banner'.

In fact, the band were concealed from the audience at first and then suddenly revealed in a blaze of light and an explosion of sound, adding in that moment both the dimension and the impact of a rock concert.

To my knowledge, this was the only one of Bill's productions to use canned music. The songs of the period were thought to be so evocative, so much a part of the world of the play, that it was decided to use the original recordings at certain key moments in the action.

The helicopter effect was most definitely a *coup de théâtre*. It would seem to come swooping over the heads of the musicians, deafening the audience with the pulse of its engines, blinding them with its searchlight, land on the stage and then (loaded down with Marines and reporters) take off again into the night sky. All it was, in fact, was a board about six feet square, hoisted up on wires in a diagonal direction, a searchlight and a sound effect. The rest was imagination.

Every night in performance, I'd sit on stage waiting for the helicopter to arrive and never entirely sure whom I'd be playing the scene with when it did. The part of the black Marine about to disembark from the helicopter was being shared by two actors: Clarke Peters and Guy Gregory. Guy would come at you like a snake, quiet, mean, and with a green aura. Clarke, on the other hand, would start burning so much aggression, so much pure energy, he'd seem to be almost dancing the part.

I worked with Clarke a few times over the years that followed, but I never saw Guy again. Before we said goodbye, he gave me a book on how to be a wizard, full of very precise instructions. I never found out why.

If there were more black actors than was usual in this

production, it reflected the large numbers of black Americans drafted into the Marine Corps, rather than a shift in National Theatre policy. In those days, black actors were not as integrated into the system as they are today. Don Warrington used to argue that race shouldn't necessarily bar actors from playing the great classical roles. He looked forward to the day when a black actor could play Hamlet, say, without anyone worrying unduly if Gertrude and Claudius were both white. He was ahead of his time. The Globe has operated a multiracial policy since its beginnings in 1996.

There were many great parts for Marines in this story, or 'grunts' as they were known. Oliver Cotton played Orrin, a Southern American going out of his mind with problems back home. Oscar James was a permanently stoned Marine called 'Daytripper' and Micky Feast a *very* stoned one. Not forgetting Derek Thompson, who played his 'grunt' with a real sense of authenticity, years before he was absorbed into the *Casualty* series on the BBC. But the focus of the play was essentially on the Correspondent and his associates in the media: Tim Page, Dana Stone and Sean Flynn.

The real Tim Page drifted in and out of rehearsals, acting as a secondary adviser. Ten years before, he'd been a war photographer, an Englishman in Vietnam at a time when – mainly on account of the Rolling Stones – being English was a very hip thing to be. Tim had been blown up, hung on to life against the odds, and miraculously survived the war with a reconstructed skull. On the first night he had to be restrained from jumping down on to the stage to shoot the action.

Sean Flynn and Dana Stone were reporters, both presumed dead. They'd gone into Cambodia to cover events there and never returned. Both men were searching for greater *involvement*, no longer content merely to observe. They'd been seduced by the glamour, the existential knife-edge of war, into taking more of an active part. Sean was the son of the legendary Errol Flynn, and very much a chip off the old block. Brian Prothero effortlessly filled the role. A squat and sardonic Trevor Ray took the part of Dana Stone. Page was played by John Salthouse.

A few weeks into the run, one of our company went 'absent without leave', failing to turn up for the evening performance. Kevin McNally, who was playing a smaller part – his first with the company – stepped into the breach. Someone covered for him. Someone else covered for *him*. And so it went on, until most of the cast were, at some point, playing a part they were hardly familiar with. When the absentee returned to collect some things he'd left behind (a guitar, things like that) he was literally captured by Trevor Ray and Derek Newark, forced into sobering up and bundled on to the stage against his will.

I had stayed well clear of this drama, focusing on the performance that lay ahead, which was a mistake as it turned out, since in those moments leading up to the absentee's entrance, I could hear what sounded like fighting going on under the stage. A few moments later, bang on cue, he was pushed on, landing at my feet like an old coat dropped off a peg. I said the line as usual, *didn't* throw him the can of lager as I usually did, guessing he was in no fit state to catch it, and waited for a response. He looked up, tears streaming down his face, mingling with the snot from his nose. 'Sorry, Jack,' he said, 'I'm sorry . . .'

The audience were very quiet that night, but we got through the performance. The actor in question, not surprisingly, was absent for the rest of the run, though it's good to report that at the time of writing, twenty-five years later, he's playing leading parts in the theatre and probably in the best form of his life.

The night the 'Vets' were in we all felt rather subdued, intimidated almost, feeling that our right to tell this story was being called into question. They sat in a bunch, like a black cloud. They were overweight men in early middle age, with straggly hair and long moustaches, laughing at things no one else in the building found funny. It was kind of sinister.

Dispatches was one of Bill's most successful epic productions, thrilling, popular, funny, glamorous even. And it said something important about the world we live in. What he'd stumbled on was a form of *documentary* theatre. And it still surprises me that he didn't follow it up in any way. *Dispatches* was never revived, the text was never published, and, more surprisingly, the *form* of it was never repeated. No other epic plays with a contemporary theme were attempted in the future. It was the closest we got, I suppose, to an Impossible Play about our own times.

It seems to me now, looking back, that *Dispatches* was perhaps the end of something, rather than a beginning. Perhaps Bill felt he'd finally realised the vision he'd had twelve years before, when he'd shown me that photo of the Abbey Road studios. Perhaps he felt that he'd finally got there and there was no further to go.

One final memory: Bill in rehearsal, talking about the helicopter flying in.

'When the punters see it . . . coming down . . . they'll think it's *real*. No question. It – it – it's a goal I'm telling you. A fucking goal.'

And it was.

19. Opportunities and Dilemmas

The Long Riders: Keith Dewhurst

Dispatches was a great theatrical happening, and it is ridiculous that it was never restaged or exploited. But then, the failure to exploit anything, really, except *The Mysteries* was ridiculous. It is explained by Peter Hall's wish to keep hit shows in the Cottesloe for which they had been designed, by the high cost of the shows, and by Bill's attitude to what he wanted to do. Things were rolling. Why wouldn't they go on? There was time, wasn't there? When Joe Papp's New York Theatre in the Park asked him to direct *Dispatches* with American actors he refused, on the grounds that he would only do it with his own company. Laudable-seeming at the time, maybe, but in retrospect a missed rung on the power ladder; not least because all through those years he was dreaming of Hollywood and the movies. In early 1979 they seemed, however amazingly, to have come within his grasp.

For some time the director Walter Hill had been trying to set up a film about Jesse James with the brothers Carradine, Keach and Quaid playing the three sets of brothers in the gang, but nobody could agree on a script. The actor Brian Cox had been a friend of Stacey Keach since drama school, and when told about the film situation said, 'Bill Bryden wrote a script about Jesse James. Why don't you read it?' Keach did. The script was then accepted as a compromise by the other parties, Bill was paid for it and Walter Hill went into production with Twentieth Century-Fox. Bill's original was very long and historically penetrating. Hill's inevitable shortening made it a more orthodox action movie, under the title *The Long Riders*. In September 1979, Bill went to America for a couple of weeks, and visited Hill on location. Before he left, because work in the Cottesloe had to continue, he set in motion the process whereby we would do *Candleford* as a companion-piece to *Lark Rise*.

Candleford: Keith Dewhurst

Flora Thompson's trilogy, *Lark Rise*, *Candleford Green* and *Over to Candleford*, charts the childhood and early youth of her autobiographical heroine Laura, and it seemed sensible to set a second play around the post office and smithy where Laura went to work, and to contrast the *Lark Rise* events of a day in summer with a day in winter.

This time, John Caulfield, Bill Dudley and I went to Fringford, the Candleford Green of the book, where the building that housed the smithy and post office still stands, and I just about finished the script in time for Bill's return and rehearsals at the end of September. *Lark Rise* would open first, and the plays run in tandem until after Christmas.

I found *Candleford* hard to write, partly because we had to live up to *Lark Rise* and partly because I had to assimilate the difference between the two phases in Flora Thompson's development. Nor could I find a proper end to the piece until we had done at least two previews. Then I had a brainwave and in an afternoon rehearsal knocked off the scene between the adult Laura and her husband.

There were good promenade effects in the Hunt, the Snowball Fight and the Hunt Ball, but Dudley closed off one end of the house set with a Welsh dresser, which made viewing harder for the audience. He has a wonderful talent, but he will bring on scenery wherever he can, whereas I would always throw it out.

At the time *Candleford* seemed a bit of a let-down, and yet when I saw it recently for only the second time in twenty-odd years I was pleasantly surprised. It is more naturalistic and less epic than *Lark Rise*, darker but also funnier, and Laura becomes a more aware observer. She grows into the knowledge that she herself will have to deal with the problems and potentialities of womanhood. The real postmistress, Mrs Whitton, was a widow, but Flora Thompson fictionalised her as the unmarried Dorcas Lane, and in consequence wrote an early study of a non-privileged but self-aware independent woman. Morag Hood was well cast in the role, and Valerie Whittington, who had been found by Annie Robinson of the Casting Department, amplified her sweet, true and luminous Laura. For the first time the company included none of the original midfield, which in one way made it less cohesive, although there was a recall for Dave Hill, a magisterial injection of star quality by Peggy Mount, and smart young chaps who had been in *Dispatches*: Kevin McNally, Brian Protheroe and John Salthouse, whom I met on *The Bomb in Brewery Street*.

There were one or two emergencies during the run, notably when J. G. Devlin went home for Christmas and slipped on the ice outside the Belfast Arts Club; going in, as he was at pains to point out, and not coming out. Newark, who had earlier deputised for James Grant, replaced him on one night and Michael Gough on another. A point of comic contention with Michael Gough had been that when, in the original *Passion*, he played John the Baptist, he often had trouble with the words of the opening speech which, as Bill liked to point out, sets up the plot for everybody. Now he arrived at a few hours' notice to replace Devlin and bumped into Bill, who said, 'Are you OK on the lines, Michael?' 'Absolutely,' said Gough, and gave a word-perfect rendition of his speech as John the Baptist.

Martin Carthy returned for both plays, and his Postman Brown in *Candleford*, when he sang a revival hymn that Bill recalled from his childhood, was a very sturdy performance. Tams was joint MD with Ashley. As things got worse in the folk world, so the Albion Band's NT gigs became more of a haven, and the longer the plays ran in this final season, the more people turned up to play in the band. 'It's like Spector's Wall of Sound,' said Ashley, grinning, as though he would have done it all the time if integrity had allowed.

On the last night all the singers went on for the *Lark Rise* pub scene, and before the last verse of the Holmfirth Anthem one of them called, 'On your feet, lads,' and as they rose they removed their hats in tribute to all England's singers before them. The emotion of it swept the audience.

Despite its hold on the audience *Lark Rise* was difficult to get published, although since it was it has never been out of print. It was also hard to get anyone interested in a recording of the music until my wife and agent Alexandra Cann involved the producer Mick McDonagh, who, after both shows had closed, raised the money to cut an album. In February 1981 he secured its release through Charisma, run by Tony Stratton-Smith, whom I had known years before – when we were both football reporters.

Plans and a dilemma: Keith Dewhurst

Bill, Sebastian and I always talked about possible projects and knew that we should try to do something about the Industrial Revolution. At one time we thought that George Eliot's novel *Adam Bede* might give us an angle, but I doubt that it would have, and the idea came to nothing. What had mainly excited us, I think, was the fact that the book begins with a stage-coach journey through England, and we dreamed that we could do this on video screens set around the space. Then Bill had the idea, long before Michael Mann filmed *The Last of the Mohicans*, to do all four of Fenimore Cooper's Leatherstocking novels, on successive evenings, which would have been a panorama of the early American frontier and the spoliation of the wilderness; we saw McManus as the hero, the promenade as the forest and prairie, and were tickled by the idea of Jack Shepherd gliding up in Huron warpaint. At one point Bill leaked this project to a newspaper, but it did not materialise.

The project that came nearest to happening was *War in Val d'Orcia*, a proposed adaptation of Iris Origo's diary written on her Tuscan estate during the Second World War. It is a small masterpiece which when I found it in the London Library had been out of print for years. Iris Origo's father was from American railroad money, and had married an Anglo-Irish aristocrat. When he died young Iris was brought up by her mother in Italy and married the impoverished Marchese Origo, whom she set up on an estate. Origo had fascist inclinations, Iris was liberal and the estate was at a historical crossroads of partisans, British prisoners of war and eventually the front line of battle. When Iris and her amanuensis Hallam Tennyson came to meetings at the NT, and to see *Lark Rise*, she was about eighty. Hallam told me later that she didn't really like *Lark Rise* (the music was too noisy) but saw no harm in us proceeding. Unfortunately nothing happened, although eventually Mark Shivas and I held the film rights, which in the end, and with Iris's approval, we sold on.

Other aspects of future promenade work that we discussed were the use of backpack video (easy with today's digital cameras), scene changes which would alter the walls of the theatre, contemporary subjects in which the actors would look like the audience, a project about the Blitz (still viable, I think) and an attempt to face up to the questions raised by *Candleford*. That is to say, whether a more naturalistic drama of individual psychology was truly suited to the promenade, and what would have to be done to make it so. And I always believed that Bill should have tried to lure Finney into Falstaff, and play *Henry IV* in the promenade; but I usually suggested it too late at night, after too many drinks, and in the middle of tracks by Stephen Stills or Neil Young. The Bill Bryden Record Hour, as we called it, when his enthusiasm made him a DJ in his own sitting-room, commentating as he snatched discs on and off the turntable, was one of the most annoying and funny things I have ever known.

It may be asked why none of these schemes matured, and the answer I guess is that they would have taken time, and Bill was suddenly not sure that he had any, or not in the short run, anyway, because *The Long Riders* seemed to promise that his movie dreams could come true. How, therefore, was he to manage things?

His dilemma points to a little-mentioned aspect of subsidised theatre, which is that although the power is in the hands of directors, they do not have the same capacity to make

141

money as the top or even average writers and actors. Writers and actors have access to films, radio and television; a director running a building has to stay in the building. In the decade under discussion, Bill Bryden was the major innovative director in British theatre but his jobs were staff appointments. He certainly made less money than me, his chief collaborator, less than a star like Rikki, and probably less than the senior actors in his company. At the same time he had a wife and acquired a mortgage and two children. The same was, and is, true for most of his fellow directors, and over the years these imbalances have caused much hidden but festering bitterness, envy and revenge, and have been a major unstated reason why some plays have been put on and others not, why art houses have done commercial musicals, and why talented people have been forced to compromise. And once they have compromised, it can be harder for them to win the jobs in which they need not.

Bill Gaskill once said to Bill Bryden, 'you will find as you get older that directing is a homosexual art', and he did not mean anything to do with gender. He meant that a single man might survive with integrity on theatre wages, when one with a wife and children might not. And does not the abuse hurled at Peter Hall by other directors look different when we realise that he had access to the profits of transfers, but they did not?

When Bill received a Hollywood fee for *The Long Riders* it was a great fillip, and who would not have wanted to move their career towards the prospect of it happening again? Chances come when they come and must be taken. Others had juggled a career between theatre and cinema or television. Why shouldn't he? Meanwhile, in early 1980 there were theatre commitments: the first of them was a season in the Cottesloe of plays by Eugene O'Neill.

Summer manoeuvres: Keith Dewhurst

By the time the O'Neill season had ended, *The Long Riders* was ready, and Bill wanted to be free to take advantage.

Productions by Lindsay Anderson, Athol Fugard and Christopher Morahan were put into the Cottesloe until September 1980. Bill went to see the film at the Cannes Film Festival, and in July the Cottesloe Company were invited to a screening at the Fox Theatre in Soho Square. In between Bill went to Hollywood. The film was a fair success and Bill's script well received. He met the studio executives at Fox and they were customarily cautious. They offered him a writing deal, to work on one of their projects. He accepted. His need then was for time to fulfil the deal, because he had already agreed with Peter Hall to work on *The Mysteries*, take it to the Edinburgh Festival, and mount Arthur Miller's *The Crucible* in the Cottesloe.

20. The O'Neill Season

The Sea Plays: Jack Shepherd

In the early part of 1980, three plays by Eugene O'Neill were brought together under the heading of the O'Neill Season. There were two new productions – *Hughie* and *The Iceman Cometh* – and *The Long Voyage Home* was brought back after a successful run the year before.

Just before we started rehearsal for Eugene O'Neill's *The Long Voyage Home* in 1979, Bill Bryden took us to a screening of the film John Ford made of it in the early 1940s. It tells the story of a young sailor tricked into serving on a merchant ship against his will, 'Shanghaied' in other words, and thereby setting out on the long voyage home of the play's title.

As will be apparent by now, John Ford had been a powerful influence on Bill. And though he made plays and not films, to a certain extent Bill was travelling along the same road. He had a company of actors, just like Ford. Men he drank with. And it used to be said that Derek Newark held the same position in Bill's company that Ward Bond had in Ford's. It's an interesting parallel, though one which can be taken too far. For one thing, Derek didn't share Ward Bond's extraordinarily right-wing political convictions. The Cottesloe Company was an anarchic bunch, by and large, veering to the Left rather than the Right. And of course there was no John Wayne in the company, though Brian Glover did work with him on one celebrated occasion.

The way Brian used to tell it was that he was in a room with a group of people all working on a John Wayne movie. Wayne himself was perched on a 'special chair', a saddle, in effect, supported by four tall wooden legs, surveying the assembled people. When he saw Brian, he eyed him up in silence for a while – as a former professional wrestler, Brian was still a very fit man – and then introduced himself: 'Well, you little cocksucker, what's it feel like to meet a super-patriot?' Brian's reply is not on record.

O'Neill's four sea plays must have seemed naturalistic when they were first produced, but what seems like naturalism to one generation can often seem like melodrama to the next, and what once looked new and fresh can appear fusty and quaint. This was the essential problem we had to overcome when we started work on these plays in the spring of 1979. They were not difficult plays to stage or to act, so our challenge was to give them the naturalistic impact they'd had when they were first performed.

The Moon of the Caribbees was the least problematic. As the title suggests, it's an atmospheric piece, concerning events on board a merchant ship at anchor in a West Indian bay, when a group of women come aboard. It was clear that *Bound East for Cardiff* would also come alive through the mood it created, in this case a sombre one, concerning the death on board of an American sailor. And the final play, *The Long Voyage Home*, still told an entertainingly picaresque story. It was the third play in the series, *In the Zone*, that created the most problems.

In the Zone is a tense little drama about an English sailor suspected of being a spy, on board a merchant ship during the First World War. His secret stash of love letters is mistaken for a bomb and plunged into a bucket of water in a misguided attempt to render the 'bomb' harmless. What had once been heartbreaking, now seemed sentimental. And try as we might, we couldn't entirely suppress the audience's need to laugh.

The night O'Neill's widow came to see the plays, we did our damnedest to bring the drama to life in a way of which her husband would have approved. We didn't get the chance to talk to her afterwards. She left early, distressed by the fact that we were playing it all for laughs.

Hughie and Stacey: Jack Shepherd

Hughie is close to being a one-man show. It's a very one-sided conversation between the Hughie of the title and the desk clerk of a hotel. And although Howard Goorney from the company played the desk clerk, it was hardly a company play; more a vehicle for Stacey Keach, who took the central role. It's common enough now to have an American celebrity featuring on the London stage, but back then it was much more of a rarity.

Although the setting was naturalistic, the performance was not. Instead of exploring Hughie's shifty psychology as an interaction with the desk clerk, Stacey played it as a kind of aria, facing out front most of the time. He was very assured and poised as an actor, in a way the character was not. It was as if he was owning up to the *real* reasons the audience were coming to see the play, 'You came to see a film star, didn't you? Well, here I am!'

Hollywood stars often show a reluctance to portray negative emotions. They don't want ugliness and treachery and so on to get in the way of their self-image. Perhaps there was something of that in Stacey's performance, or perhaps it was simply that the 'Broadway style' was incompatible with our own. It's hard to say.

A Comment: Keith Dewhurst

Stacey's performance was indeed indulgent. It was also true to something in O'Neill. O'Neill's father, the James Tyrone of *Long Day's Journey into Night*, was a barn-storming star actor who played huge theatres. This was the influence to which as a boy O'Neill was exposed, and it is surely reflected in the high rhetoric of his dialogue. What Stacey gave was the Broadway solution to the gap between O'Neill's naturalistic situations and what the characters say. The highbrow solution is more difficult to sustain, although Bill's actors achieved it in the Edinburgh *Iceman*, much more than Jack fears, I think, in these productions.

The Iceman Cometh: Jack Shepherd

Everyone involved, I think, was under strain, from the first day of rehearsal to the very last performance. It wasn't just the length of it (the play runs five and a half hours uncut), it was the energy required just to get it off the ground, and then to keep it airborne. It was like a very large propeller plane. It was a thing of wonder. *Iceman* is a drama about broken dreams, failed idealism, the collapse of the American Left, alcohol, murder. And in performance, at least, it is surprisingly hilarious.

In my own case, there was also something in the nature of the part which made the experience particularly demanding. Hickey, the character I was playing, is deceiving himself, in the grandest manner imaginable.

Hickey arrives in a bar full of drunks, and, in a strangely euphoric state, he sets out to persuade them all to renounce the bottle and face up to the world. When his attempts begin to founder, it finally emerges that his euphoria, his new-found teetotalism and his evangelical zeal, are all attributable to the fact that he's just murdered his wife.

When you're acting this part, when you *identify* with this degree of self-deception, every little problem of your own starts to magnify, inflamed seemingly by the extraordinary nature of the role.

I wasn't the first actor to be disturbed. The very first Hickey in the very first production had been replaced after a few weeks. And in the Royal Shakespeare version, a few years before our own, Ian Holm was found in a foetal position in his dressing-room, unable to continue with the role. My own disturbance wasn't anywhere near so profound, but there were times when I felt like a disoriented and very old man, dragging myself breathlessly towards the stage.

I wasn't Bill's first choice for the part. The text specifies a fat man of about fifty, bald with a putty nose. I was thin, turning forty, with a mass of black hair turning grey at the temples and a fair-sized nose. As a matter of fact I looked not unlike O'Neill himself, which gave an odd postmodernist slant to the production, to those who knew what the great man looked like.

Bill told me that he needed an extrovert to play the early section, when Hickey works his charismatic magic, and a troubled introvert to play what follows. Bill's feelings were, I think, that I was going to have to work very hard in that earlier section. His original idea was that I should play Rocky the barman and that Robert Stephens should play the title role. Robert backed out at the last minute and I took the part over almost as a last resort.

There seemed to be a Catch 22 at work here, or maybe even a Catch 23. Only a fifty-year-old alcoholic would have the background to play the part. Yet if you happened to be such an individual, then the chances are you wouldn't be in any fit state to survive it.

Derek Newark seemed to recognise this. He eyed me suspiciously throughout the run as if I was a kind of imposter. 'You're not a drinker,' he'd once said to me. 'You don't understand.'

A Comment: Keith Dewhurst

After Robert Stephens pulled out, Bob Hoskins volunteered, apparently, and of course he does look very like O'Neill's description of Hickey, but Bill shied away. In a way this was a pity. But could Bob have come up with the variety to sustain a huge stage role? Who knows? All in all I think this production was affected by the relentless pressure of work upon the company and by Bill's uncertainty over what Walter Hill's film of *The Long Riders* might mean for him.

The demon drink: Jack Shepherd

The drinking on *The Iceman Cometh* was fairly spectacular, but there were extenuating circumstances: virtually all the characters in O'Neill's play are alcoholics. It's a drama saturated in alcohol, reeking of cheap whisky, soiled clothing, sweat and tobacco smoke.

At the beginning of the play, pretty near everyone is happy drunk, awaiting Hickey's arrival. In the middle of the play they are most definitely sober, but by the end they are quietly sodden with alcohol. Stocious. Blootered. All they are required to do in that last act is listen, as Hickey confesses to murdering his wife. I wasn't surprised to discover, therefore, that in many performances of that final act I was the only truly sober person on stage.

I've never found alcohol of much use when performing, unlike other Hickeys: Ian Bannen, for example, first played the part back in the 1950s and, as a roaring young alcoholic, he took London by storm. He played Hickey again at the Lyceum Edinburgh, in the mid-1970s, which Bill Bryden also directed, the earlier of his two attempts at the play. Bill tells me that Ian found it much more difficult the second time around. He'd quit drinking years before, and some nights the magic was there and some nights it wasn't. It's also possible that the Celtic actors who played the supporting roles in that first production were a good deal closer to what O'Neill had in mind.

All these supporting roles are well defined, big enough to be leading roles in a play of normal length, an international array of drunks: South Africans, Europeans, Americans. Brian Glover (who, whatever he did, always seemed to come from Barnsley) was a bent cop. Derek Newark a circus man. Gawn Grainger a faded newspaper correspondent. Each character is hanging on to a dream of who they once were and what they might still do with their lives, and they drink to avoid facing up to the truth. This sense of disillusion grimly held at bay isn't just personal, it's political too: the American Left at the dawn of the twentieth century is seen to be as washed up as the drunks and the whores of Harry Hope's 'last chance saloon'.

Three of the characters have backgrounds in the anarchist syndicalist movement. Tony Haygarth played Hugo, a one-time anarchist, now pickled in alcohol, dreaming of Utopia 'beneath the willow trees', and fast asleep through much of the action. Actually, to combat the boredom brought about by the long periods of inactivity and also to keep himself from *really* falling asleep, Tony rigged up a device whereby he could suck up drink through a straw, while apparently comatose.

Niall Toibin played Larry, the disillusioned revolutionary, now in hiding from the police. Throughout the run, Niall held the political centre of the play together with ferocious concentration, and was very well supported by Kevin McNally as the treacherous Parrit, not for the first time displaying a seemingly effortless talent for acting in the American idiom.

All this effort took its toll, however, for just before the end of the final week at the Theatre Royal Bath, in the very last seconds of the play, Niall finally snapped, convinced that someone was laughing at him behind his back. As soon as the curtain came down, he started cursing and throwing the furniture about, demanding to know who it was. But the moment it went up again, Niall – and the rest of us – carried on smiling and bowing as if nothing out of the ordinary was happening. It was as if the play were by Eugene O'Neill and the curtain call by Alan Ayckbourn.

Since I was leading the company, I felt it was my duty to go to his dressing-room afterwards and try and sort things out. The door was opened by J. G. Devlin, who was sharing the room with Niall. Caught in the act of injecting adrenalin into his bare chest on account of the frailty of his heart, J. G. was utterly unperturbed, unmindful of the tornado still cursing in the corner.

As it turned out, it was Kevin, white-faced with fear and contrition, who confessed to *causing* the laughter. He'd said something to Geoff Chiswick, just before the curtain call, and made him laugh. Nothing to do with Niall's performance, he hastened to add. Geoff Chiswick, it has to be remembered, was on the edge.

As I've already said, the play put us all under a lot of stress.

J. G. Devlin: Jack Shepherd

J. G. played Harry Hope, the proprietor of the hotel. And looking back, it's hard to imagine his performance being bettered. This is how O'Neill describes the character: '*Harry Hope is sixty, white haired, so thin the description bag of bones was made for him. He has the face of an old family horse, prone to tantrums, with balkiness always smouldering in his wall eyes.*'

J. G. himself was not dissimilar, except that he didn't have the face of a horse; he had the face of a very old and irascible leprechaun. He was a great teller of stories and a sociable man, though he had an aura about him that kept people respectfully at a distance. He liked a drink, too, even though he knew that it might kill him in the end. And despite his wife's determination to keep him alive, he would still on occasions get roaring drunk. But only on his days off.

By this time he was well over seventy years old, reaching the end of his theatrical career, enjoying an Indian summer of definitive performances with the Cottesloe Company.

He reminded me of one of those old actors, who used to come over with the great Continental theatre companies in the 1960s, such as the Berliner Ensemble, or the Moscow Arts. After watching such productions, the talk was always about the old men in the company, actors who'd spent a lifetime in the theatre; how adept they were, how relaxed, so consummately skilful, they truly inhabited the stage. J. G. was one of those.

He played Giles Corey in *The Crucible*. A brilliantly crotchety Noah in *The Mysteries*. As Quince in *Midsummer Night's Dream*, he didn't patronise the character, didn't satirise his pretensions, he played it from the heart; a self-taught man operating at the limits of his knowledge. And as Harry Hope in *The Iceman Cometh*, he was playing a part he'd been born to play; despite looking very frail, his will was resolute and he survived more happily than others half his age.

J. G. didn't transform as an actor, he didn't move towards the character but he pulled the character in towards him. Perhaps he felt that his hump-backed shape – brought about by a diving accident when he was a young man – was always going to make any physical transformation impossible. He was always resolutely J. G. Devlin in whatever part he played, spitting out the lines in his gut-bucket Ulster accent. In fact, he was the very epitome of the actor David Mamet talks about so succinctly: the actor who doesn't allow the characterisation to get in the way of the text.

He was a wily old bird, who knew a lot about Irish history and the old religion. He'd been a serious Republican when a young man; in fact, he'd been sent to Israel, he told me, in the 1940s, to learn how to make bombs. But by the 1970s, like the characters in O'Neill's play, he'd grown distant from the ideals of his youth. Not disillusioned necessarily, more wearily phlegmatic, and on occasions twinkling with irony. He was enough of a Republican, in 1983, to turn down an invitation to Princess Margaret's ill-fated reception, during the tour of *A Midsummer Night's Dream*.

Derek Newark: Jack Shepherd

The first time I saw Derek on stage was in *Man is Man* at the Royal Court. He was playing a soldier. It was a role I'd seen him play before in several, now only dimly remembered, television dramas of the 1960s. Derek had in fact been a Guardsman, and seen action in Malaya in the mid-1950s. He was very proud of his military connections, and this 'soldierliness' was something he carried with him for the rest of his life. (Asked by a fellow actor if he'd seen the Trooping of the Colour on television, he roared: 'Seen it? I've been in it!')

He was also a drinker. That's how he saw himself. Not a 'drunk', a 'boozer' or a 'lush', but a '*drinker*'. In other words, he was willing to recognise the truth about himself, but only if it was defined in that particular way.

Drunk or sober, he prided himself on the fact that, on stage, he could always be relied on to deliver the play. If there was a laugh to be had, Derek could usually find it. But in all other respects, he saw himself as the rock around which the more chaotic elements in the production could ebb and flow. Like a good NCO, he was the man who would carry out the director's orders, to the letter if necessary. He liked to think of himself as Bill's captain on the field. And I suppose he was, but more in a military than in a footballing sense.

He was invariably as steady and reliable on stage as he was paranoid and unpredictable in the bar. I say 'invariably' but in the 1982 production of *Don Quixote*, he was not at his best either on or off the stage. For one thing he was drinking brandy at the time, which he always claimed made him behave badly. Though it's more likely that he drank brandy *because* he was behaving badly and not the other way around. He was certainly professionally frustrated and bitter about the fact that he'd played a lot of supporting roles in the company and hardly ever a lead.

In one scene, the pair of us were shackled one behind the other in a long chain gang. Some nights when we all trooped off stage, Derek would be so preoccupied, he'd forget about the shackles and stride away as if he were on his own, sending the person directly behind him, me that is, flying in all directions. Derek didn't pay much attention to my rather diffident complaints and so when it happened again, I jumped straight up on his back, got him round the throat and begged him in a terrible whisper to stop doing it. Derek fought back blindly and we fell wrestling to the floor.

Paul Scofield, who was playing Don Quixote, was standing way downstage. He turned his head majestically in our direction, the ghost of a smile on his lips: 'What *are* those men doing?' And we toppled off the back of the stage and into the scene dock.

Derek's bark was worse, much worse, than his bite. One night in the bar, after a performance of *The Mysteries*, he launched into Sylvester McCoy, who'd just been to see the play, with a stream of insulting repartee. This was too much for Jim Carter, who'd had enough of Derek's bullying and knocked him down. Jim was bigger and stronger than Derek. Keeping him pressed to the floor, he held a fist to his face. 'You want some of this?' he said, making it clear that if Derek didn't clear off there and then, he'd certainly get some. Derek got up and left without a word. The fit young man of twenty years before may well have fought on to the death, but Derek was past fifty by then. His knees were bad and he was getting tired.

As it turned out, the period which followed *Don Quixote* was a golden one for Derek at the National. He was finally playing leading parts: Bottom in *Midsummer Night's Dream*, Shelley Levine in *Glengarry Glen Ross* and Tom Murphy in *Golden Boy*. His mood lightened and his drinking steadied down.

Derek's mood was always very difficult to predict. He'd greet you in the bar with a stream of insults, angry and suspicious, and then the clouds would blow away in a second and he'd continue the conversation as if you were the friend he'd been longing to see. He could be very beguiling, and very funny when he chose to be. He'd been a comedian in fact, in the late 1950s, under the name of Jacky Stiles. Like other comedians of the period – 'comics' is the word Derek himself used – he was fond of the odd catchphrase.

'Don't you give me a bad time', was one of his favourites. 'What *is* your game?', was another. And if he was imagining somewhere terrible, it was usually a place 'where the birds don't shit'. He talked a lot about 'bottle' meaning nerve or courage, often adding, if he'd found a situation on stage particularly frightening, 'Two bob – half a crown', making little twitching gestures between thumb and forefinger. He would say this in the expectation of a laugh, as 'comics' tend to do.

By the time I arrived at the National, he'd already done a platform show about Groucho Marx, of which he was very proud. And he talked a lot about another one, in which he impersonated W. C. Fields, though I'm not sure if this one was ever performed. I remember him once showing me his hands, big swollen powerful hands, saying: 'When W. C. Fields was dying, he could see flowers growing out of the ends of his fingers. I'll go the same way I shouldn't wonder.'

He still had another twenty years to go, as it happened; led by his appetites into an increasingly chaotic lifestyle, retaining a bullish, hot-blooded sexuality right to the end. He was essentially heterosexual, though he could at times give off the most surprisingly ambivalent signals. When it came to playing the Dame, however, in the company production of *Cinderella*, in 1984, he didn't seem entirely comfortable with the travesty, the half-world of pantomime; which was surprising really for someone who could be so dangerously ambivalent off the stage. He was playing an Ugly Sister, in tandem with Robert Stephens; drinkers both. Robert acted his 'sister' with the frantic petulance of a spoilt child; Derek was like one of the boys having a bit of a frolic in the sergeants' mess.

He once talked about a story he had in his head, where the murderer turned out to be some unacknowledged part of the narrator's mind. He called it 'The Enemy Within'. He talked about it being a play, seeing if he could get me interested in the idea, but I also sensed he was trying to tell me something else and can only guess what that was. But an extraordinary encounter I had with him in 1978 did give me an insight.

We were sharing a dressing-room. I was in *American Buffalo* at the Cottesloe, Derek was in *Bedroom Farce* at the Lyttelton; the curtain came down in that production about twenty minutes after ours.

On this particular night, I came off stage feeling very tired and sat slumped in a chair, staring into the mirror, too drained to wash off the fake blood, now drying a dark red, which on stage had been streaming from my nose and across my face.

I knew Derek was in a dangerous mood. He'd been drinking throughout the day and at the interval one of his fellow actors had likened him to an unexploded grenade rolling about the stage. Nothing prepared me, however, for what happened next.

I heard him come in through the door behind me. I heard him cry out. And the next thing I knew I was on the floor, his heavy black coat wrapped around my head. Derek was hanging on to me like a bear, suffocating me with the coat. I fought to get free and, still in shock, yelled out for him to stop. After a few desperate moments, he loosened his grip and I broke free. We sat facing each other on the dressing-room floor.

Derek was confused. He was apologetic and his eyes were full of tears. 'I'll try and explain,' he said. What followed was a kind of confession. He talked about his time as a Guardsman, fighting with his regiment against the 'insurgents' in Malaya. He told me how hungry he was for a commission. And how, after a series of interviews, he was finally offered one. Unfortunately, there were strings attached: one or two 'little jobs'.

After training in assassination techniques, he told me, he was dispatched into the jungle on various missions, to eliminate certain specified targets: individual insurgents the army wanted out of the way. He then confessed that, on his last mission, things hadn't gone according to plan. There'd been a fight. He'd given the man a gaping stomach wound, but he hadn't managed to finish him off.

The man's face had been covered in blood, in much the same way that mine had been when Derek came in through the dressing-room door. He then admitted that he'd begun to regret what he'd done, telling me how he'd spent the rest of the night consoling his victim, trying to nurse him back to life, but by the morning the man was dead. And when he finally got back to base, he decided to confront his commanding officer, telling him that he'd had enough, that he couldn't take any more.

As a result he lost his commission and left the army at the earliest opportunity. He became a comic for a while: Jacky Stiles. He joined a Masonic lodge somewhere in the city, and then he went to RADA.

I see no reason to disbelieve Derek's story. To see him as a casualty of war puts a very different spin on the way he carried on. When in 1979, a crowd of Vietnam Vets came to see *Dispatches* and laughed in totally different places to the regular audience, Derek was almost certainly the only actor there who knew why.

21. Extending the Cycle

Creation: Jack Shepherd

After the success of *The Passion*, it was only a question of time before an attempt was made to extend it and so in the summer of 1980 work began on an adaptation of the earlier plays in the York cycle. This new production, together with *The Passion*, was to play in repertoire at the Assembly Hall of the Church of Scotland for the entire Edinburgh Festival that summer and then transfer to the Cottesloe Theatre later in the year.

Rehearsals for this new production were some of the most creative I have ever experienced. It's true, of course, that a lot of the key decisions had already been made, but there was still work for the company to do.

Bill Dudley was once again in charge of the design, and although there was a greater reliance on technology in this new production, the unifying concept of the earlier one was still in evidence: the exposed cable representing the apple tree in the Garden of Eden, for instance, clear evidence of the cable-maker's art. There was the same gloom and smoke. The same configuration of tiny lights. But whereas *The Passion* was in black and white, the new creation was very definitely in colour.

Mark McManus was missing from this production and in his absence the part of Jesus was played by Pip Donaghy. Pip's Jesus had a very different aura to Mark's: with Mark you felt there was a lot he wasn't telling you, whereas with Pip, you felt he was telling you everything.

The first rehearsal began, as Bill's rehearsals invariably did, with a leisurely cup of coffee and a song from the band. As the day progressed, it became clear that Bill was taking a leaf out of Roger Planchon's book and making the realisation of this production more of a *collective* responsibility. In the absence of Tony Harrison, John Russell Brown was roped in to adapt the Cain and Abel play and the more celebrated comedy of Mak the Shepherd. I was to work on the early plays and the scenes involving Herod. And Bill himself was to be responsible for the rest.

Most of the work consisted of editing the plays down to size and, while being careful to keep the rhythm, find more comprehensible alternatives for archaic words. There was a real problem, however, with the structure, in that all the plays are inexorably moving towards the Crucifixion. And in our version of *The Mysteries*, that wasn't due to happen until the end of the second part. So how were we to end part one?

The evening began in a burst of radiance with the creation of the world. Should we then end it with the Massacre of the Innocents, which was the point in the cycle we had actually reached? Plays shouldn't end on a deepening downward spiral; there has to be a glimpse of hope.

As the rehearsals progressed, a solution began to emerge. We began to perceive the story we were telling in increasingly dualistic terms; that is to say, as a battle between the forces of light and the forces of dark. We already had an angel descending from heaven, dazzling humanity with reflected light, so why not also hint at the forces of darkness creating an equally powerful shadow?

Eventually a final scene was stitched together, in which the Prince of Darkness rises up from the carnage of the Massacre of the Innocents, spitting out a triumphant text gleaned from one of the Coventry plays: his challenge is met by God (also atop a forklift truck), affirming that the imminent sacrifice of his 'only begotten son' will indeed save mankind from sin. While below, Joseph, Mary and Jesus make their escape into Egypt, followed by a long line of people, common people, dancing their way between the two towers, unaware of the cosmic struggle going on above.

It was a truly collective experience and, looking back, it's not easy to say who in 1980 exactly originated a particular idea. Was it Brenda Blethyn who conceived the notion of Mary 'making' the infant Jesus out of folded bits of cloth, or was it another of Bill Dudley's ideas? Again, when faced with the problem of creating a serpent in the Garden of Eden, who exactly had the idea of linking hands and dancing a snake dance?

Brilliant as they usually were, not all of Bill Dudley's ideas actually came off. There's a sequence, for example, where Noah sends a dove in search of land. Bill's idea was to launch an origami bird and send it flapping up a wire, but, try as we might, it couldn't be made to work. This had all been left until the technical rehearsal, so there wasn't much time to come up with a new solution. And then someone suggested (it may well have been Tony Haygarth, he was always good at this sort of thing), 'Why don't we use one of the umbrellas? I mean, we've all of us got one.' It should be remembered at this point that a wall of umbrellas had been used to create the sides of the ark. 'And while Noah's going through the motions of throwing the bird up in the air,' he went on, 'why doesn't someone do this?' And he flapped his umbrella open and shut a few times. And it sounded very like the beating of a bird's wing.

It was certainly Kenny Ireland who then suggested that since the bird was a dove, why don't we use a solitary white umbrella? A truly elegant idea, but in performance it was a navy-blue umbrella that was flapped, the same colour as all the others.

A popular success: Jack Shepherd

Success always comes as a surprise. When you expect it, more often than not, you don't get it. And when you're not expecting it, it can sometimes sneak up behind you and tap you on the shoulder. Most times you have to wait for the reviews to come out, to know if you're a hit or not. Not so with this production. You could feel the joy of the audience as they joined in the dance at the end. And from my vantage point on the tower, through the smoke and the twinkling lights, I could see them swaying around below me, laughing, shouting. It was as if I was watching them from the top of a helter-skelter, like revellers in a fun fair. We were very definitely a popular success.

This wasn't the kind of theatre where the audience sat

attentively in the dark, appreciating the work they were being shown on a brightly lit stage: with *The Mysteries* as with *Lark Rise*, they always felt a part of it all. As I stated earlier, you had to *include* the audience in your performance: they could be appealed to, shied away from, harangued. But they were always there. In *The Passion*, for instance, they were the crowd condemning Christ to death, shouting *'Crucify him!'* with the players. And who could forget the nuns, during the procession to Calvary, trying to touch the hem of Mark's robe? It was as if the act of coming together to tell the Bible story had restored a sense of community to all the people taking part, a feeling of belonging, that had been displaced by the sheer scale of modern-day urban life. It showed, too, how deeply ingrained the Bible story is in our cultural identity, hinting at a level of belief, lying just below the surface, subverting the rational processes of our daily lives.

I think it's true to say that we were carried away a little by our success and sometimes the celebrating got out of hand. I remember a trip to the seaside, to celebrate Sarah Parkin's birthday when, after far too many bottles of red wine, Tony Haygarth, Brenda Blethyn and myself walked fully clothed into the sea.

After the show that evening I was anxious to know if the effects of our celebrations had marred the performance, and I asked Dave Hill for an appraisal. 'I *was* good, though, wasn't I?' I said defensively. 'Oh yes,' he replied. 'You were good. *Very* good. But also, I have to say, you were very, very slow.'

The outdoor performances: Jack Shepherd

Not everything, however, lived up to the heady excitement of those performances at the Assembly Hall. Both Bill Bryden and Bill Dudley had been intrigued by the idea of reconstructing the feel of Corpus Christi, the day on which the plays had been first performed, five hundred years before. With this in mind, Bill Dudley had designed three latter-day versions of the original carts, lorries actually, with a wooden construction on the back, suitably carved and decorated, with platforms for the actors to stand on and holes for them to stick their heads through.

Bill Bryden's idea was that the carts should be set up at different parts of the old town, where, at noon, open-air performances would be given of each of the original three plays. There was a 'Last Supper' cart, another depicting the creation of the world, and a Noah's ark.

It was to be an event, something Bill was usually very good at. Jesus and the Apostles were to walk through the streets in a long line (hopefully drawing a crowd) and, on reaching the cart, perform the play; sitting down behind the long table it contained, like the figures in Leonardo's well-known fresco. In a different location, and with the aid of ingenious mechanical devices, Brian Glover was to create the world. And somewhere else again, J. G. Devlin and Edna Doré were to board the third cart as Noah and his wife, arguing with each other in a kind of slapstick Punch and Judy show.

It didn't work out too well. It didn't attract large crowds. And those it did attract couldn't hear very much over the traffic noise and were unsure of how they were supposed to respond. It was a bit of a let-down, really, after the rapturous response we'd been getting indoors.

Sixty crop pruners: Jack Shepherd

The success of *The Mysteries* was essentially due to the coming together of four exceptional talents: Bill Bryden, Bill Dudley, Tony Harrison and John Tams.

John was the melodeon player with the Albion Band and the lead vocalist. When he approached the microphone in those days, with his shoulder-length hair and drooping moustache, he looked like a reincarnation of the gunslinger Wyatt Earp.

John had been involved from the very beginning; at first only as a musician, but as the project grew, the scope of his contribution grew with it. He not only sang in this production, he acted as well, playing one of the Shepherds. And given his background in the Derbyshire hills it was a part he was ideally suited to play. He also contributed ideas; in fact, he was so full of ideas that he began to function as a kind of creative co-ordinator, linking the music, the staging, the acting, the design even, with a constant stream of suggestions. He had so many good ideas, it often seemed an embarrassment to him.

The music in this show was a natural development of the music from *The Passion*: essentially electric folk, with medieval elements woven in. And, like Bill Dudley's design concept, a celebration of working-class culture. Not everyone was happy with that. For some reviewers, folk music had no place in 'high art'. One critic wrote that he would have preferred the music to sound more like Verdi's Requiem, describing the band as 'sickly pop crooners'. John, who evidently took the criticism to heart, responded by making a pun of it, which he pinned to the door of his room: 'Sixty crop pruners. If you want to talk to one of us, knock here.'

The one new development in the music, however, was a Country-and-Western song, written by Bill Caddick, as a backing to the Cain and Abel play. It was a song that was to prove controversial when Tony Harrison came back on board in 1985. Tony certainly approved of the medieval music used in *The Mysteries* and all the music in the English folk tradition, but he drew the line at Country-and-Western.

I spent a lot of time with the musicians on the Edinburgh trip, wandering about the town, chatting, drinking with them in the pubs (I even sat in with the band on one occasion, playing saxophone). I found the rhythms of their conversation much quicker than I was used to, their comments sharper, the subtext deeper and much more barbed, but all said with a smile, usually, in a light-hearted sort of way.

Actors, on the whole, are more cagey about offending each other, intent on smoothing over any differences. It's this kind of behaviour that has created the media stereotype of the 'Luvvy'. And, yes, it's true, people really do come up to you after the performance and say, 'Oh, you were super, darling,' when you plainly weren't. An acknowledgement, I've always supposed, that it's hard enough *surviving* on stage, without making enemies of the rest of the cast.

162

Just before the Festival got under way, the company was asked to contribute to the opening procession winding its way around the streets of Edinburgh. I found myself sitting on a float, joining in with the band, playing the music for our 'hobby horse' dancers. Peter Hall was sitting in, too; playing a small piano and looking very happy in a white jacket and panama hat.

The hobby horse dance is an exhausting one, each dancer encased in a heavy tarpaulin drum, with his head sticking through the top, enclosed in a conical mask. And by the end of the afternoon, they had pretty much danced their way around the entire city.

Dave Hill was playing the 'fool', that is to say, prancing around among the hobby horses, walloping people from time to time, with a bladder on a stick. He lurched up to the side of our float as we neared the end of our tour of the city, looking very pale and clammy, anxiously stammering out, 'Jack. You play football. You know about these things. Do you have your heart attack while you're *doing* the exercise, or do you have it *after*?'

Men without women: Jack Shepherd

Throughout our stay at the Festival the company lodged in Pollock Hall, a large modernist building, which functions as a student hall of residence during term time and during the Festival as a kind of hostel.

Only Bryan Pringle declined to remain there, paying for his own room, in a hotel. Bill Bryden too. The accommodation was perfectly adequate, though, the breakfasts fine for those who could get up in time. Everyone had a room of their own, but the only problem was that the beds were so narrow you'd wake up in the morning, gripping the sides with your knees and clinging on for dear life.

After the show, in the absence of any kind of bar, people would drift into the laundry room, for a last bottle of beer or a cup of tea and a bit of a chat, as we all tried to wind down after the elation of the performance.

It was always very hot and noisy in the laundry room – a room without any windows. Everyone would want the evening to continue, but not know quite how to do it. It was like a 1950s B-movie in black and white: *Men without Women*. Edna would be there some nights, Brenda too. But in the main, there was too much testosterone flying about as the men in the company, including the band, outnumbered the women by about six to one.

One evening, people started dancing, but of course there weren't enough women to go round. So Brian Glover started dancing with John Salthouse, the way French people used to in Parisian *bal musettes*: holding each other by the waist and vaguely sort of jigging up and down. I can still see Brian, a glistening satyr in a damp T-shirt, murmuring in John's ear: 'Well just *pretend* then . . . Go on.' And then adding even more archly: 'You know you want to.'

Brian Glover: Jack Shepherd

I last saw Brian in the winter of 1996–97. It was at an informal dinner party given for him by Oliver and Irene Cotton. He was recovering from a brain operation and was cheerful enough, though not optimistic about his future. 'Another ten years would've done me, Jack. I've no wish to be an old man.' He shook his head as he said it, and then rapidly drew in his breath, in a way that was characteristic of him.

He died that summer, in a hospice overlooking Clapham Common. The last thing he said to me was, 'All those years I spent running round Battersea Park, trying to stay healthy, and when it comes, it's a bloody brain tumour.' He was smiling when he said it, but there was bitterness in his voice.

Brian had been an athlete all his life. He started out as a boxer but, on realising his limitations, he switched to pro-fessional wrestling. In one of the schoolboy comics of the 1950s, there was an ongoing adventure about a schoolteacher with a secret identity: at weekends he would transform himself into a professional wrestler known as 'Blockbuster Brown'. At the time it seemed very unlikely, yet Brian was just such a phenomenon, wrestling at the weekend – in Iran as often as not – and flying back to Barnsley in time to teach his class on a Monday morning. Brian was a qualified teacher with a degree in geography – a fact that often surprised people.

In the ring, Brian was an animal. Balding, with a heavy physique, broad shoulders and bow legs, he'd devised a way of fighting that was pure slapstick. 'Get out of that, then!' he'd shout boastfully, locking his arms around his opponent's head, challenging him to escape, which, to Brian's increasing frustration and the crowd's delight, his opponent was repeatedly able to do. The routine would come to its climax in the final round, when Brian's opponent would unexpectedly turn the tables on his tormentor, gripping his head in the same hold, causing the once braggardly Brian to beg for mercy and start crying like a baby. The punters would naturally yell out in delight, mocking the cringing bully with chants of, 'Get out of *that*, then!' It was a kind of theatre.

Brian, incidentally, didn't wrestle under his own name. Early on in his career he'd stood in for a wrestler who'd missed his plane, and the name stayed with him: Leon Arras, from France. In some parts of the country he was regarded as a hero, in other parts as a villain, and the outcome of the bouts he fought would be stage-managed accordingly; though Brian would always get quietly angry if anyone tried to suggest wrestling was bent. 'All sports are bent,' he would retort. 'Even cricket.' And so it proved to be.

He had very sharp reflexes, and sometimes when the tension of rehearsals was dispelled by improvised games of indoor cricket, Brian proved to be a dazzling slip fielder. He'd played football for Barnsley Schoolboys and it was as a footballer, in fact, that he first came into the public eye. There's a scene in the film *Kes*, where the games master takes a penalty, triumphantly booting the ball past a hapless fourteen-year-old goalkeeper. The games master was played by Brian Glover, and the scene captured the national imagination.

It was entirely due to the success of this film that Brian came to the attention of the Royal Court Theatre in the early 1970s, where Bill Bryden was quick to cast him in *Pirates*. This was the first time Brian and I worked together. We even wrestled together, very briefly, in *Corunna!* a year or so later. But the bout we fought, in a live television performance of Howard Brenton's *Skinny Spew* a short while later, was a more protracted affair. We were a mismatch, of course: a banana versus a pumpkin. I was a playing a schoolboy, Brian a headmaster. And when the schoolboy finally triumphed by throwing the headmaster over his shoulder in a 'Flying Mare', it was entirely due to Brian's acrobatic skills that the move looked remotely authentic.

In performance, however, the adrenalin levels were running high and when it came to the 'Flying Mare' Brian threw himself a good deal higher than he ever had in rehearsal. As he arched himself through the air, he quite forgot that he would be landing on the studio's concrete floor and not on the yielding canvas surface of the wrestling ring. He hit the deck with a terrible splat, landing on the flat of his back, the air coming out of his lungs in a long protracted hiss. His face was grey, wrinkled up with pain, his breathing shallow. But this was *live* television, after all, and he still managed to spit out the next line.

In the first run of *The Passion*, Brian's primary role was that of Caiaphas, the high priest. When I saw the production he was playing most of his scenes with Albert Finney, as a kind of northern double act. In the scene following the trial of Christ, for example, Caiaphas was given a flagon of wine to drink, in its entirety, to the accompaniment of a drum roll. Brian told me that, on one famous occasion, Albert substituted the grape juice that normally filled the flagon, with the contents of a very expensive bottle of red wine. Albert was clearly expecting Brian to sense that it was *real wine* he was about to consume, *good* wine, pause in his action, smile in gratitude and then sip the contents with *real* delight. Brian sniffed the liquid in the flagon, came to terms with the deception and downed the lot, without pausing to draw breath. He then hurried to his dressing-room, vomited it up again and, to Albert's astonishment and relief, returned to the stage apparently none the worse for wear.

In his work with the Cottesloe Company Brian was at his most secure playing the northern working man. At the end of *The Passion* he played a character bearing witness to Christ's death on the cross. A collier still in his pit gear, the dead Christ hanging above him, lit by a beam of light from his helmet, testifying that when Christ died: 'corses crept out through t' earth's crust and cursed'. He had real authority in that part.

He was much less comfortable in the role of Pat McGloin, the one time police chief in *The Iceman Cometh*. Not that he didn't look every inch the part; he simply couldn't get to grips with the accent. Brian had a tin ear and a surprisingly light tenor voice and always struggled to stay in tune. (His was the voice, incidentally, of the Tetley Tea man in the 1970s TV advert, and the reassuringly northern presence that informed us that Allinson's bread was the bread 'Wi' nowt tekken out'.)

It was as God in *The Mysteries* that he achieved his true potential as an actor. Presiding over the creation of the world like an omnipotent baby; descending from heaven to have a word in Noah's ear, with all the cosy familiarity of a neighbour dropping by to borrow a cup of sugar.

In the millennium production of *The Mysteries*, twenty years later, the part of God was played by David Bradley, a lean and weathered eremite, newly emerged from his Christian cave. Brian was something altogether more priapic, hardly a Christian God at all.

Brian didn't have the kind of talent that would have got him into RADA; he simply applied his intelligence to the demands of the role and then set his imagination free. At one point in *Don Quixote*, Brian and I played a lion and a lioness respectively, pent up in a cage, both of us wearing dun-coloured lion suits. Brian had no difficulty with the part, he simply *imagined* himself to be a lion. He hardly moved or changed his expression, yet there was no doubt about it: he *was* a lion.

At some point in the 1990s he went on the pilgrimage to Santiago de Compostela, walking westward across northern Spain. He was not only keeping a diary for the newspapers, he was also keeping an eye open for a possible film, wondering if he might uncover a latter-day *Canterbury Tales* in the circumstances of his journey. As time went by, he fell in with a woman on the pilgrimage. They became friendly, and one night at one of the hostelries on the way, they stayed up talking and drinking until the early hours. And then the woman suddenly astonished Brian by confessing that she was in fact a nun. I was led to believe that the relationship had finished at this point, as quietly and as politely as it had begun, but there was a look of absolute bewilderment on Brian's face as he told the story and just the hint of a smile.

In his later years he grew to resemble Silenus, the old wine-drinking God from Greek mythology, not only in spirit, but in features as well, with his bald head, flushed face and eyes misty with drink and desire. It was easy to imagine him, sitting in the shade of an olive tree, wineskin in hand, eyeing the nymphs and the dryads as they went by, remembering happier days.

In his last few months, Brian was visited by Dave Hill, who offered to take him on one last trip, anywhere he'd like to go. This was an act of understanding on Dave's part, who knew full well what Brian was going through. He'd once been misdiagnosed with cancer himself, and even gone as far as looking for a property on the Isle of Sark, where he'd fancied he might spend his last days. And so they took off to the West Country, for one last look at the world.

Brian was buried in West Brompton cemetery in the summer of 1997. There was a brief humanist service in the cemetery chapel and a brief (and at times hilarious) celebration of his life. The Albion Band played a slow march as the coffin was carried to the graveside and Brian was laid to rest. Standing there with the band playing and the people milling around, I had the strangest feeling that Brian hadn't really gone. His appetite for life was so great, I couldn't see him giving up that easily. I could almost see him standing by the graveside, rather bewildered as he watched himself lowered into the ground.

22. Choices and Changes

Crazy Horse: Jack Shepherd

People have asked why, in the company's eight-year history at the National Theatre, so few plays by British writers were attempted, why the emphasis was on American drama. Bill had, in fact, directed John Osborne's *Watch It Come Down* in 1976, but this was with a regular National Theatre cast, a year before the company came into being. This production apart, the only British writer to get a look-in – apart from Bill himself – was the co-author of this book.

It's Bill's claim that since the *established* writers, the writers he most wanted to work with, were already 'teamed up' with a particular director – as David Storey was, say, with Lindsay Anderson – it was almost impossible to break into such partnerships and get hold of a new play by one of these writers. Furthermore, it seemed to Bill that the playwrights who wrote for the West End invariably wrote with a star performance in mind, when what he was always searching for was a play written for a group.

Although it's true that Bill was personally drawn to American culture, particularly to the Hollywood film, to the street life of the big city, the world of the conman, the boxer and the gangster, it's also fair to say that in the works of O'Neill, Mamet, Miller and Odets, he found the well-written kind of group drama he was searching for. So it was hardly surprising that he turned to *The Crucible* by Arthur Miller.

The play is concerned with the events surrounding a witch trial that took place in the town of Salem, during the seventeenth century. The play's hero is John Proctor, a man of integrity brought down by the hysteria and the recriminations generated by the trial as it runs its terrible course.

Before rehearsals began, Bill met Arthur Miller at the Algonquin Hotel. The secret of a good production, he was told, lies in the casting of the girls who are supposedly possessed by devils. They have to be young, Miller told him, below the age of consent yet knowing enough to create a dangerously erotic charge. With this in mind, Bill cast the girls as youthfully as he possibly could.

It was no surprise when Mark McManus accepted the part of Proctor. Mark excelled at playing men of integrity. He had a way of delivering a line that was honest to the point of naivety. As it happened, this was his last performance with the company, before he left to make a name for himself in the television series *Taggart*. Diana Stabb played his wife. She had already been involved in *The Mysteries* and *Lark Rise*. And although she wasn't in *everything* as Edna Doré was, she was one of the few women who could consider herself a member of a very male-orientated company.

When the production transferred to the West End, Jimmy Grant took over the leading role. Jimmy, like Mark, was good at playing decent upright people, but in Jimmy's case they usually seemed to be carrying more than their share of guilt.

The run at the National had been very successful, so there was no reason to suppose that the West End run at the Comedy Theatre wouldn't be equally so. The production was thrown into disarray, however, when one of the cast quite literally lost the plot. Everyone began to realise something was wrong when the actor playing Hathorne started making up his own lines. Hathorne is the lesser of the two judges in the trial scene, and on this particular evening Geoff Chiswick, who was playing the part, seemed intent on redressing the balance. It wasn't that he was trying to change the outcome of the play exactly, it was more that he was trying to bring the trial to a conclusion a long time before it should. 'Guilty!' he kept shouting. 'The man's guilty!' And banging his fist down on the table in front of him.

Geoff Chiswick was in fact going mad. He had shown signs of mental instability the year before, when during the production of *Candleford* he'd earned himself the nickname 'Crazy Horse'. In the hunting scene, he'd been cast, together with several other broad-shouldered actors, as a horse: each 'horse' patiently bearing its rider as the hunt assembled before the morning's jaunt got under way. On the day the play opened, Geoff suddenly astonished everyone by throwing his rider and making a bolt for it into the open air.

He was eventually found wandering down-river, up to his knees in water, among the wastelands of the London dockside. He recovered quickly enough, but the nickname 'Crazy Horse' stuck with him. Up to the time of his breakdown he had been a supporting player within the company. He wasn't in any sense a theatrical type, which meant, of course, that he perfectly fitted Bill's credentials for a good company member. He was strongly built, bald-headed and prematurely middle-aged. The word saturnine comes to mind.

He was usually reticent in rehearsals, keeping well in the background. Thoughtful, polite and occasionally quietly subversive. But when the demons were clamouring inside him, he could be dangerously manic.

The last time I saw Geoff was in the Green Room bar at the National. It was in the middle of the afternoon and the bar was on the point of closing. As soon as he saw me come in, he ordered six vodkas, which he lined up on the bartop. Fixing me with a baleful stare, he drank them, one after the other, roaring with laughter between each mouthful. Up until then I'd only ever seen him quietly sipping a pint of bitter. He was clearly trying to tell me something, but I never found out what it was.

Geoff will be remembered as the 'Jewish Father' in the BT adverts of the time, on the receiving end of Maureen Lipman's long-distance phone calls. The money he made did nothing to stabilise his fractured personality. He died of a heart attack a few years later.

Bill's choice: Keith Dewhurst

Although *The Nativity* and *The Passion* were the triumph of the 1980 Edinburgh Festival, and went from a 17 per cent advance to capacity in three days, I made myself unpopular by saying that I thought that the work was much coarser than the purity of old, and that everyone was having far too much of a good time. When I discussed this at the time with Jack Shepherd he said that it was broader because there were too many people on the promenade floor, and I expect he was right; also, pure epic players like Newark, Ray and McManus were missing, and the audience were divided. It was not possible to have access to all parts of the auditorium, which I think was another factor.

Ironically, while the actors and Bill Dudley found it their most creative experience, off-stage politics were calling the very existence of the company into question.

Peter Hall's visit to the production in Edinburgh, ostensibly to share his army's victory, had other purposes. He wanted to persuade Bill Dudley to work with him on Wagner's Ring Cycle at Bayreuth, and Bill Bryden to hold the fort at the NT during his absence. There was an implication that this would stand Bill in good stead to become Director of the NT when Hall moved on.

Not that Bill ever articulated a desire to be the Director of the NT. He was not suited to a desk job, he said, he did not want to make enemies through refusals, the higher politics were too high, et cetera, et cetera. And he had so far been very lucky. At both the Royal Lyceum and the Cottesloe he had wielded the artistic power of a theatre director without most of the other problems. How he expected that luck to hold for ever, I do not know. Neither, I suspect, did he. (Ironically, when he took a desk job as Head of BBC TV Drama in Scotland he was very good at it.)

Bill was now faced with a choice in a form he had not anticipated, and its timing was thrust upon him. Hall wanted an answer 'within a day or two'. This was at the end of August and on 19 September, the day *The Nativity* opened at the Cottesloe, it was announced by the NT that Bill would remain an Associate but give up his post as Director of the Cottesloe Theatre. Instantly, wolves sniffed at the door.

Of Bill's confidants Sebastian had left and gone into TV, not least because his private life was difficult, John Caulfield was more a support than an equal, and I was at once too close and too distant. Our dreams and ambitions and debts to each other were too entangled. We had let them ride and not talked about them, and now we were both proud and it was too late. We drank too much, of course, and some things festered. It is the way of too many collaborators.

So Bill never really discussed his dilemma, or how things might be made to work, or, indeed, whether an end to it all would be the best. I think he was torn: one part of him wanted to cruise along at the Cottesloe, write another movie script, see how that went, and then make a decision; another part was tired of being responsible for other people's dreams, and wanted to be free. He believed that he did not have time for administration and wanted to write another movie.

Questions may be asked, and no doubt should have been asked at the time. Was a studio project the right way to kick off a movie-writing career? The Greenock novelist Alan Sharpe, a Scots hero to Bill, had made a reasonable shot at Hollywood, but he had gone there to live, like many others before and since. Should Bill have taken the same risk? Should a person who wanted to direct not have held out to direct his own script, another labour of love like *The Long Riders*? Would that have been possible? Could Bill, who relied so much on the energy of a moment, have endured the planning that is the real basis of movie-directing success? Whatever the answers to these now rhetorical questions, he was set upon a course, and on 6 January 1981, Caulfield and I went to the Bistingo in Shepherd Market and waited for Bill to join us for lunch. He had been to a meeting with a West End producer. This was in the trough of the West End's fortunes, when the post-1956 Osborne-cum-Royal-Court-cum-RSC effect had worn off, but before the musicals arrived to give it a new, blander level of work that brought great affluence. What the producer suggested was that he investigate a scenario whereby he took on the Cottesloe Company, turned the stalls of his theatre into a promenade, and presented and toured the old shows while we rehearsed new ones. Would this have filled an evident gap? Could it ever have been made to work financially? Would the NT have cooperated? Could the dream of the work pleasing a wider audience have come true? Nobody knows. Bill backed away from the idea, and suggested a one-off project in which the producer was not interested, so the chance was lost.

On 20 January, the last night of *The Nativity*, there was a leaving party for Bill in Rehearsal Room 2. I bumped into the actor Don Warrington. 'What's happening here?' he said. I could have asked the same question myself when, two weeks later, I went with Ashley Hutchings and a road man to promote our *Lark Rise* album on local radio stations. We finished in Edinburgh and came back on the sleeper. I bought Ashley breakfast at the Great Eastern Hotel. Then we shook hands rather solemnly, and went our ways. I did not see him again for twenty years, because a day or two later, when the Albion Band were about to go on a short promotional tour, Tams and others could contain their feelings no longer and announced that they were splitting. It was a bizarre rerun of the *Battle of the Field* débâcle: no tour, irate record company, and some years before a folk band could get a record deal. The hard work of Alexandra and Mick McDonagh in setting up the first folk band album in a long time was half-wasted. Alexandra also negotiated with the Perth Festival in Western Australia for a world tour of *Lark Rise*, but that too came to nothing.

Cologne and Rome: Jack Shepherd

In the autumn the production returned to the Cottesloe Theatre and played there right the way through until the New Year. The first part, with its torchlit nativity scene, made a perfect Christmas show. There was even a Demon King.

After a few months' respite, the company was reassembled in the summer for a tour. Around the time of its inception, it was referred to as the 'European Tour', but all it entailed, finally, was a week at the Cologne Theatre Festival during the summer of 1981, followed by another week in Rome. It was basically the same show that had played at the Edinburgh Festival, the previous year, but with a few changes in the cast.

Kevin McNally took over the part of Jesus, Paul Young, one of the few crossovers from the Scottish company, the part of

Cain, and Caroline Hutchinson the role of Mary. Caroline, whose north-eastern accent was perfectly suited to the poetry of the play, had the look of a da Vinci Madonna. She died a few years later, after a desperate struggle against cancer.

The plays were to be performed in the vastness of Cologne Cathedral and we all worried about the acoustics. Added to that, no one was very sure how well we would be received. Would many people turn up? And would those who did be able to understand what was going on? The language of the plays was often difficult for a British audience to understand, never mind the Germans who'd be the basis of our audience in the cathedral. And again, Bill had always encouraged the poster designers back home to think of the piece as a celebration, whereas the German poster had as its image the solitary and skeletal figure of Death, the designer clearly appealing to the dark side of the German imagination. What kind of a show did they expect?

As it turned out, the show was an extraordinary success. We performed in the transept of the cathedral, facing an enormous wedge of seats constructed in the nave; 'bleachers' the Americans call them, low at the front and very high indeed at the back. On the first night, these seats were taken not by festival-goers in the main, but by the citizens of Cologne, respectable, God-fearing people, most of them middle-aged.

That afternoon we had learned that our production was to be the first 'event' to take place in the fully reconstructed cathedral since the destruction of the original building by the RAF in a bombing raid twenty-five years before. Many of the audience that night could remember those terrible events.

The atmosphere throughout that first performance was highly charged. The acting was powerfully energised, as we tried to fill the cathedral's immense space, and much more emotional than was usual. It was strange. Something seemed to be happening beyond the mere performance of a play. In the dying moments, during the singing of the carol, Clarke Peters nudged me, pointing upwards. The lamps hanging from the ceiling way above were swinging very slowly, like dowsers' pendulums, each describing a great arc and moving in a different direction to its neighbour. And the applause when it came was rapturous.

It's always difficult to analyse these collective feelings, where everyone's individual unconscious unites in a pool of meaning and resonance, but I would guess that on this occasion it had something to do with forgiveness.

We were a sell-out for the rest of the week, the hottest ticket of the festival. We were all avidly looking forward to playing Rome: If this is the response of staunch Northern Protestants, we thought, what's it going to be like when we get to Rome and perform in front of all those volatile Southern Catholics? As it turned out, we were to be very disappointed.

Our troubles began at Heathrow, when we were delayed on the tarmac for a good two hours before take-off. Drinks were available throughout the delay and on arrival in Rome, Derek Newark, for one, had clearly over-indulged, serenading some embarrassed and increasingly angry Italian passengers with repeated choruses of 'Just One Cornetto', a song from a successful advert of the time, based on the Neapolitan love song 'Santa Lucia'. Derek knew he was out of order but, like Bernard Manning, whom he sometimes resembled, he didn't seem able to contain his inner devilment.

We were to perform the plays at a film studio, not a normal venue for theatrical events, so the publicity was clearly going to have to be very good if we were to get any kind of an audience. The publicity wasn't very good and consequently the audience on that first night wasn't very large. A few people sauntered into the auditorium in their summer clothes. Most of the men possessed leather handbags, either hanging from their shoulders or clutched protectively in their hands, and as the evening wore on, they seemed to be paying more attention to the design of their neighbour's handbag than they did to the play, which they probably couldn't understand anyway. To be fair, the audiences did build as the week progressed and if we'd gone on for a while longer, who knows what the response might have been?

Enforced changes: Keith Dewhurst

During 1981, apart from his tour revamp of *The Mysteries*, Bill Bryden worked on his script for Twentieth Century-Fox. But in the early autumn he seems to have realised that his Hollywood gamble was failing – probably when he delivered a draft and the studio bosses were not enthusiastic. To his credit he acted swiftly, both for himself and the dispersed acting company.

On the film front he sought to use his position at Scottish Television to write and direct a project. Scottish Television had appointed him a non-executive director some time before, in what they freely admitted to him was the use of his name to gain brownie points in the campaign to have their licence renewed. They succeeded in this, and one or two projects had been discussed, including a life of Robert Burns. What Bill secured was *Ill Fares the Land*, a film about the evacuation of St Kilda in the 1920s, to be written forthwith and shot in the summer of 1982. At the same time he looked to the theatre, where he was soon reminded that to have a flow of work you need control.

From March 1978 to September 1980 Bill directed eleven new shows plus revivals in the Cottesloe; from September 1980 to April 1983 he did three, plus three in other theatres. He had lost the control and needed to hustle, and to hustle ideas you need a bait. Bill's plus was that he persuaded Paul Scofield to rejoin the National by offering him Don Quixote, in an adaptation I would write for the Olivier, and Oberon in *A Midsummer Night's Dream*. Bill was also in touch with David Mamet, who was finding it hard to persuade Broadway producers to invest in his latest play *Glengarry Glen Ross*. They wanted extensive rewrites. Bill suggested that the play should première at the Cottesloe, where people could see whether it needed to be rewritten or not, and this is what happened in late 1982. Bill's production was a great success, as were a subsequent Broadway presentation and the Hollywood movie. In the meantime, the first of Bill's hustled projects to be realised was *Don Quixote*, in the summer of 1982.

23. Endings

Don Quixote: Keith Dewhurst

Don Quixote, which might have been a huge success, turned out a mess. It was planned to be a show that would stay in the repertoire for some time, tour, and be revived to go to the Mark Taper Forum as part of the celebrations during the Los Angeles Olympics. It had a lot going for it. Dudley would design the set and Deirdre Clancy the costumes. The cast included Glover, Newark, Shepherd, Ray, James Grant, J. G. Devlin, Karl Johnson, Edna Doré, Tamara Hinchco, Tony Haygarth ideally cast as Sancho Panza, and Scofield as the Don. Tams assembled an excellent band that had Martin Carthy and Maddy Prior as singers. New people in the cast included Julie Legrand, Billy McBain and Vicky Ogden. We were not short of talent. So how, then, did we mess it up?

When James Fenton, whom I knew and liked, reviewed the play in the *Sunday Times*, he said that it looked as though Bill, Bill Dudley and I had never met and spoken about it, which was a pretty shrewd appraisal. Although we seemed to prepare with thoroughness and had ample time to do so, there was not much listening to one another. There was less talk about *Don Quixote* than about any of the so-called Impossible Plays; fewer of those repetitive discussions about what it should be like and how it should strike the audience.

Bill and I had talked at first and were agreed that on the open stage it would have to be an Elizabethan-style play with epic scenes that changed swiftly from one to the other, and with two acts to correspond to the two halves of the book. The second half, in which Don Quixote is recognised everywhere as the hero of the novel, is a very early alienation device. We agreed also that I should use the first English translation, made by John Shelton in 1610. James Fenton's review pooh-poohed this, but was wrong. Shelton's Jacobean was a language familiar to the actors, it was of the period, and it solved the old problems of accents. Some dialogue I had perforce to invent, and more often than not stole phrases from the translation's straight narrative.

But as things drew nearer we seemed to talk less, and when Caulfield and Dudley went to Spain to see La Mancha, Bill and I did not join them. This was a mistake, because in situ we would have had to face up to some problems. Sebastian was missed here, I feel. Had he still been with us he might well have brought about a proper trip, because he was a great one for talking things through. As it was, people were left to their own devices.

My contribution to the confusion, apart from becoming slowly pissed off, was that the script was far too long. In the past, Bill and the actors expected an Impossible Play to be too long, so I would deliberately leave some things to be resolved in rehearsal. The advantage of doing this was that what came through the rehearsal period and the previews was tried and tested. The drawback was that if people misbehaved, or took advantage, or something beyond our control went wrong, the work on the play was difficult to do. The time lost on *The World Turned Upside Down* is an example.

As success mounted and drink flowed, the actors did get cocky, and were more ebullient in rehearsal. In *Don Quixote*, curiously enough, although we must have thrown out a huge chunk of something like half an hour's material, it was not in the end the text or its construction that suffered from what happened; they were tuned and tightened.

Clancy's costumes were a great evocation of Spain's Golden Century, but Dudley's set was somehow at odds with the play. The Olivier was a pig of a theatre and Dudley's attempt to master it involved a steep rake and huge flats, painted the colour of the La Mancha earth, that moved hydraulically to make different settings. The band were in a sort of Spanish village at the side of the stage opening. To solve the problem of a lighting man with whom Dudley would work, Bill Bryden brought in the great veteran William Bundy.

The obligatory technical problems of the play were the

windmills, which the Don charges, his horse Rosinante and Sancho's donkey. Dudley's notion of representing these with tricycles was typical of his inspiration: a penny-farthing for the Don and a small one for Sancho. Similarly, he had the actors on roller-skates to simulate a flock of sheep. Alas, on the rake none of these devices was stable. Sancho's tricycle was by far the easiest to manage, but the actors hated the roller-skates and the penny-farthing wobbled and Scofield fell off. The windmills were equally hazardous and Scofield fell there as well.

At the technical rehearsal things took for ever and the new computerised lighting-board played up, so that even during the run of the play a lighting state might change for no reason in the middle of a scene. After a bad tech, the first preview was a nightmare. The play was too long. Its momentum was lost every time the hydraulics moved with numbing slowness. Seat backs banged as people left for their trains, and at one point Haygarth had to ask the audience to be patient and allow a stagehand to come on and remove a chair.

We had to cut and we had to speed up. Bill threw himself into it but the price of fluent scene changes was that much of the set's movement had to go, which left it stranded, somehow, like ruins in the desert of the Olivier.

Gawn Grainger, a veteran of the Cottesloe, where he had both acted and seen plays he wrote directed by Sebastian, watched one preview and at the interval came up to me. 'What's wrong?' he said. 'It's all there but somehow they aren't doing it.'

They weren't, and what finally threw them, because nobody could do anything about it, was the fact that when he fell from the penny-farthing and the windmill, Scofield injured himself and could not go on. Previews were cancelled and the date of the first night put back. When Scofield was fit again, it was too late. The first night had the unmistakable atmosphere of a production that lacks conviction because it has not solved its problems, and the reviews and subsequent public reaction reflected this.

Things got better, of course, and there were times when in

their scenes together Scofield and Haygarth were sublime. As Scofield got into it, some of the things he did were remarkable, and his performance could be different from night to night as he tried to keep the inspiration fresh for himself. Some of the best things he only did once, and some of the least effective also, as when one night he took the whole thing at about two and a half times its proper pace.

When we were in rehearsal, I ran into Bill Gaskill, who said, 'Has Paul given up the book yet?' He hadn't, and was the last to do so. 'Those people are always like that,' said Gaskill. 'They soak it up more than the others.' And, indeed, Scofield did sometimes hold the script right up to his face, as though he might suddenly drink it. He was modest and charming and he loved the roughnecks, turning up in the bar when one of them had a birthday. It took them longer to be at ease with him, I think, which was perhaps another unspoken reason for the production's sense of unease.

Bill was less focused when he directed *Don Quixote* than on any other show I did with him. The dreaded Olivier had defeated him again, in some measure I suppose because he was thinking about his TV film *Ill Fares the Land*, which he went off to direct soon after the play opened. This resulted in the most ludicrous situation of our entire adventure, because he had booked some of the *Don Quixote* actors to appear in the film, and the dates clashed. As the actors arrived at Heathrow from Scotland, Frank Nealon, our staff assistant director, met them at the gate, demanded their return tickets and refused to allow them to go back. There were furious phone calls with agents, and a suggestion that the NT would take legal action against Scottish Television. When it was realised that they were each represented by the same lawyer, the conflict of interest seems to have ended the matter.

A difficult stage: Jack Shepherd

Don Quixote was one of the few productions we attempted which was not a box-office success. There were two main reasons for this. In the first place, the book doesn't really have a narrative. It consists of a series of adventures, each one fascinating in itself, but hardly bound together into a suspenseful story. Second, Bill's epic events thrived best in an *environment*. *Don Quixote* was performed in a set, constructed what's more on the Olivier's notoriously difficult stage. And despite Bill Dudley's ingenuity, I always felt we were performing in an art deco cinema.

Nor was the acting as effective as it had been in the Cottesloe. There wasn't the same intimacy and the amount of detail lost in performance was considerable. Most of us felt as if we were just shouting. Only Paul Scofield and Tony Haygarth seemed comfortable with the cavernous proportions of the theatre.

Departure: Keith Dewhurst

Don Quixote opened at the end of June. As a consequence of my divorce and paying for two households, I had a huge overdraft. Alexandra and I had already sold our London flat, and had been living in Italy. At the end of August we borrowed a friend's house in France. We were in England for three weeks in January 1983, for the rehearsals of a TV play I wrote called *The Battle of Waterloo*, and then we went to Australia for four years, where we repaired our finances by working in the last days of the tax shelter film boom.

In 1985 I visited England for two weeks and saw Hayden Griffin and Derek Newark, but I did not meet Bill again until a christening at Southwark Cathedral in 1988. We embraced and he launched at once into an analysis of team selection at Old Trafford. My disappearance without warning had hurt him, I think, as I guess it had me. On the other hand, our friendship was so intense that it had burned most of itself out, leaving the bedrock, which said that it was wiser to slip away in silence. So it has proved; and, of course, I knew that the dream was over on the day we had lunch at the Bistingo.

A threat to family life: Jack Shepherd

It's my feeling that we were at our most creative during the period 1977 to 1981. During this time the company briefly threatened to take over my life. What followed, from 1982 onwards, for me, didn't have the same intensity.

I did a good deal of other work at this time. I played a gay South African terrorist in a TV play by Rose Tremaine, I devised a play for Joint Stock and I got sacked by Bernard Miles at the Mermaid. Bernard was a cricket fan. He wanted the Mark Antony in *his Julius Caesar* to be more of an Ian Botham, he told me, and less of a Geoff Boycott.

I returned to the National in 1982, to play in *Don Quixote*, intrigued by the possibility of working with Paul Scofield, and I stayed on for *A Midsummer Night's Dream*. But from this point on, I wasn't as *immersed* in the thing as I had been and didn't approach the work with quite the same commitment.

For one thing, I was pulling away from the culture of *the bar* and all that it represented, perceiving it as a threat to family life, not to mention my health and general equilibrium. This also meant that I was pulling away from Bill's meetings, which inevitably took place with a drink in hand, steadily losing whatever influence I had had with the company. I was still enjoying the work, I was still involved, but I wanted to take a step back and get a perspective on the whole thing.

24. *A Midsummer Night's Dream*

Playing the *Dream*: Jack Shepherd

I've always suspected that the tobacco first brought over from America was laced with marijuana, and that *A Midsummer Night's Dream* is the result of a long afternoon spent lounging in some aesthete's ornamental garden, smoking Sir Walter's latest consignment.

The designer for this production was Bob Crowley, who took as his inspiration the ambience of a ruined castle with lichen-covered walls, broken masonry, weed-encrusted court-yards and dead leaves blown by the wind. Thousands of leaves, each hand-made, cut from fabric, brushed with paint, and swept up and bagged at the end of each performance. It was the kind of place that might well be inhabited by the last few survivors of an ancient fairy race, a magical place.

Apart from Grant Hicks's junk shop set for *American Buffalo*, the Cottesloe design had been pretty much shared between Bill Dudley and Hayden Griffin. As a general rule, Bill designed the events and Hayden designed the plays. Bill would create an environment where the piece could happen, Hayden would try to create a perfect set.

The most telling feature of Bob Crowley's set for the *Dream* was the simplest: there was no raised platform. The line between spectators and performers had been deliberately blurred. Most of the audience sat in the balconies and the stalls, but some of them sat on cushions, which were partly in the auditorium and partly in the set. It was a sort of sitting-down promenade.

Titania and Oberon were played by Sue Fleetwood and Paul Scofield. These two actors had been working in the building for a number of years, but this was only Paul's second venture with the company and Sue's first. They each spoke the verse in very different ways. Sue tended to invest the word with the quality it defined. If the word was 'beauty', say, she would try and say it 'beautifully'. If the word was 'ugly', her face would wrinkle as she spoke, with a sense of the word's 'ugliness'. I felt that this approach tended to make the character rather precious and self-regarding, which I'm sure was not intentional; it was more a side effect created by her approach to the verse. Added to this, the quality of her enunciation would have made a 1960s voice teacher purr with delight.

Paul's voice, on the other hand, was very much his own. The poetry emerged through the *clarity* of the speaking, the pulse of the metre and the ability to sustain the thought to the end of the phrase. His ability to listen was also in evidence. In some performances he would become so involved in what I was saying, that he would forget it was his turn to speak.

In rehearsals Paul exerted a very serious moral influence on the way we worked. Usually dressed in tweeds and corduroys, he was a massively avuncular presence. He didn't betray any kind of vulnerability until the technical rehearsal, when he suddenly appeared in the auditorium, dressed in housecoat and slippers, having just given himself a full 'Robert Helpmann' ballet make-up, sensing it was inappropriate, yet feeling obliged to give it a try. Paul was in his early sixties and I guessed he felt anxious about being too old for the part. He needn't have worried as it turned out. The costumes and wigs were designed to make all the fairies look thousands of years old. I had a grey wig that stuck up – punk-style – a good six inches into the air. I was described in Michael Billington's review as a truly 'ancient Puck' (and I was only forty-two).

Paul had a natural majesty in the part. He was clearly a king of the fairies, unlike Robert Stephens who in time took the part over. If Paul was a monarch, then Robert was a pirate chief, swaggering up and down the boardwalk in some fairy Port o' Spain. It was also true that Robert's idea of the relationship between Oberon and Puck didn't always agree with mine. The scenes between us would often develop into an unseemly struggle, as Oberon tried to manoeuvre Puck under his voluminous cloak and Puck in turn dodged around trying frantically to avoid the experience.

The lovers were clearly a product of the Edwardian era. A generation of bright young things, dreaming their way through that seemingly endless summer before the outbreak of the Great War; their equilibrium shattered on this midsummer night by the inadvertent absorption of consciousness-altering substances. Karl Johnson, I remember, drifted through the play in a state of the most languid confusion. I have a clear image of him, his expression a perfect balance of terror and delight, sitting next to a loudly guffawing Edward de Souza, as the Mechanicals danced their Burgomask at the end of the play.

Our Burgomask was a re-creation of a sand dance routine, popular in the music hall for many years, danced on this occasion not by 'Wilson, Kepple and Betty' but by Newark, Grant and Petcher, each wearing a fez, shuffling in a tray of sand and adopting positions that must at one time have been lifted from an Egyptian frieze. It was very very funny.

Mechanicals and Princess Margaret: Jack Shepherd

It was the Mechanicals who were at the heart of this production. The Cottesloe Company was essentially a working-class company, and in the last act there was a palpable tension between these working men, clearly out of their depth with the play they'd chosen to perform, and the upper-class characters watching the performance.

The class tensions evident in the play were comically mirrored in real life, when the company was invited to meet Princess Margaret at a reception after one of the performances at the Theatre Royal Bath. It was thought to be exactly the sort of production the Princess would enjoy, but as it turned out events didn't run anywhere near as smoothly as the organisers had hoped.

J. G. Devlin, given his Republican sympathies, decided to

stay well clear. As did Jimmy Ellis, another Ulsterman, who was playing Hermia's father. But most of the company turned out, intrigued by the idea of royal patronage and intent on having a good time. It was a party, after all. I arrived a little late, when the festivities were in full swing. At the top of a broad stone staircase that led up to a very spacious flat, I was briefly vetted by a group of overweight, mostly middle-aged security men in suits, not in the best condition of their lives. They were to feature prominently in the evening's events.

The Princess was standing at the end of a long dimly lit room, drink in hand, one eyelid drooping very slightly. After a while I was introduced to her. On being told who I was, she lowered her eyes, making it very clear she didn't want the conversation to continue any further. I retreated. Out of the corner of my eye, I could see Derek Newark, looking every inch the Guardsman, eagerly waiting his turn in the queue.

It wasn't very long before I was approached by one of the security men: could I possibly have a word with one of the company who was causing something of a disturbance? It was Steve Petcher. He was standing on the stone staircase, faced by a posse of security men, his entrance to the party denied. Could I either calm him down, or persuade him to go away.

Steve was very drunk, and probably stoned as well. Though out of his mind, he was intent on having a conversation with the Princess. 'I just want to *talk* to her, Jack.' His voice was a high-pitched whine, breaking with emotion. 'There's people in this country living in terrible conditions. And there's people like *her*!' Steve was from Bradford, whippet-thin, dark hair framing a pale face. 'I just want to *talk* to her, Jack. Just so she *understands*!'

I did my best to calm him down. But as soon as I took a step up the staircase, the security men fell on him, carried him down to the door, and threw him into the street.

One down. One to go.

Back at the party, Derek had successfully engaged the Princess in conversation. From where I was standing it looked as though they were getting on pretty well. And then the

Princess dropped something on the floor, bending forward to pick it up at exactly the same time that Derek bent forward to do the same. Their heads collided. From a distance it may have looked as though Derek had inadvertently nutted the Princess in the face, but I don't think this was the reason why he was thrown out of the party. What seems to me to be much more likely is that Derek managed to retrieve the situation after the clash of heads and then resume his conversation with the Princess. And then, after drinking far too much, far too quickly, suddenly chancing his arm.

What Derek actually said to the Princess will always remain a mystery, but he certainly intimated to Bill Bryden a few moments later that things had been going well. 'I think I've pulled, Bill,' is what he said, giving him a surreptitious thumbs-up.

The fact remains, however, that he was bundled out of the building in a most unceremonious fashion a short while later, his arm locked painfully behind his back, a security man murmuring in his ear, 'Be a brave soldier', as he was danced down the staircase on the tips of his toes and then propelled into the street below.

It seems unlikely that Princess Margaret was too put out by the company's behaviour at the infamous Bath reception, because a short while later another party was arranged for her, this time at the National Theatre itself, after a performance of the pantomime *Cinderella*. This second occasion proved to be a good deal more relaxed than the first. The security forces were not as oppressively in evidence and the Princess seemed to be enjoying herself a lot more. At one point I remember her happily joining some of the company around the piano for a sing-song. Everyone was a little self-conscious, however, and you couldn't escape the feeling that the gaiety was being stage-managed for the Princess's benefit. And if Derek Newark and Steve Petcher were present, they were keeping a very low profile.

A flashback: Keith Dewhurst

Some years earlier, Bill Bryden and I sneaked into an NT hospitality room to plunder the drinks cabinet and were startled by the arrival of Christopher Morahan, Prince and Princess Michael of Kent, the Austrian Ambassador and a retinue. They had come to see a play by Schnitzler. 'What are you two doing here?' hissed Christopher, but he needn't have worried. The Royals assumed that we had directed and/or written the play, offered very warm congratulations, and turned their backs. So far as I remember, we did likewise, and kept on drinking.

25. *Glengarry Glen Ross*

Jack Shepherd

I think it was Harold Pinter who first read the play and instantly spotted the quality and the originality of the writing. The language comes fizzing off the page at you, like street jazz; slang so intense it almost seems like a different language.

One lunchtime, Bill took the company to a Southwark restaurant to meet David Mamet. When we arrived, he was already deep in conversation with Harold Pinter. This wasn't the time for introductions, so we shuffled off to another table and waited. I watched them for a while, intrigued by the fact that they were getting on so well when they were such profoundly different writers. There was Pinter, who'd been living in the surreal twilight of the subtext, and there was Mamet with his 'what you see on the page is pretty much what you get' approach, who was later to say that he didn't want the actors to infer anything from the text, he just wanted them to say it.

Glengarry wasn't an easy play to rehearse. Written in the sharp-toothed jargon of American real estate sharks, salesmen living on the edge, working exclusively on commission and in such ruthless competition with each other that two of these sharks are driven to burgle the very office in which they work in order to get hold of the best 'leads', the names and addresses of potential buyers.

It was a nerve-racking process. We knew exactly where we wanted to go, but we were falling over ourselves in our haste to get there. We were all of us strung out.

One day there was very nearly a fight. All I now recall is losing my temper and, in order to make my point, throwing over the table in front of me. Well, that's what I *meant* to do, but in that moment I released so much energy that the table went flying across the room, catching a very startled and wholly innocent Derek Newark full in the chest.

Bill immediately set about calming everyone down, standing in the middle of the room like an evangelical minister, trying to steady a congregation suddenly possessed by demons. 'We don't do this,' he kept saying, trying to make calming gestures. 'The Cottesloe Company just doesn't *behave* like this.' And as we started to realise how genuinely upset Bill was, we began to steady down. And no one finally got hurt.

We *were* a company by then, for better or for worse. Most of us had been working together regularly for six years, and on and off for thirteen. We knew each other's strengths and weaknesses. And crucially, in the group scenes, we knew precisely when to take the focus on stage and when to give it to somebody else. It was this ensemble playing that made the productions so successful. Companies are so short-lived these days that true ensemble playing is something audiences rarely see.

When the film of *Glengarry Glen Ross* came out a few years later, it seemed to me that although the individual performances in the film were, in the main, much more sharply defined, as a *group* we had the edge. Film is different, of course; it usually has little to do with group dynamics. It's a medium where the actor takes each moment as it comes. And the actors in the film were very very good at seizing the moment. They also had an advantage over us in that they were saying something about their own country. They knew what real estate salesmen were really like. In other words, they knew about things at first hand, that we could only glimpse from the outside.

Yet when John Caulfield went to see the film, he was heard to say on the way out: 'Who'd've thought Derek Newark was a better actor than Jack Lemon?' And there was some truth in that statement. As Shelley Levine, Derek probably gave the performance of his life. It's usually true that when an actor plays a character very close to himself, he's the last one to realise it. The psychic tension that this brings about is often the chemistry of a great performance. Derek wouldn't have wanted to admit that there was anything in him that was like Shelley Levine. And yet there *was* something of the salesman in Derek: the easy jokes, the charm – when he cared to use it – and the sense that when he talked to you, he could make you feel honoured to be taken into his confidence. And there was one other thing: Derek, like Shelley Levine, was living his life desperately.

Years later, Alan Arkin, who played Aaronow, told me a story about Jack Lemon's performance in that film. They rehearsed for several weeks before shooting began, ending with a run-through on the final day. 'Jack Lemon was so good,' he told me, 'so convincing, so *unlike* Jack Lemon, we applauded him off the set.' He then added, however, that as soon as he started work in front of the camera, he went back to being Jack Lemon. Not a trace remained of the originality and brilliance of his rehearsal performance. It sounds to me as though he was trapped inside his 'star' personality, reluctant to express a side of himself that he sensed the public wouldn't like; nervous about revealing a true vulnerability.

The problem with the worst of American film acting is that it can be very self-referring, relating more to the experience of *acting* than to the experience of *life*. Some actors often seem to be doing little more than advertising their talent: 'You want to see crying? I can do crying.' And they cry. 'You want to see *stillness*? Now *this* is stillness.' And so on.

These were not our problems, however, as we struggled through rehearsals. We had few fears about bringing the play to life, but we were anxious about the authenticity of our accents. Did we all sound like we came from Chicago? A problem, incidentally, that didn't seem to worry David Mamet. He even said it would be OK for us to use English accents, so long as we kept to the rhythm of the text. The *rhythm*, as far as he was concerned, was the key to it all. We weren't so sure; to have played the play with English accents would have felt like getting on the wrong train. In the end, the accents weren't half bad.

So much of our popular culture these days comes from America, people are tuning in to the accent at a very early age.

It's now almost like a second language. It's a process, of course, that's been going on for a long time. When I was growing up in the 1950s, like all my friends, I found that I was identifying more intensely with the heroes in American films, than I did with their British counterparts of the same period. In other words, there seemed a greater gulf between us and the invariably upper-class heroes of British films than there did between us and an actor like James Dean, say. So we copied the way they dressed (Chesterfield Box raincoats were the big thing in 1955), the way they walked (Americans seemed to have a much looser walk than the stiff-backed British) and, of course, the way they talked. So, later, when it came to playing Americans, the accent was almost second nature.

Mamet didn't say a lot during rehearsals, observing for the most part, letting the director get on with the job. There was one thing, however, he was determined to impress upon us: the importance of 'closing the deal'. 'It's like making a woman,' he told us. 'You talk to them, about this and that, blah blah blah. But there's just one thing in the back of your mind.' He didn't talk about the play in terms of what it might mean or the ideas it contained, though he did talk about the salesmen he'd once worked with, saying how good some of them were at 'closing the deal'. Good at that one thing to the point of genius.

I don't know what he made of us as a company. He usually seemed a little wary.

The production won two awards that year: the best new play, and I won an award for the best performance in a new play. It was an award that Derek Newark had been tipped to get. People had been slapping his back in the bar, telling him how good he was, saying that when the time came for the awards, they fully expected him to get one. I think it was a bitter pill for him to swallow, but he was very civil and generous with his congratulations when the news came out.

26. *Cinderella*

Jack Shepherd

For Christmas 1983 Bill Bryden had the chance to undertake a project that had eluded him in 1978: *Cinderella*, an evocation of the classic British Edwardian pantomime. It turned out to be a mixed experience.

It's Bill's belief now that he didn't spend enough time working on the text before the start of rehearsals, believing that there was enough talent in the company to tailor the script to the strengths of particular actors, as we went along. The problem was, of course, that there were so many different things to do in rehearsal – songs to learn, dances to practise, routines to develop and so on – there wasn't time to worry about the text.

When we opened, it was clear that the children in the audience were enchanted, and the middle-class parents pleased and perhaps a little relieved by the absence of any vulgarity. It was charming, moderately funny and absolutely harmless. But when those people who fancied they knew about pantomime came to see the show, they were sneeringly dismissive. We had apparently completely missed the point.

What was it we had missed? There is a clue to this, I think, in the fact that a routine taught to us by one of pantomime's great performers, Jimmy Jewell, proved not to fit into the style of show we were developing, and so it was dropped. Now I had seen this routine as a child, when Jimmy Jewell and Ben Warris brought their *Babes in the Wood* panto to the Leeds Empire, and I remembered it as being hilarious. Thirty or so years later, Jimmy taught the routine to John Tams and me – we were playing the Broker's Men – and I suddenly saw it in a different light.

The basis of the routine is this: one half of the double act (the straight man) enters with a mouthful of water, and the clown is encouraged to say, 'Busy bee. Busy bee, deliver all your honey to me.' And when he does, he gets the mouthful of water full in the face. When the clown has a go at playing the same trick, everything goes wrong. It's a very physical routine, requiring enormous energy. John and I managed to learn it, to Jimmy's evident delight, but we couldn't make it fit in with everything else in the pantomime and the routine was dropped. This hurt Jimmy's pride, I think, and he took no further interest in what we were doing.

It was the sheer vulgarity of the routine that made it stand out. And *vulgarity*, I now realise, is the quality that our pantomime was most definitely lacking. This is why there was no real conviction in what we were doing. We lacked authenticity, because we lacked vulgarity and all the energy that comes with it. What you remember from childhood is the enchantment of pantomime. The vulgarity passes you by.

There are two Principal Boys in the pantomime of *Cinderella*: the Prince himself and his valet Dandini, traditionally the more worldly of the two. In our production Sue Fleetwood played the Prince and Marsha Hunt, Dandini. I think Sue was flattered when she was offered the role. She had all the qualities necessary to make a good Principal Boy, all, that is, except one. She didn't have a singing voice. And in her duet with Cinderella, Janet Dibley often had to sing along with her, as she lurched towards the end of the chorus, like an exhausted athlete being helped over the line.

She was a handsome woman, tall with a great figure and very long legs. Exactly what was needed. But sexually the Principal Boy role is rather ambiguous. On the one hand, the character is supposedly a man and yet the woman playing the part is very much on display. This seemed to make Sue rather self-conscious and you always felt she was hiding timidly behind the character: acting the part of a Principal Boy instead of simply *being* one. If she'd just let go she'd've been terrific.

Marsha, on the other hand, carried on as if the whole thing was a great joke, which of course it was. And in consequence she seemed much happier in her role, swaggering about the stage, shrugging off the historically accurate, but potentially uncomfortable, fact that she was playing the black servant of a white 'master'. Marsha could sing too.

It's always been a puzzle to me why Derek Newark and Robert Stephens were so subdued in their roles as the Ugly Sisters. Admittedly, they didn't get the flying start that Bill's 1978 notion of Gielgud and Olivier would have had in the parts. With those two the audience would have laughed as soon as they saw the dresses and the make-up. There's always tension in the air when someone very famous and rather dignified dresses up in the clothes of the opposite sex, a tension that's invariably released through laughter. But with Robert and Derek, neither of whom was really celebrated, you felt there was more a sense of the audience sitting back and saying, 'Come on, then. Let's see what you can do.'

There's an art to wearing 'drag', a knowingness, a sexual ambivalence. To succeed, the actor has to enjoy playing around with the masculine and feminine within himself, implying depths to his character the audience has never guessed at. And, what's more, enjoying doing so. Neither Robert nor Derek was prepared to go that far. There was no vulgarity in their performances, no release, no innuendo, no real enjoyment. You simply felt they were gritting their teeth and getting on with it. This was a surprise to the rest of us, and a disappointment, since, privately and individually, the pair of them could be utterly outrageous.

Tony Haygarth, on the other hand, as Buttons, seemed to be in his element. Tony was one of the few actors in the company who could generate the warmth and the sentiment that pantomime requires. Tony has always been very much at ease on stage and he was entirely comfortable in a world where the audience are invited in to the very heart of the action. So relaxed is Tony in performance, on forgetting his lines, he's been known to stroll down to the front of the stage and address the audience: 'Do you know, something extraordinary has just happened. I've forgotten my lines. Isn't that amazing?'

Finally, I think it's true to say that the company members were getting tired. There wasn't much left in the tank, as they say. And we weren't prepared to invest the last of our fuel on something as frivolous as a pantomime. Around the time of the trip to Edinburgh in 1980, the energy on stage had often been incandescent. We felt, rightly or wrongly, that we could do *anything*. Four years later, the enthusiasm and commitment were nowhere near as intense.

A pantomime is physically very demanding. And when it came to it, the company as a whole wasn't prepared to put the hours in. In the dance sequences, of course, it's doubtful if hard work would have been enough. Although a few specialist dancers had been brought in, the choreographer, David Toguri, had to work with actors in the main and no matter how hard they worked, they were never quite going to come up to scratch.

Companies can only live for a certain amount of time. And we were reaching the end. There would be *Golden Boy*, one last effort with the final version of *The Mysteries* in 1984–85. And that would be it.

A Comment: Keith Dewhurst

I still have the old Victorian and Edwardian playbooks that I would have used to write *Cinderella* in 1978. Pantos change over the years, and even from city to city. To judge from those I saw in wartime Manchester, provincial pantos were more vulgar than those in London, and the Rikki Fulton shows that Bill and I saw together in Edinburgh were slapsticky but not as vulgar as the routine Jack describes. So when Bill says the script was the problem, I guess he's right. He should probably have settled on the style of a specific time, and made everything integral to that.

27. The Boxing

Jack Shepherd

Over the years, I suppose, we'd got used to performing in the intimate space of the Cottesloe Theatre, and when we rehearsed *Golden Boy* by Clifford Odets in the winter of 1984, there was a feeling in the back of our minds that the Lyttelton would be similar; if not quite so intimate, then very nearly so. We were wrong.

When I first tried out my performance at the technical rehearsal, I soon realised that very little was actually getting across. I was playing Eddie Fuseli, a New York mobster. And the quiet, dangerously introverted man I'd developed in rehearsal was hardly registering. I was clearly going to have to restructure the performance, from introvert to extrovert. In other words, I wasn't going to be able to draw the audience into my world, I was going to have to project outwards, revealing the character I was playing in a kind of display.

Part of the reason for this is the nature of the Lyttelton stage. Like many other theatres designed at that time, the building had been conceived as a rectangular box, with a stage at one end and an upwardly sloping auditorium. The problem with such a design is that the energy is scattered, diffused. The auditorium can seem strangely lacking in atmosphere, bland, like a concert hall or a cinema, from which source I suspect the inspiration for the design was unconsciously drawn.

I think it's true to say that *Golden Boy* had not worn well in the forty-odd years since its first production, but this didn't really become clear until we were well into rehearsals. In fact, the criticisms levelled at O'Neill's sea plays might also be levelled against this one: what had once seemed naturalistic and 'moving', in a later context appeared heavy-handed and melodramatic. Bill, of course, was motivated by his passion for boxing and may well have been blind to these weaknesses.

Bill always referred to it as 'the boxing'. 'I went to the boxing last night,' he would say. 'A great fight.' And because he enjoyed it so much, he had a real expectation that a play about 'the boxing' would be popular. He was mistaken.

In the Cottesloe the audience would have been so much closer to the boxing, the sweat and the pain of it all, that the play would have fared a good deal better. Or perhaps it was always a mistake to imagine that a piece about boxing, a sport traditionally supported by the proletariat and the aristocracy, would appeal to the National Theatre audience of the time.

Be that as it may, by 1984 the company was very comfortable with the American idiom, and this was the tenth American play we'd attempted in the past six years. Derek Newark was again well cast as Moody, the fight manager. This was one of his most accomplished performances and his last leading role with the company before the sad decline of his later years. Jerry Flynn was drafted in to play the hero of the title, the 'Golden Boy' himself. Jerry's grip of the American idiom was very secure. He was self-possessed throughout and, like a good boxer, he took his chance with both hands.

Lisa Eichorn played his girlfriend, Lorna, a character with something of the femme fatale about her. Lisa, a real American, was very comfortable with the glamour of the role, though I'm not sure how she got on with Bill's oblique style of directing.

Bill's qualities of reticence and sensitivity have never inclined him towards playing the Svengali in rehearsals. Bill's process always involved casting well and allowing the actors to develop the performance in their own way, fearing that if he interfered with the mechanics of the process too clumsily, he might be a destructive rather than a creative influence. It's easy to see how an actress, struggling to fit in with the masculine and occasionally macho ambience of a Cottesloe Company rehearsal, might be looking for a more supportive, one-to-one relationship with the director, something Bill studiously avoided throughout his directing career.

A Comment: Keith Dewhurst

Yes. But let's face it. Bill *was* a Svengali, and hypnotised us all into following him. The outcome, we believed, would be triumphant recognition for doing what we most enjoyed. On the other hand, his rehearsal method did seem far from impositional. He did not interrupt the actors much, or give line readings. When he did interrupt it was because an idea had struck him there and then – or because he was very good at acting the part of a director to whom an actor had revealed something. He would let people act and then almost off-handedly sculpt what they did with phrases like, 'I have the feeling that maybe what should happen here is . . .' He would allow moves and staging to emerge in the same way, although it would be a mistake to assume that he did not have very clear ideas of what he wanted. As far as scripts were concerned, he was imbued with the Royal Court notion that the writer must see his text respected: that is why virtually all rewrites were done in rehearsal or previews, when something had been *shown* not to work. A writer who could not think in this way, and mend things under pressure, was not for Bill.

28. *Doomsday*

Following the score: Jack Shepherd

In the autumn of 1984, work began on the final part of *The Mysteries*. It was given the title *Doomsday*, and once it was added to the two existing works – *Creation to Nativity* and *The Passion* – the cycle was complete.

On the first day I was very surprised to be handed a script, and after glancing through it I realised that Tony Harrison had produced a finished draft, complete in every detail. I, for one, had mixed feelings about this. There was no mistaking the quality of the verse and the integrity and the strength of the interpretation, but I found myself disappointed that, this time, all the creative work had been done in advance of the rehearsal. There was little left for the company to discover. What had inspired me about the earlier productions was the collective involvement, the harnessing of the creative energy of everyone taking part, the sense of commitment it produced: the feeling of ownership.

This time we would return to more traditional procedures. The cast would interpret the text and the direction the production was taking would be decided by people sitting on the outside. The days of democracy were over. It was a return to absolute rule.

I remember a conversation between Tony Harrison and Harrison Birtwistle that had taken place a few years earlier during the workshops for Tony's version of the *Orestia*. Tony had been grumbling about how difficult it was to get actors to speak verse properly, how the interpretation often got in the way of the verse itself, especially if it was over-emoted or if the pulse within the verse was ignored. What was the best way, he wondered, of getting them to speak it correctly, with the right rhythm and intonation; drawing attention to the *poetry*, as opposed to the performer's feelings about what it might possibly mean?

'Why don't you score it?' Birtwistle had replied. 'Find a way of annotating the text, so there's only ever going to be one way of saying it. That's what I'd do.'

Tony disagreed. I think he was a little shocked. Music's different, he said. The speaking of verse was more than a technical discipline, and couldn't be limited to the following of a precise set of instructions. Because poetry conveys meaning, the speaking of it should not be absolutely fixed.

Despite my misgivings about the process of rehearsal, it was clear that the text that Tony had produced for this final part was beautifully wrought, in keeping with the medieval spirit of the original, yet with powerful resonances that would strike a chord with a contemporary audience.

> This space about us all, no corpse shall need as much.
> The roof of thy hall, thy naked nose shall touch.

Tony has never been one to shrink from a challenge: faced with the choice of making demands on an audience or giving them an easy time of it, Tony has always taken the former option. Aware that the attention span of a modern audience seems to be considerably shorter than it once used to be, he has always taken delight in challenging this capacity and stretching it to the limit.

It was no surprise, therefore, to discover that by far the longest speech in the trilogy came at the very end. After a good two hours of drama (a whole day, in fact, when the three parts were put together), and just at the point where people were beginning to glance at their watches, Jesus began to weigh mankind in the balance. Long as the speech was, it was only a fraction of the original, delivered almost certainly in the early hours when, under the torchlight's hellish glare, the last cart pulled up at the final 'station' and, in front of an exhausted crowd, God's terrible judgment was given.

Karl Johnson had to face up to the challenge of this final tirade. He had the good sense to leave his ego at home and surrender to Tony's influence. He was consequently always in control of that final speech, picking his way through it with clarity and wit; frowning with anger and then grinning suddenly like Simon Rattle in the midst of a standing ovation. But Tony was right. It was the sheer length of the speech, the fact that he didn't stop, that he went relentlessly on and on, beyond the point at which a character in any other play would have called it a day, that made it momentous.

At the beginning of the judgment and at the close, a great wheel was visible, spinning behind the figure of Christ, its axis more or less level with his head. The wheel was as high as the theatre itself and almost as broad; concealed from the audience up to this point by a huge black drape. It was a truly spectacular device. An image of the earth, fashioned like a Ferris wheel out of metal rods, spinning slowly at first, with the souls of the damned hanging from the struts. Later, when the souls had been judged, it was still and empty of any life.

Clearly, the production had moved a long way since the earliest days, as Bill Bryden and Bill Dudley both searched for increasingly conceptual ways of realising the *mise-en-scène*. In Part Three these ideas were taken even further. In the first scene, Satan was hoisted up from hell by a series of ropes and pulleys and then deposited on top of a street-cleaning machine, and in the second scene, instead of being laid in a tomb, Jesus walked into a conjuror's cabinet, shutting the door behind him. The cabinet was then bound up with chains, which duly fell away as the door opened again and an angel stepped out in his place, to greet the grieving women on that first Easter morning. The logic of Part One was still in place, all the protagonists in the New Testament story were definitely being played by working men; but there was no longer a sense that each play in the cycle was being sponsored by a different trade union.

I'm not saying that there was any betrayal of the ideas that had made *The Passion* such a success, it's more that the project gained its own momentum as it went along; that the inter- pretive logic that lay behind the first production began to develop and then change, as it became evident that the text of the later plays was posing a new sort of challenge.

The resurrection scene was a case in point. As the last trump sounded, the resurrected dead erupted through trapdoors, cut like graves in the floor of the theatre; the bad souls shrinking from the judgment that was to come and the good souls joyfully reuniting with their families in expectation of paradise. The inspiration for this scene was taken directly from the Cookham paintings of Stanley Spencer, and I think it's fair to say that, as the trilogy developed, it moved from simplicity into spectacle.

A Comment: Keith Dewhurst

Personally, I loathe design-concept theatre. It does not transform the space but clutter it with decorative, fake-intellectual objects. Just as narrative is not really the point about painting, so decoration is not really the point about the theatre. Although I fully recognise that it is crowd-pleasing. Alas.

Rehearsal strategies: Jack Shepherd

Whenever we started out on a run of *The Mysteries*, introducing a new group of actors to the techniques of the promenade, Bill would always assemble the entire company and after a short introductory speech would ask: 'Could I have the blue cloth please?'

Stage management would then produce a large rectangular expanse of blue silk, which was to symbolise the River Jordan. The actors would then be instructed in the art of unfurling it and spreading it out, holding it just above the auditorium floor, fluttering it slightly to indicate the rippling surface of the river.

Once Jesus and St John were in place for the baptism and the band was ready to play, an approximation of the scene could then be attempted, revealing to the new members of the cast not only the style of the production, but also demonstrating that this was going to be a group venture where no individual would dominate for very long, where everyone had a part to play. And since all this would be played in the midst of a large standing audience, it also introduced them to the ways in which that audience were going to have to be moved and manipulated and (when it came to the fluttering of the blue cloth) encouraged to join in, a paradigm in fact of all that was to come.

Another of Bill's strategies was to rehearse the first few minutes over and over again, until he felt the actors had got it right, and then suddenly relinquish control, allowing them to go all the way through to the end without any interruption at all. The thinking behind this is straightforward: You're not going to complete the journey successfully if you set off on the wrong foot.

He'd sit close to the action, coiled, with his legs crossed, smoking heavily in those days (untipped cigarettes), ready to spring out into the arena, eyes blazing, arms whirling, crystal clear in his intent, if not his language.

A furious row: Jack Shepherd

It was during this run of *The Mysteries* that Bill and I had a furious row, about the only serious one we ever had. It was one of the few occasions when Bill passionately confronted an issue, rather than politically giving ground and maintaining good faith. That night on the balcony of the Cottesloe Theatre, just after the audience had gone, Bill and I both lost our tempers and really let rip. What we didn't know was that the microphones in the Prompt Corner were still active and our frantic argument was being relayed to anyone in the company with their dressing-room loudspeaker still switched on. When we finally retired to the Green Room bar, I could tell by the sheepish nature of the smiles we were getting that most of the company were fully aware of what had happened.

What sparked the row was my concern over Robert Stephens's increasingly erratic behaviour on stage, which that evening reached crisis point. Robert was playing Pontius Pilate and his first entrance was on a gantry high above the bandstand where, in the company of his wife, Dame Precious Percola, he would announce his presence to the audience crowded below: 'Pilate am I. Prince of great pride.'

I was playing Judas, and standing below the gantry as usual, hidden in the crowd, ready to betray my master for thirty pieces of silver. But on this occasion Pilate lurched up to the balcony, blurted out something wholly unintelligible and disappeared again, leaving his wife Percola, played by Brenda Blethyn, to face the consequences alone.

There was a very long hiatus. Brenda smiled and nodded for a while and then with amazing presence of mind, announced to the crowd below, as though referring to a defective boiler: 'I think my Pilate's just gone out.'

This produced a roar of laughter from a very knowing audience. I can't remember now how we got out of it. Maybe I shouted some of my lines up at her, or maybe we simply carried on with the play, thinking that the audience probably knew the story well enough to get on without the missing scene. Thankfully Robert managed his next entrance, but with a hangdog look that left the audience in no doubt about the reasons for his earlier disappearance.

'Death' takes the stage: Jack Shepherd

Besides being the sole creator of *Doomsday*, Tony Harrison revised and to some extent rewrote the first part, *Creation to Nativity*, which he had not been involved in when it was first conceived. He replaced the final scene, which had been devised by the company back in 1980, with a play from an existing canon. A life-affirming dance gave way to the spectral figure of Death scything down an unrepentant Herod, still exulting with his court after the killing of the male children. I was to play Death.

This was a very dark experience. Strange. Wholly negative. With a feeling of cobwebs in the eyes. I had to come on stage to make people realise how *vulnerable* they were, how *mortal* and, if possible, scare the living daylights out of them.

When an actor comes off stage after a long and highly energised speech, lathered in sweat and charged with adrenalin, there's usually an accompanying sense of euphoria. Not so with this part; there was only fatigue and emptiness. You don't *play* the part of Death so much as are *consumed* by it. It's as if your system turns against your feelings (feelings that would normally be released in performance) and starts to devour them, like an exhausted athlete burning up his own body fat.

I think it's worth pointing out that Tony Harrison, at whose insistence this scene had been added, was not himself immune from the odd spasm of anxiety when it came to the subject of death.

On one occasion, a technical rehearsal, he was watching the scene where Christ returns to the disciples and, to their astonishment, eats a plate of fish that's put before him. Herring, actually; a fish that Tony was particularly fond of. When the cast broke for coffee, I noticed that Tony stayed where he was, in the gloom of the auditorium, underneath the side balcony. When I asked him what the matter was, he smiled. Or tried to. 'I've just had a bad moment,' he said. 'I've just realised that when you're dead, you won't be able to eat anything.' He was ashen. 'For some reason, I don't know why, it really got through to me.'

Tony had also added the play about Abraham and Isaac and embellished the scene between Herod and his son, pushing it further into the realm of music hall. Robert Stephens played Herod and Tony Trent his son. Newcomers both to the production and its style, Robert was never very comfortable with the music hall approach. And after the first few performances, he started launching himself into a more heroic version of the role, leering at the audience and gratuitously baring his breast, overwhelming them with a demented kind of narcissism. In part it was a bold attempt to realise Herod's ludicrously boastful identity, but I also think that in the back of his mind he was confusedly trying to recapture the sexual charge of his earlier performances at the National, when, for example, as Atahualpa in *The Royal Hunt of the Sun*, he had been the talk of the town.

Robert, it always seemed to me, was torn apart by the extreme contradictions within his character: the introvert and the exhibitionist. The masculine and the feminine. He veered wildly between kindness and disdain, sensitivity and bragadoccio, humility and arrogance. His outward vanity was matched by an inner despair.

Edna Doré, on the other hand, was unusually modest, both in herself and in her approach to acting. She was nearly sixty, her hair was white and her voice was deep (she smoked too much, as we all did). She enjoyed the occasional gin and tonic and, in keeping with Bill's casting principle, looked like someone who worked for a living.

Edna had played Mary in *The Passion* and so it was inevitable she should continue with the role in the *Doomsday* play, where the now aged virgin dies and then ascends to join her son in heaven. Her performance touched everyone who saw it, especially those old enough to be anxious about their own mortality. It was a straightforward account of a very old lady at the end of her life, played with simplicity, dignity and a true largeness of spirit.

The trilogy was now complete. We opened each part in sequence, played them in repertoire for a while and then put them all together every Saturday for the remainder of the run: *Creation to Nativity* in the morning, *The Passion* in the afternoon, *Doomsday* in the evening.

If Part One was in black and white, Part Two in colour, then Part Three was fashioned in those strange hallucinatory colours at the ultra-violet end of the spectrum, often seen in the visionary paintings of William Blake.

Part Four

Reputations

29. The Wrap-up

Keith Dewhurst

The Mysteries was a huge feel-good hit in the Cottesloe and when it transferred to the Lyceum's historic if somewhat dilapidated auditorium it was, for its brief season, a mainstream triumph. It was also an end. Plays at the Cottesloe had been heavily subsidised, which is why, being so lavish, they could be mounted at all. But now Margaret Thatcher's arts policies had begun to bite, and after *The Mysteries* left the Cottesloe in April 1985, Peter Hall closed the theatre for five months, partly for lack of money and partly in protest. This closure marked the end of the great age of subsidised theatre, and in effect of a flowering of English drama that was bettered only by those extraordinary years between the 1580s and Shakespeare's retirement.

Bill Bryden lost his power base when he gave up the Cottesloe in 1980, and had been in negotiations to join BBC TV in Scotland before *The Mysteries* hit the stage. *Ill Fares the Land* had not been a success, but Scottish Television had retained their licence and could afford to be gracious, and gave their blessing to Bill's move to the opposition. At about the same time they signed Mark McManus to be in *Taggart*, which showed too late in the day that he could always have been a genuine star.

As his introduction to BBC Scotland, Bill set himself up to direct a film written by Peter Macdougall and starring Harvey Keitel, but before he could start his life's contradictions came to a crisis and he broke down. Jack Shepherd visited him in the Priory, where, for once, he remembers, Bill was quiet and Jack did most of the talking.

Happily Bill soon re-entered the world, where he was an outstanding Head of TV Drama in Scotland. He gave the Keitel gig to someone else.

Since leaving the BBC he has done two epic theatre projects in Scotland, one of which, *The Ship*, created one of the greatest *coups de théâtre* in living memory, Bill Dudley engineering the illusion of a great ship sliding down its slipway into the water. At the Cottesloe he did a Dutch classic and in 2000 a millennium re-creation of *The Mysteries*, in which Jack Shepherd, Trevor Ray, John Tams, Don Warrington and some Albion survivors all appeared. Jack says that it was like footballers of another era appearing in a charity game, but the magic of the event was still there.

Bill has also directed three or four plays in rep or the West End, several radio plays, a couple of operas and has lectured at an American university. In other words, during a decade and more, he has done what before would have filled eighteen months.

In the same period, less gifted contemporaries have achieved fame, fortune and high honours, and the work that Bill championed, the attempt by Brecht, Tyrone Guthrie, Stephen Joseph, Ronconi and Vilar to take popular theatre outside the proscenium and have it encompass the postmodern world, has been halted. Whether it could have been a lifeline through a more shallow and cost-conscious time nobody knows, because today's young audience hardly know that it existed.

To what extent Bill's personal ambitions and the behaviour and reputation of the Cottesloe Company contributed to this ignorance of what they did is another open question.

30. Reputations

Jack Shepherd

'The road to excess leads to the palace of wisdom,' wrote William Blake, and most of us trod it. But as this book shows, it is a very dangerous road.

Most theatre companies, then as now, have maybe one actor who is inclined to over-indulge; the thing about the Cottesloe Company was that there always seemed to be about half a dozen, no matter how much the personnel might change.

I remember the whiskies lined up on the piano in Rehearsal Room 3, at 11 o'clock in the morning, ferried through from the bar as soon as it opened. It was a phase that a few of the more roisterous members of the company were going through. It didn't last, of course. And it wasn't long before they started to realise that drinking whisky during the daytime wasn't necessarily a very good thing. One company member woke up one morning to find that much of his hair had fallen out. And when it grew back again, it was white. Such was the shock that he stopped drinking whisky from that moment on, limiting himself thereafter to the consumption of wine. Another suffered a busted pancreas and had to stop drinking altogether.

Brian Glover liked a glass of scotch, but he only ever drank it after most of us had gone to bed. And then, of course, he was up at the crack of dawn 'training it off' as he jogged round the track at Battersea. Bryan Pringle had the eyes of a dragon, blotched with all the colours of the rainbow, but he wouldn't allow himself a drink until he'd made his final exit. Barry Rutter enjoyed a pint of beer but was ruthlessly abstemious before the performance, which was true of most of the company.

The discipline on stage was invariably very good. We were gaining a reputation and we were proud of that reputation. People came to see the company, the way it worked, not the individuals within it. We were a kind of organism, each actor relating to the other, giving and taking the focus on stage in the twinkling of an eye.

Derek Newark drank a great deal, but his attitude to the work might be summed up as follows: 'You can stay up as late as you like, drink as much as you like, do whatever you have to do, but once you get out on to that stage, my son, that's where it counts. And what you don't do, what you don't ever do, is let the side down. I'm telling you.'

There were lapses, of course, but for the most part people didn't let the side down. One such lapse occurred during a performance of *The Passion* in the autumn of 1978. As fate would have it, it was the night Lindsay Anderson came to see the play.

The four Knights had been drinking all afternoon in the company of Jesus. All five were well oiled. They had no problem with the lines. They were a little loose-jointed, maybe, and perhaps a bit over-confident, but everyone was making complete sense. Everything was going fine, until the moment came when the four Knights, having secured Jesus to the cross, had to haul it into an upright position. The manoeuvre was a tricky one at the best of times, but on this often-talked-about occasion, any kind of proper coordination eluded them completely.

The cross swung about alarmingly. The audience gasped like a circus crowd. It looked very much as if Mark was going to fall headlong into the audience, crushed by the weight of timber behind him.

It was at this very moment that an incensed Lindsay Anderson came hurtling out of the theatre and into the upstairs bar, where a group of us were congregating before making our last entrance. 'Those men are drunk!' he said, bristling with indignation. 'All four of them, drunk.'

He bought himself a stiff drink at this point. He was genuinely rattled. 'They're so drunk, they can't get the bloody cross up. They're going to kill someone before they're done.' He may even have gone back briefly for another look. 'And what makes it worse', he said, settling down on one of the

214

barstools, 'is that the man playing Jesus' (he knew perfectly well who it was) 'is even more drunk than they are!'

But as I say, such lapses were very rare.

It seems to me now that the company gained its reputation because of the amount of time spent in the Green Room bar. The bar doesn't open at lunchtimes any more, it hasn't for years – a legacy, I'm sure, of the way its facilities were taken advantage of by the Cottesloe Company in the distant past.

There was another reason why we all used to congregate in there, aside from the drink and the casual conversation; Bill Bryden tended to hold court there, lunchtimes and evenings before the show. It was almost literally a court, with its own hierarchy – those who had 'the King's ear' and so forth – and its own protocol for that matter. In those days, for instance, it was difficult to say, 'I'll have a Perrier, please' and then expect to be taken seriously. This was where the previous night's performance would be discussed, where grievances could be aired and notes given. It was where dreams about the future could be shared; attainable dreams and fantastical dreams, but dreams none the less. It was where people waited, trying to catch Bill's attention, ready to petition him with their ideas about the next production. And since this was a bar, it was only natural that a certain amount of drink was taken. The enthusiasm generated was invariably high octane, boisterous as opposed to rowdy and spirited as opposed to drunken, but looking back it becomes clear how intimidating our group must have seemed to many of the other people working in the building. And annoying, too, for those who simply wanted to talk through the business of the day over a quiet drink.

This very masculine, occasionally bullish behaviour went against the notions of both the 'sensitive artist', and the rose-tinted West End world of 'Oh, you were wonderful, darling'. I can see now that a lot of the more traditionally minded people working within the building must have found the Cottesloe Company rather strange and disagreeable. Hardly actors at all. More like a rugby team, which is in fact what many people called us. 'Oh, God. The rugby team's in again,' they'd say as they spotted us from the doorway, rapidly retracing their steps.

I suppose if they'd said 'soccer team' we'd've taken it as a compliment.

And Derek Newark didn't help matters. He was to be found, as often as not, sitting on a barstool, invariably clutching a brandy and soda when he was in a bad mood – vodka and tonic when his mood was good – glaring at anyone who dared approach him, his features stiffening in a grimace of paranoid disdain, muttering darkly, 'What *is* your game?' And then, after the uncomfortable silence that invariably followed, 'What *is* your fucking game?' To which there was never any possible answer.

It has to be said, though, that from the summer of 1978 right the way through to the winter of 1980, the company worked very hard: performing on stage six nights a week and then returning to the building most mornings to rehearse the next production. There was very little time off, little time to relax, so people took their leisure when they could. In the bar, usually.

And so a pattern began to emerge, a seductive one too, of working throughout the morning, congregating in the bar at lunchtime, getting one's breath back (some people then ate, others didn't) and then rehearsing throughout the afternoon. This was followed by that difficult period for an actor when the body has to gather energy for the coming performance, which can often feel like falling into a black hole. Everyone prepared in the way that suited them best: taking a nap, eating a meal, going through the lines. Some would have a drink before they went on, but most would not. And then, of course, after the show everyone would congregate in the bar once more, this time in a celebratory mood, often moving on to the Village Taverna in Chelsea for a meal, before falling into bed in the early hours.

I don't think there was anything particularly remarkable about this life we were leading, except perhaps the intensity of it all, the commitment required. And the fact that it was sustained over such a long period of time, producing as we did a string of successful and for the most part wholly original productions.

216

The problem was, there seemed to be no time for other things. There was only the play you were doing, and the play you were going to be doing. Home life began to feel like a distraction. We were a community, a world within a world. It was like being consumed by a warm slightly drunken thing that pulls you into itself and then starts to suck the life out of you. For a brief while our lives and our art were in danger of becoming one.

I once met a German actor called Kurt Raab, who had travelled a great deal further down this particular road than we ever did and found only disillusion at the end of it. Kurt had been the film director Rainer Werner Fassbinder's producer, art director and lover. For years his life and his art and been fused together. 'Life was a party,' he told me, 'every day.' But when Fassbinder died suddenly, he had been cast adrift into a life without purpose. He became a lost soul.

I didn't go with *The Mysteries* when it transferred to the Lyceum, so I missed out on the final party. No one was aware of it of course, but this last celebration marked the end of it all. The tombstone. The epitaph.

31. Something Happier

Keith Dewhurst

In the years since the end of the Cottesloe Company there have been our own lost souls, disillusionment and drink-related deaths. The dream had not been delivered, the triumphs not realised, the point not acknowledged to have been made. So this section of our book is about something not made much of at the time but happier in the long run: the actresses.

If they have not figured in our story as much as the men, it is because they did not have the same continuity. Morag Hood worked for Bill in both Scotland and England but other regulars joined halfway through, at the Cottesloe, when the agenda was set. Even then they came and went a bit, and Susan Fleetwood's elusiveness is perhaps symptomatic of the fact that women in general, perhaps, were less swayed than men by Bill's rhetoric and dreams.

At the same time, the women Bill cast resembled the men: they were high-energy, realistic and centred character players, although they came from a wider range of social backgrounds than the men. They were without exception rock-steady in performance and Edna Doré, a working-class striver who began as a showgirl and loved the company almost as much as her garden allotment, is probably the only person one will ever meet who could act Bill Gaskill's 'an old woman going down to the river'. Indeed, in *Dispatches* she actually did.

In terms of worldly success, the women did as well as the men. Brenda Blethyn won international acclaim, and Anna Carteret and Edna Doré became big TV favourites. Peggy Mount was a hugely popular West End seat-filler, and Fleetwood was after all a star of sorts. June Watson, like Newark, deserved far more recognition than she achieved. Celia Bannerman of *Pirates* became a voice-coach on international movies. In the folk firmament, Maddy Prior is a star.

Several of the others led independent and unorthodox lives with a great deal more sense and success than the men, but that is what women do, is it not, so they are less likely to be undone by disappointments. And the girls whom Caulfield picked for his stage crews were as tough as the actors but with less bombast. 'Do you want to speak the proper dialogue or not?' Sarah Parkin once famously said to Derek Newark when she was on the book.

In rehearsal the actresses didn't need to debate at great length to prove that they too had creativity. They would ask a quiet question, receive a quick nod, and get on with it. As they did with bad behaviour. They could be as naughty as the men, but never advertised it. And they are still alive, when so many of their playmates are dead.

Jack Shepherd says that during the last performance of a play he always feels as if he is standing on the stern of a ship, staring down at the wake, and looking back towards the land he has just left; and Sir Walter Raleigh, when he was finished and in the Tower of London, wrote that his hopes were 'clean out of sight of land'. So is what was done at the Royal Court, the Royal Lyceum, and the Cottesloe. The point, though, is still the same: what the popular theatre could mean for the future.

Epilogue: What's the Score?

Keith Dewhurst

Throughout the time I worked with Bill Bryden I wrote episodes for the BBC TV police series *Softly Softly* and *Juliet Bravo*. A play like *Lark Rise* would be seen by about four hundred people a night, and extensively written-up, commented on, and reviewed. An episode of *Juliet Bravo* was listed in the *Radio Times*, but received no reviews and was seen by about ten million people. I wrote neither sort of show differently from the other: each was pitched at the same artistic level, which is the only one that comes naturally to me. Yet the style that satisfied the mass audience suited the subsidised so-called elite and vice-versa; and if some viewers switched off, no doubt some people were bored in the Cottesloe. My dual situation would be unlikely today, and it says something crucial about our notions of popular theatre: that the humanity the artists and the audience have in common is more important than whatever divides them.

To say this is to state a belief, and to make a choice, that cannot, like an advertiser's market research or Hollywood demographics, be quantified. Ratings show what people watched and focus groups what they can articulate. They tell you about yesterday. They say nothing definite about tomorrow. Even the biggest power-brokers know this, and yet the business notions of our time are so pervasive that art struggles not so much against the market itself, as against corporate pressure to manipulate that market at a low common denominator, which is always presented as consumer choice.

Popular theatre is difficult because it is not about these attempts to find certainty. Its subject-matter may be yesterday but its soul is tomorrow. It is about the spark that is in everyone, the feeling that they do not know how to express. It is about what people will rise to, and not what they will accept. It challenges the apathy that is the other side of acceptance. It is an act of faith.

At the same time it is well aware that what it wishes to say must be comprehensible. Popular theatre beats its brains out to be accessible without loss of integrity, because that is the point: to combine what everyone can understand with the highest possible quality of writing, acting and production.

That such issues of taste and integrity have existed for centuries we know from Hamlet's speech to the Players. What he called tearing a passion to tatters can still be seen every night of the week, mostly in the work of famous people who are praised for it. Wankers, Derek Newark would have said, and I have no doubt that Hamlet and his writer would have agreed with him. Wankers now, and wankers in 1601.

Bill Bryden was not, like me, an Oxbridge highbrow. He was a working-class person who knew two things from the life around him as he grew up: that ordinary people could be manipulated, and that they had dignity and deep feelings, which could be addressed in stories and dramas they would appreciate. He believed that to cheapen the story in the hope of ensuring its effect was cheating, and an insult to those anonymous lives. From the boxing match in *The Baby Elephant* to the launching of *The Ship*, he went for many spectacular effects yet never lost his loyalty to the narrative line. 'This isn't boring enough,' he would say in *Lark Rise* rehearsals, as he sought a true way to depict the tempo of other lives. His half-back line, for all their rampaging, had similarly simple things to offer.

'What we're fighting is beasts in human form,' said Brian Glover's character in *Corunna!*, a looter and rapist who was himself the victim of an atrocity; and for years Bill, Sebastian, Caulfield and I called the actors 'The Beasts', because the aggression in the company, the intense competitiveness, the merciless jokes, the energy level, the sheer excitement of striking sparks off like minds were an essential part of their creativity: it was the grit in the rehearsal room oyster.

Jack Shepherd taught everyone about the space, and Glover that what is popular need not be vulgar. Newark was the lightning-conductor: the other actors laughed at his nerves to cure their own. Then on stage he had more bottle than anyone. Lucky Bill and me, to have had such fidelity at our disposal. McManus was in retrospect a wonder: taken young to Australia, he worked on oil-rigs off New Guinea, married the Federal Prime Minister's daughter, and starred in films. My mother-in-law was his Sydney agent. After Tony Richardson cast him in *Ned Kelly* he went not to Los Angeles and movies, but to London and highbrow theatre. What he showed was that poetry and heroism need not be bourgeois. He was a glorious womaniser, and when he carried the cross as Jesus in *The Passion*, girls shoved their phone numbers into his hands.

For the rest, actors and actresses fucking in the dressing-room showers seem innocent, really, and it is pointless to apologise for arrogance, drink and insults thirty years ago. The people who hated the company, and have tried to airbrush it out of history, hated and feared the work which had ten times more power than their own; our behaviour was their excuse, and was enough, I guess, for the world of 'Darling, you were wonderful,' which is always to hand with its platitudes.

Popular theatre is not like memory plays or domestic dramas. It presents stories in action, which is expensive. In a bad time there are always reasons not to take the risk, and what is not performed can soon fall out of fashion; so can people, as Bill discovered when he gave up his power base and could not find another, dooming his work thereby to a long twilight. But the idea that we have called popular theatre cannot be lost for ever, because it springs irresistibly from our nation's soul.

As for me and Bill, well, he annoyed me more than anyone else in the world, actually, and probably vice-versa. But when you have heard Carthy's voice open one of your plays, and said exactly what you thought and howled with laughter in restaurants and so on and so forth you have to admit that it was a drug, and you were addicted, and came out of it, as I came out of alcohol, with a fine calm but something missing. Recently Bill and I boarded a tube train at Leicester Square, each of us using his bus-pass, and I asked him about the time he suggested we apply for the Stoke City managership. 'Were you serious?' I said. 'Of course,' he said. 'Why?' I said. 'Because you have to start somewhere,' he said. Would that we could.

What's the score? Search me. All I know is what Matt Busby said: keep on playing football, and the goals are bound to come.

A Glossary of Terms

Keith Dewhurst

Admiral, the
The director William Gaskill. 'Take my drum to England, hang it by the shore, beat it when your powder's running low.'

Alienation
A concept initiated by the German playwright Bertolt Brecht. The audience maintains the suspension of its disbelief but, at the same time, knows that it is watching a play and being fed information outside the narrative. From one point of view this is so simple a postmodern notion that it is strange how many people still object to it.

Antelope job with them paying, an
On critical occasions, such as a first meeting with a writer, or getting him to accept an actor he didn't want, Royal Court assistant directors were allowed to use the dining-room above the Antelope in Eaton Terrace. More often they would ask the writer to lend them a pound so that they could buy him a drink.

Ashoka, the
An Indian restaurant on the corner of Sidney Street and the Fulham Road. No longer extant. Used by Royal Court directors of an evening.

Attendance money
A cash per diem paid to a writer for attending rehearsals of his play at the National Theatre. Intended to pay his fares, et cetera. *See Float.*

Ball-winners in midfield
Actors who embody the essential energy of a play's narrative, keep it at the right level and tempo, and make it live for the audience.

Beasts, the
Cottesloe actors. *See* Epilogue. Derived from a line in *Corunna!*: 'What we're fighting is beasts in human form.'

Bench, the
The director, writer and stage-management, who watch the performance and hope to have influenced it; as opposed to the actors who are the players on the field. Another football analogy, and, of course, it is the Bench who most need a result.

Beulah
The distinguished actor and film star Brian Cox.

Blanding
The process whereby a power-broker such as the Director of the National Theatre influenced his colleagues.

Boat people
An obscure Bill Brydenism, derived originally from his suspicious view of a play about the Chinese Agrarian Revolution. It came as with most Brydenisms to have shifting nuances, and could be used as a noun, an adjective, or as an indication of an ambience. The root of it was a working-class unease at liberals who make moral statements about things of which they have no direct experience. Although the last time he said it to me was in 2004, when he realised at a funeral that I was wearing a black Issey Miyake suit; actually he mistook it for Armani, but by now the astute reader will have caught the drift.

Bodger, the
The distinguished theatre director Michael Bogdanov.

Bottle
Everybody knows what bottle is, but not many actually have it. 'Bottles will be popping tonight!' was a classic Brydenism.

Can you see me now, lads?
Oft-repeated Brian Gloverism, first uttered during a sexual escapade that this book is too highbrow to describe.

Captain, the
John Caulfield, Bryden's stage-manager at the Cottesloe Theatre. Died in July 2005.

Chelsea Tandoori, the
A more expensive Royal Court restaurant on the Fulham Road. Trading now as 'Love India'.

Claw, the
The writer Keith Dewhurst's gesture of emphasis and argument, employed not least against actors who juxtaposed words or seemed incapable of standing still. Some, such as Brian Glover, would misbehave in order to witness the effect.

Commander, the
John Coleby, sometime Literary Contracts Manager of the National Theatre. A Royal Marines officer and gentleman on Mountbatten's staff during the war, a talented amateur cartoonist and a great friend of the Cottesloe Company.

Como Lario
Still there in Holbein Place. An Italian restaurant near the Royal Court, much loved when there was cash to spare. In 2003 a waiter who had worked there in the 1970s hailed Sebastian Graham-Jones by name in Washington DC.

Constance Spry
Flower-shop account maintained by the old Royal Court, and operated under instruction by an assistant director. Bill Bryden, for instance, ordered flowers for Vanessa Redgrave on

the birth of her first child. Robert Kidd is reputed to have used the account to take bouquets to actresses who had failed to win a part, but whom he wished to chat up.

Diagonal
Placement of actors on the opposing top and bottom corners of the stage. If they face each other or turn heel, it is the *diagonal of passion*. Half-turning the body to look back makes it the *diagonal of regret*. A sideways up or down eyeline is the *diagonal of vision*.

Dipstick
Fundamental Bill Brydenism, used originally to describe a type of person: a planner or technician who is important in the bureaucratic structure but whose connection to the artistic activity is tenuous. As decades passed *Dipstick* became a shorthand cover-all for more or less anything or anybody, according to context. More recent uses would include a phrase like 'Rupert Murdoch clocked the dipstick'. That is to say, he understood how to promote his satellite television interests in every country of the globe.

Doing white wine
A desperate attempt by a spirits-drinker to be, or at least to seem, more responsible.

Don't give me a bad time
Essential Derek Newarkism.

Early panic
What it says. People want to rewrite, to cut, and to change performances before anything is proven either way. Endemic in today's television.

E. G.
A Bryden cat, named after the American actor E. G. Marshall.

Elephant Trousers

The Cottesloe actor Trevor Ray, so named because his build made the fall of his trousers resemble the back legs of an elephant.

Energy

The vital ingredient in writing, acting and directing.

Fat boy in your life, you've got to let this

Advice offered by Keith Dewhurst with regard to a child understudy who Bill Bryden prayed would never have to go on. It is a line from a Randy Newman lyric.

Fitness training

From 1971 to 1980, Fred Wardour organised fitness training in the Jubilee Gardens. Fred was very fit. Of those company members who took part regularly, Oliver Cotton was a jogger (as was Fulton Mackay). Barry Rutter and Jack Shepherd both played football, often for the same team. John Salthouse had played professionally. David Rintoul was an acrobat. And Bob Hoskins tried it once, cramped up halfway and never came back.

Float

A notional sum of money enabling the writer and director to buy drinks. *See Attendance money.*

Freston

An all-powerful wizard in the imagination of Don Quixote. Used sometimes by a very distinguished actor indeed as a flippant nickname for the Director of the National Theatre.

Frontal energy

When a performance is given directly to the audience, as in stand-up comedy, concerts, song and dance numbers and the choruses of *Oedipus Rex* et cetera.

Goal, a
A theatrical moment which captivates and astounds the audience.

Going through
Scots idiom. *See Haymarket job.*

'Has anyone seen Robert?'
Frank Nealon's plaintive cry, as the cast filed past the stage door, before performances of both *Midsummer Night's Dream* and *The Mysteries.*

Haymarket job
Phrase used by Scots actors working in Edinburgh who gave themselves more drinking time by catching the last train to Glasgow at Haymarket rather than Waverley. The journey itself was described as *going through.* There was an ice-rink at the Haymarket, in which Dewhurst and Bryden dreamed of doing a play.

Heavy duty
Serious. Extremely professional. Unforgiving. Powerful. Bill Bryden would use the phrase to describe Glasgow detectives, or theatre technicians he admired.

House, not the expensive
Sotto-voce instruction given by Sebastian Graham-Jones to a waiter at Mr Chow's, Knightsbridge, when someone who could not afford it foolishly ordered champagne. Thereafter, occasional code for damage limitation.

Jason's
A Greek restaurant in Battersea, much used in 1977 because it was an easy stop on the way to Bill Bryden's home in Wandsworth. When a play was on, everyone would go to watch and socialise in the bar, so there was a lot of eating out.

Jobsworth

See *Dipstick*. An enemy hiding in an office. As paranoia grew, so did the number of *Jobsworths*.

La Barca

An Italian restaurant near the Old Vic, still trading, and an early National Theatre venue. Sometimes referred to as the Boat.

Lad with the short arms, that

A famous lady singer's description of a distinguished Scots actor and director.

Laying down beside it

A fault in acting, when the performer does not inhabit the role, but presents instead the feelings that it is intended to arouse in the audience. For an interesting variant, see Jack Shepherd's description of the way in which Susan Fleetwood spoke the verse as Titania (Chapter 23).

Mafia, the

Brydenism for the Royal Court, and people of its artistic persuasion.

Midfield

Brydenism for the fundamental energy and impulsion of a play, that has to be made to work in performance. Actors who performed that function he called ball-winners in midfield.

Mr Guffy

The actor Michael Gough, who gave the Cottesloe an old-fashioned touch of class. As did Robert Flemyng and Richard Johnson. Richard brought as well a whiff of movie blockbusters and the Château Marmont.

Mugging

A form of over-acting: registering something in a blatantly cheap way.

Narrative line

The essential story of a play; the logic of each character's development; what is actually happening, which is not necessarily what people are talking about.

Nick

Sebastian Graham-Jones's Springer spaniel.

Own goal

A moment which causes the audience to lose concentration and interest. (*See also Goal.*)

Phoning it in

Acting without energy, conviction or the risk of finding one's true feelings. Not quite the same as *laying down beside it* (q.v.). There is a suggestion in *phoning it in* of laziness or even recalcitrance; and in *laying down beside it* of mistaken artistic notions.

Platforms

The Bench's (q.v.) favourite platform performances were both in the Olivier. In one Derek Newark, Ken Cranham and Warren Clarke were amazing in Kipling's poetry, and in the other Richard Johnson and Robert Stephens, in evening dress and with champagne in an ice-bucket, delivered the Earl of Rochester's obscene verses.

Poof's theatre

A politically incorrect vulgarism that is a criticism not of gender, nor exactly of camp acting, display for its own sake, or director/designer 'concepts'. In the eyes of the *Mafia* (q.v.) for a concept to be justified, it had to be on the same intellectual level as the original, which they rarely are. It is also interesting that, unlike operas and epic drama, naturalistic plays for the proscenium are difficult to 'conceptualise' without looking absurd. Ibsen in jock-straps, for instance, is not absolutely a goer. A known homosexual actor like Sir John Gielgud, or a homosexual director like John Dexter, never did *poof's theatre*:

they were both the real thing; and a homosexual actor like Kenneth Williams did legitimate camp, because he never pretended. *Poof's theatre* is a criticism of pretence and the pretentious, one feels: and there should be another vulgarism to cover its hetero manifestations.

Promenade
That style of theatre where the audience and the actors share the space and are intermingled, with as little scenic interference as possible.

Prosser
A basset-hound, very unruly, named after the lead in *Watch It Come Down* and presented to Bill and Deborah Bryden by John Osborne.

Resistance, the
Stanislavski's definition of what the actors must recognise and provide; the ebb and flow between the characters in a play; the conflict between different narrative lines. But really the writer should provide it in the first place.

Rubbish, tuneless
Music that Bill Bryden did not like.

Save the day acting
An actor realises that things are going wrong and ups his energy and brightness, or if colleagues are gabbling, concentrates and slows them down. If the play and direction are sound this can work; if they are indifferent it can make everything look awful. But at least the actor knows that the ship is sinking.

Snatching
A fault in acting where people have no confidence in things and do not take the time to execute them properly. A product of nervousness, which a good director should not allow to happen. It is one of the few mishaps, one guesses, that actors really do share with sportsmen.

Taxi vouchers
If real, they are very welcome. If metaphorical, they imply a rickety payments structure.

Terminal
Shorthand for terminally boring, usually with reference to other people's productions.

Theatre Wars, the
The struggle to get plays accepted, put on and properly done.

Third world
Inadequate working conditions.

Three acres and a cow, I've got
Brydenism, derived once again from that play about the Chinese Agrarian Revolution (*see Boat people*). *Three acres* is less a cover-all than a thumbnail critique of writing which asserts, and assumes thereby, a moral view, without much factual back-up. This was not necessarily a fault of the original play.

Trevved
What had happened to people blanded (*see Blanding*) by the distinguished director Sir Trevor Nunn.

T-shirts
Green Room entrepreneurs had printed, and indeed sold to the public, T-shirts and sweatshirts for most of the Cottesloe and other hits. There were also private printings. Edna Doré inspired *I'M A BRYDEN BIRD* for the Cottesloe actresses, and Keith Dewhurst and Alexandra Cann distributed *I SURVIVED THE FIRST PREVIEW OF DON QUIXOTE* as first-night mementoes. The actress Louisa Livingstone (*see Whinger, the*) was on the cusp of being murdered by Bill Bryden by interrupting him in a crisis to ask about sweatshirt logos.

Village Taverna

A Greek-Cypriot restaurant on the Fulham Road. First used by Keith Dewhurst and Alexandra Cann when they moved to Fulham Broadway in 1978, it became for years the late-night Cottesloe rendezvous. Run by Mr John, a redoubtable fish cook, and his wife Christina, its long-time waiters were Jimmy and Nikos. It witnessed drunken imbroglios, pick-ups, poetry-quoting contests between Brian Glover and Ted Hughes, visits by Al Pacino, Stacey Keach and E. G. Marshall, pre-wedding dinners and post-funeral lamentations. It moved from one side of the road to a space opposite, and in the early 1990s Mr John died of cancer. Christina continued for some years before she sold up, and retired with her second husband to Cyprus. She had kept a diary of every night's diners and happenings, including the never-explained entrance and disappearance of a naked man.

Wankers

In Cottesloe usage surprisingly specific: not so much a personal insult as one applied to people of different artistic persuasions.

What do they know?

Brydenism. A rhetorical question. Not so much arrogant as a genuine, even impotent, query about people who had not been there. (*See Theatre Wars, the.*)

What I'm saying to you is

Derek Newarkism. When it was written as a line of dialogue for his character in *Don Quixote* he delivered it without much conviction.

What's the score?

Fundamental question asked of each other by Keith Dewhurst and Bill Bryden. Is the performance working and what is the effect upon the audience? What, by implication, do we need to do about it?

What's your game?
Derek Newarkism. A comic defence that could turn beleaguered. He was at heart insecure.

Whinger, the
The Cottesloe actress Louisa Livingstone, a small woman of unique appearance who played children and juvenile character parts. Her nickname was unfair because she was loyal and rock-solid, but it came from her piping voice and gift for interjecting questions at dodgy moments (*see T-shirts*). She married the sometime Albion Band guitarist Martin Simpson.

Who's best?, the
The actor Victor Henry's name for the curtain call.

Acknowledgements

The authors and publishers wish to thank the photographers who have kindly granted permission for their photographs to be used. Acknowledgements and copyright as follows: John Haynes 1, 2, 3, 4, 5 and 13; Nobby Clark 7, 10, 12, 16, 17 and 18; Michael Mayhew 14 and 15; Brian Windsor 8; and Frank Hermann 11. It has not been possible to trace the copyright owner in every case and the publishers would be pleased to receive any information that would enable them to amend omissions in future editions.